"Everyone in America shc
plain language the extrao...
in creating close and meaningful relationships. Lisa and
confront these challenges head on, supporting their explanations with both research and narrative. Recognizing that online experiences can be both positive and negative, healthy and unhealthy, the authors strive to empower both young people and those who care about them to consciously and intentionally create lives of love and meaning both online and offline. They remind us that time is the most powerful resource we have and that we must teach the next generation to create and value time away from screens and to engage in F2F, real life interactions with one another in order to promote health and well-being."

Warren Binford, Professor of Law, Director of the Clinical Law Program, Willamette University, Internationally Recognized Children's Rights Scholar and Advocate, TEDx Speaker

"Information technology, the internet, and all the vast number of applications running in "the cloud" have exploded in numbers and capability over the last 50 years. Why? Because the internet, unlike most industries, has been largely unimpeded by government regulators. But, the absence of state or federal regulations demands a higher standard of social responsibility. Unfortunately, some tech companies have put profits above social responsibility. In *The Glass Between Us*, Jason and Lisa Frost have identified the segment of our population most vulnerable to the addictive and transformational power of the internet...our children. Their work raises some very important questions we must answer if we are to protect the most vulnerable among us, and I highly recommend *The Glass Between Us* for every parent."

Bill Johnson, U.S. Congressman, Ohio

"We aren't in Kansas anymore! Navigating the digital world is more complicated than ever. With all of its dangers and detours, we are called to steward that dimension of our lives. Lisa and Jason help the next generation of parents and children do just that."

Mark Batterson, New York Times Best-Selling Author of *The Circle Maker*, Lead Pastor of National Community Church

"Lisa and Jason Frost have offered a profound gift to parents, adolescents, teachers, and mentors. Drawing from their work in education and through a context informed by relatable stories, current data and research, they offer a template for parents and adolescents towards cultivating informed minds and compassionate hearts to build skills necessary to navigate today's complex world. The discussion questions offered are a brilliant guide to opening the doorway to self-reflecting insightful conversations that are supportive of adolescents' developmental journey of learning about themselves and identifying their personal values, that becomes part of their inner guidance to inform choices towards their goals and wellbeing. As a mother, sex educator, and mindfulness-based sex therapist, I am grateful for this important contribution and resource. *The Glass Between Us* powerfully shines light on problems while also providing myriad ways to address them and proactively prevent potential harm by giving clear direction for youth, and those who love them, to create their own inner light of awareness and wisdom to intelligently navigate our ever-changing world."

Gretchen Blycker, LMHC, LMT, RYT, Licensed Mental Health Counselor, Instructor, University of Rhode Island

"Impassioned and well informed, Team Frost gently but firmly awakens parents to the realities of life with screens, not shying away from the Web's underbelly. This practical, action-oriented book may well increase your entire family's enjoyment of life."

Gary Wilson, Author of *Your Brain on Porn: Internet Pornography and the Emerging Science of Addiction*, TEDx Speaker

"*The Glass Between Us* is essential reading for parents, caregivers, teachers and anyone who cares about today's youth. With nuance, compassion and great insight, Lisa and Jason Frost have created a relevant and modern guide which integrates research, expert advice and raw personal accounts of life in the digital age. *The Glass Between Us* successfully tackles the big issues surrounding screen-use and teens, without being judgmental or simplistic. This detailed guide empowers readers to support and understand the issues young people are facing. This book is not anti-screen but provides a framework for adults to help teens navigate the internet and live out their true potential. This truly is a wonderful resource."

Alice Taylor, Founder of The Grace Spot and Author of *Restored: A Woman's Guide to Overcoming Pornography.*

"Successfully supporting teens to navigate the digital landscape is, by far, one of today's biggest parenting and educational challenges. Jason and Lisa have done a phenomenal job laying out the realities of what's available online, the potential emotional and mental wellbeing impacts, pitfalls to avoid, and guided discussion questions. The husband & wife duo provide real-life stories, research, and practical examples to lay out a blueprint for conversations that are all-too-often avoided—including pornography and the polar-opposite, healthy sexual relationships. This must-read is for every parent seeking to positively connect with their teen and instill digital and relational values to last a lifetime."

Liz Walker, International Authority on Porn Harms, Education and Advocacy

"I am enthused about this wise book by a young couple who know first-hand the reality of the ever-evolving issues online, as they were among the first generation to grow up in the digital world. *The Glass Between Us* gives a fresh perspective that will surely equip parents and professionals to empower teens to make healthy choices online that support both their short and long-term goals."

Donna Rice Hughes, Internet Safety Expert, Author, Speaker and President of Enough Is Enough

"This is an incredibly important and timely book. Every parent knows the struggle of their children spending too much time staring at their phone, and the loss of the development of the basic skills of real, human social interaction that results. This book helps chart a path on how to (…) reverse this dangerous modern-day problem."

Adam Smith, U.S. Congressman, Washington

THE GLASS BETWEEN US

Empowering Youth to Combat Digital Exploitation

A Value-Based Approach to Screen-Driven Challenges

LISA AND JASON FROST

The Glass Between Us
Empowering Youth to Combat Digital Exploitation
A Value-Based Approach to Screen-Driven Challenges

Cover Design by Booklerk

White Fox Publishing LLC, Nashville, USA

ISBN-13: 978-1-7359100-0-0

Contents

This book is dedicated to the largest group of unsung heroes the world has ever known. They are vastly unrecognized. Who, you might ask? The fact that you are investing your valued time to read this book probably means you belong to this radical group of world changers. They are the parents, caregivers, teachers, social workers, and any other individuals who sacrifice their time and resources to support, love, and mentor this rising generation of youth.

digital exploitation

[**dij**-i-tl ek-sploi-**tey**-shuhn]

noun

digital exploitation is the selfish utilization of web-based functions for one's personal gain.

Introduction

Lisa

"The pedal was on the floor. My steering wheel started to vibrate as the engine in my little Skoda screamed with fury. Jason, my husband, had a curious look on his face as we tore down the road at a speed of 130 mph. I prayed that the slower traffic in the right lane wouldn't make any sudden moves, or it might be our last. Oops, another pesky Beemer! I moved over into the slow lane as a BMW rocketed past us. Its wake of dirty air shook our little car as it bulleted into the horizon. Jason had a flashback to his days in driver's ed in Virginia. He told me that flying down the road at this pace went against every instinct he had learned about safe driving, and following "the all-important rules." Threat of jail time, major fines, or loss of your driver's license were standard deterrents for tempted speed junkies in the U.S., he explained. However, we weren't in Virginia, or even the United States, for that matter. We were living in Germany at the time, making our regular eight-hour trip to visit my family on the North Sea.

Vehicles changed everything. They revolutionized the way we live. Suddenly, a trip to a nearby city was measured in hours rather than days. Travel dangers that once could have cost you your life, such as the elements or highway bandits, were no longer part of the trip equation. Automobiles offered a convenience that no one could have dreamed of in the last thousand years. People no longer had to live in close proximity to their workplace, birthing a whole new concept of suburbia living. However, as luxurious and ground-breaking as the eruption of the auto industry was, it came with a heavy cost. The death rate of automobile accidents in 1913 was 33.38 for every 10,000 vehicles on the road. If this ratio was applied to the number of vehicles registered today, this would equate to nearly 950,000 deaths a year in the United States.[1]

Detroit's first decade of 1900s automobile history is a prime example of cars gone wild. According to an article published by *The Detroit News*, there "were no stop signs, warning signs, traffic lights, traffic cops, driver's education, lane lines, street lighting, brake lights, driver's licenses or posted speed limits."[2] Out of all vehicle-related fatalities, three-fourths were pedestrians. One driver, who was taken into custody for mowing down several people on a sidewalk, had already been charged twenty-six times for reckless driving and suffered from a medical condition, resulting in random blackouts. Even children were put behind the wheel of delivery trucks and pressured to throw caution to the wind to meet customer demands.[3] Since the early 1900s, the death rate has improved 96 percent.[4]

Americans were more than willing to receive with wide-open arms the astounding freedom the automobile brought to their lives, but society itself was not prepared for the incredible responsibility and infrastructure needed to keep someone else's freedom from getting struck down by another.

Similarly, the advancement of the internet has created unfathomable opportunities to exercise freedom, but just like the relationship between 1900s drivers and pedestrians, unchecked freedom becomes someone else's suffering. In the case of the wild web, it leads to compulsion, addiction, and exploitation of this rising generation.

"I broke my new record!" Thirteen-year-old Emme came running towards her friends and me with her smartphone still glued to her hand. "I did it. Twelve hours straight on TikTok." "Twelve hours?" I was stunned. "What did you do for twelve hours?" Emme responded, "I stalked my TikTok crushes. I learned a few new dance moves and listened to my favorite artists." I went on to ask her if anyone at home would interfere. She told me, "Not really. I just pretend that I go to bed and then I get up again. I know my way around the parental controls. Me and my friends, we chat all night long. Besides, I have to have my phone nearby. My best friend has been making her favorite pasta lately." "Her favorite pasta?" I looked confused. "It's our code language for struggling with anxiety and depression. She is suicidal. I have to have my phone next to me in case she has an emergency."

Enslaved to their Phones

The high school teens we interviewed felt that their generation is enslaved to their phones.[5] They were disconnected from people in the present moment. They felt exhausted by their own insatiable appetite for media consumption. The drive to stay connected and maintain the perfect curated digital appearance was a demanding chore. Many of the students came from elite, upper-class families. Their schools were rated among the best in the country. Their academic performance was exceptional, yet somehow, they felt out of control when it came to the digital devices that were seemingly invented to enrich their friendships and upgrade their social status.

The smartphone generation is hyper-connected, but incredibly lonely. Despite having the world at their fingertips, teens are losing the art of building meaningful real life friendships. Online, they are blasted with values that attack their body image, hypersexualize their world, and promote pixels over people, which is pushing their mental health to the brink of disaster. Like the child delivery truck drivers of former times, the introduction of high-speed internet to the world has placed children in the driver's seat of their very own digital universe. They are often left to their own devices as they explore relationships, plug into immersive gaming worlds, and awaken their sexuality through the limitless opportunities of the web.

Despite having the world at their fingertips, teens are losing the art of building meaningful real life friendships.

Digital media is not evil in itself, but most parents and professionals guiding youth are not equipped to combat the challenges that come with this vastly unregulated territory. We do not have the luxury to experience first and teach later. The lightning-fast advance that tech has made into our homes and our teens' pockets has left many of us feeling like we missed the train. Our teens are seen as the *digital natives*; born into a virtual world unto themselves.

The Pandemic Effect

There has never been a time where we were more grateful for our devices than during the Covid-19 pandemic. The ability to see the faces of our loved ones through our screens while protecting each other by keeping distance made life in quarantine bearable. The coronavirus pandemic has undoubtedly led to an exponential spike in screen time. Yet, while being virtually connected, teenagers have struggled with loneliness and anxiety like never before.[6] COVID-19 pushed us all into isolation, leaving teenagers alone with their screens and vulnerable to the exploitive side of the digital world. Cyberbullying rose by fifty percent during the pandemic.[7]

When Kate's 13-year-old son decided to trade the video game *Grand Theft Auto* for *Minecraft* and *Fortnite*, she was relieved. About six weeks into his gaming adventures, Kate made a horrific discovery on her son's phone. She stumbled upon a video of bestiality involving a young boy. When scrolling through the game's chat function, she found that her son's account was filled with sexual acts and graphic language.[8] Predators have taken advantage of teens who are logging record amounts of screen time during the lockdown, which has resulted in a sky-rocketing amount of online exploitation, even on mainstream social media sites like Instagram and TikTok.[9] By the time this pandemic is over, we will inherit the most tech-addicted generation in history.

With unhinged access to the curated lives of others, infinite entertainment options, and a never-ending stream of sex on demand, we need to fight for core values to guide our teenagers' media choices. The screen habits adolescents develop today have a fundamental influence on their health, happiness, and success in the future.

The screen habits adolescents develop today have a fundamental influence on their health, happiness, and success in the future.

You have to Have RUMB

When you have finished reading this book, you will have the tools to equip your children, students, and mentees with the knowledge and wisdom they need to steward a healthy, value-driven interaction with digital media. It all starts with R.U.M.B.: relationship, understanding, mentorship, and boundaries. "Rumb" is an old navigation term used by ship captains to journey long distances.[10] It is the bearing that navigators use to help keep them on course. In a similar way, we use the acronym R.U.M.B. to help you navigate your teens' online interactions and empower them to make healthy media choices.

- **R**elationship: Our most valuable asset, regardless of wealth or social status, is the time we set aside for our teens. Being fully present with them builds meaning into the relationship, where acceptance and open communication about digital habits become possible.
- **U**nderstanding: We need to uncover the "why" behind our children's media habits. From a place of understanding, we can relate to their draw to digital media without condoning poor media choices. Approaching their media consumption with empathy removes shame and allows teens to feel seen and known.
- **M**entorship: The aim of mentorship is to help teens identify the values, both good and bad, that drive their online choices. The tools in this book will lay the foundation for mentors to guide teens to establish a healthy, value-driven interaction with digital media that leads them towards their goals.
- **B**oundaries: If healthy values become an integral part of a teen's identity, their online choices will be driven by who they are, rather than what they are told to do. When teenagers learn to live by their values, boundaries surrounding tech protect what they have said "yes" to in life.

This book is designed to help you establish your own RUMB journey in your family or professional career working with teens. We believe that the most powerful form of learning takes place when teens are given the opportunity to ask questions, draw their own conclusions, and feel activated in the context of informed guidance and caring mentorship. Throughout the book, you will find "RUMB Challenges" and discussion questions at the end of every chapter. We encourage you to take on those challenges, along with the teens you mentor. As you journey through each chapter, RUMB will outline a path to equipping your teens to learn how to make healthy and sustainable media choices that protect their relationships and wellbeing.

A Value-Driven Approach to Digital Media

Finding our voices as leaders in the digital age has left many of us feeling sidelined in our authority to mentor this generation. In our day and age, teens have Google, Siri, or Reddit to answer their questions. However, there has never been a more critical time in history in which teens so desperately need our guidance and support. Teenagers may be able to Google the answers to any question they would once have looked up in an encyclopedia, but they do not have the wisdom and maturity that are forged through the fires of life experience to plug their knowledge into.

It is the values that we live by that lead to successful careers, the building of healthy relationships, or starting a family with a committed partner. In the same way that teenagers need the proper training to safely operate a vehicle, they also need our mentorship and support to empower them to develop their own value-driven approach to using digital media. Our mission is to equip you with knowledge and understanding so you can ask the right questions and fuel meaningful discussion. With this knowledge, we will raise digital pioneers and launch this generation into a successful future. Now is the time for parents and professionals to rise up and provide the mentorship and wisdom that these *digital natives* so desperately need.

Part I

Relationships: Our connections to friends and family are the backbone of a healthy, thriving life. Our brains are wired to be social, making healthy relationships the most critical component in protecting our mental health.

Understanding: Digital media is engineered to hack the primitive functions of the brain, which leaves many teens feeling shameful about their online struggles. The long-term gains of placing people over pixels greatly improves mental health and increases the likelihood of personal and professional success.

Mentorship: We have to help teens identify values that prioritize face-to-face interactions. Teens need to understand how tech can exploit their healthy desires for friendship and intimacy by offering instant gratification for their time and attention. We should confront feelings of shame by empowering teens to rewire their brains, to build healthy coping mechanisms, and to use the internet as a tool to succeed, instead of a place to escape.

Boundaries: Teens need to identify practical ways to protect their mental health from the exploitive side of the internet. It is important that teens come to recognize time as their most cherished and valued asset. We need to empower them to set boundaries that protect how they spend their time online.

Chapter 1: Tweens, Teens, and Screens

Lisa

"I was teaching at a small high school in the middle of a quaint college town nestled in the Black Forest in Southern Germany. One Wednesday afternoon, Ben and Jenna, both in ninth grade at that time, sheepishly came to me after class. I could see it in their faces. They had something important to say, but were not quite sure how to approach me. Ben, calm and polite in nature, awkwardly stammered, "I told Kerry I didn't want to see those pictures!" I wondered what he meant. What pictures? He continued, "I really didn't want to look at them, but it's so hard when they are right there on my phone." It suddenly became clear. Just a few days prior, a social worker in my school approached me concerning a student named Kerry. She had been sending nudes to various guys in school, followed by invitations for oral sex. As one of Kerry's teachers, I wasn't sure how to confront this issue. When I approached Kerry, she was in complete denial. What was I supposed to do? Find proof to show her? A teacher could lose their job or face criminal charges for having any misunderstood involvement in such cases. From a legal perspective, Kerry, as a minor, had created her own child pornography, correctly referred to as Child Sex Abuse Material (CSAM) or Child Exploitation Material (CEM). Should I get other teachers involved, despite it being a private matter? Would it be appropriate to call the police? Should I remain silent to protect her from possible backlash and public humiliation? Or was this just normal behavior among today's youth? As the conversation with Ben and Jenna unfolded, the severity of the situation became more apparent. Ben shared that Kerry had entrusted him with a dark secret. He insinuated that Kerry was struggling with severe depression, and that if things got bad enough, she had a plan in place to end her life.

Shock overwhelmed my body; I felt helpless. While I spent years getting equipped to become a teacher, nobody had ever taught me how to address issues concerning digital media. I didn't take any courses on how it influenced my students' social interactions, internal worlds, and sexual expression. While most of Kerry's escapades unfolded behind a screen, they obviously affected her interactions at school. Did the smartphone simply reveal underlying mental issues Kerry struggled with, or was it the source of her mental anguish and depression? Maybe she considered suicide because she knew there was no going back. Her most intimate moments were now and forever available to the masses on the wild plains of the digital frontier. ”

The New Digital Frontier

Without a doubt, new technology has drastically altered the way young people live their lives, express their sexuality, experience love, and maintain friendships. The smartphone readily at hand is now integrated into the lives of nearly half of the world's population.[11] As Melinda Gates, American philanthropist and former general manager at *Microsoft* profoundly stated, "I spent my career in technology. I wasn't prepared for its effect on my kids."[12] What started with Steve Jobs premiering the iPhone in 2007 has now defined an entire generation. In many ways, the iPhone has created a smartphone arms race of epic proportions. Bigger screens, sharper photos, lightning-fast data plans, and the ability to be constantly connected have transformed the social fabric of society. The smartphone provides highly stimulating forms of social media, the most gripping and immersive online gaming platforms, and a virtual red-light district that offers an unlimited selection of sexual experiences to anyone holstering the pocket-sized powerhouse.

Kerry never knew a time without the internet. She is part of Generation Z, born after 1996, a generation that has had media technology readily available since infancy and entered their teenage years with a smartphone in their pocket. It is the first generation that finds it completely normal to talk through a screen, date through

RUMB Challenge

Before you jump into any discussion, we encourage you to set aside one week to intentionally observe and take note of any screen activities your teens engage in.

Pay close attention to the games, social media platforms, influencers, and apps they interact with to gain a better understanding of the draw of online entertainment.

The goal is to relate, not to be judgmental.

a screen, and even have sex with the help of a screen. According to *Common Sense Media*, Generation Z spends a staggering nine hours a day consuming various forms of online media entertainment.[13] This is more than the average time spent sleeping, and far more than the physical time teens spend with one another.[14] The number of teens who meet up on a regular basis has plummeted by more than forty percent between 2000 and 2015. Today's youth are learning that the screen is the modern-day portal into community living. "I think we hang out less," confessed seventeen-year-old Mia, "cause you talk with them on social media and you don't feel obligated to go out of your house to see someone if you have been talking with them every day." Generation Z is less social than Baby Boomers, Gen Xers, and Millennials were when they were the same age.[15] Typical teenage activities, such as getting together to hang out, going to the mall or the movies, cruising around, and even dating and having sex have become increasingly less common.[16] One *Pew Research Center Survey* found that thirty-five percent of twelve- to seventeen-year-olds admitted that they seldom interact with their friends face-to-face, while sixty-three percent relied on texting as the primary form of communication.[17]

When teenagers hang out, smartphones dictate their time, interaction, and activities. Conversation tends to revolve around a screen, and digital media interruptions are the norm. Navigating between different apps, tabs, texts, and the constant stream of information, updates, and entertainment make it virtually impossible to fully focus on the person right in front of you. According to a study published in Environment and Behavior, merely the presence of a smartphone negatively affects the quality of a conversation.[18] Like a cowboy and his six-shooter, the smartphone is drawn with the snap of the wrist and the tap of a finger, always at the ready, armed even at one's

RUMB Challenge

Assess the relationships in your life by using the UCLA loneliness scale. You can find the quiz here: https://psychcentral.com/quizzes/loneliness-quiz/

Reflect on the question: Does tech strengthen my core relationships? Why? Why not?

bedside.[19] There is a war over our attention as work, school, friendships, free time activities, and volunteer work are streamlined through one device. In a study conducted by Cigna in 2018 that surveyed 20,096 adults, Generation Zers (eighteen- to twenty-two-year-olds) expressed that the relationships in their lives aren't meaningful and they don't experience true companionship. Almost seven out of ten Gen Zers feel that the people they interact with are not fully present when they are together, and admitted that they do not have anyone in their lives who knows them well. About six in ten Gen Zers feel an absence of closeness with the people around them.[20] Boring moments, awkward situations, stress, anxiety, as well as family and friends fade behind the screen of the ever-present smartphone. Can anybody compete with an unlimited supply of engineered stimulation designed to activate our brain's reward system and deliver immediate results?

"I wish I lived in the 80s!" Emilia proclaimed. As a tall, strawberry blonde twenty-one-year-old girl with an inviting smile, I was surprised by her statement. She went on to tell me, "It's that time before new technology like social media existed. People actually hung out. They went to parties and danced. They talked until early morning without any smartphone interruptions. There wasn't that constant pressure to always be on, post a *selfie,* and immediately respond to the online chatter." She explained that her friends would get upset if she didn't comment or like their stuff on social media. If she wanted to fit in and be a part of the group, she needed to play along.

The Loneliness Epidemic

An epidemic of loneliness has been sweeping through Western societies.[21] According to *Cigna*, Generation Z is the loneliest of all generations, followed by Millennials. Six in ten generation Zers feel isolated and alone.[22] More than half of them reported feeling socially disconnected from the people surrounding them.[23] While they are hyperconnected, their lives are a relational wasteland. Vivek Murthy, an American Surgeon General, writes, "We live in the most technologically connected age in the history of civilization, yet rates of loneliness have doubled since the 1980s."[24] In January 2018, the U.K. appointed a Minister for Loneliness as they became aware of the crisis among young and old alike. It would be wrong to blame the present loneliness crisis solely on technology. Loneliness arises out of a complex mix of underlying social currents such as growing individualism, increased single households, economic and academic pressure, and less time available to spend with loved ones.[25] However, the unlimited supply of engineered stimulation that connects us with each other tends to be more about sharing than deeply caring. This bombardment of digital stimuli has taught a generation to first turn to a device, rather than another person. Loneliness decreases one's ability to self-regulate,[26] which is why people who often feel lonely are more prone to eating fatty foods or seeking out sexual encounters to numb their pain.[27] In a similar way, digital media can become the band-aid of choice to cope with feelings of isolation. I talked to a professional counselor about this rising generation. She shared her understanding, that "If people do not learn how to build healthy attachments with a human counterpart, they are much more prone to developing an addiction." A recent study published in the *Journal of Preventive Medicine* analyzed social media use and perceived social isolation among 1,787 U.S. adults ages nineteen to thirty-two. It found that the more time people spend on social media, the more isolated and lonely they felt.[28] In other words, putting a digital device into the hands of someone who feels isolated is like pouring gasoline on the fire of loneliness. Posting a picture of yourself when feeling lonely might initially soothe the pain of not feeling seen, but most often intensifies the feeling that everyone knows how you look, but nobody truly knows you.

By the time kids reach middle school, they can connect to digital outlets in myriad ways. At the beginning of the school year, I would ask my fifth grade students about their free time activities. Hardly anyone could think of a hobby apart from gaming or social media. The peaks and valleys of their days were conveyed through status updates, filters on Instagram, and quick check-ins on Snapchat. Ninety-five percent of teenagers ages twelve to seventeen are now online. Eighty percent of those teenagers use social media sites[29] such as Facebook, YouTube, Instagram, TikTok, Whisper, Omegle, Snapchat, Reddit, and Twitter. Nine out of ten teenagers play video games daily.[30] Their lives online dominate their social interactions. As Gina, a sixteen-year-old high school student, told me, "We don't really meet in person anymore. We just message each other." Jean

Twenge, a renowned demographer who has researched generations for decades, even goes as far as to say, "Online friendship has replaced offline friendship."[31] For many, life in the digital world feels more real than life offline.

Nomophobia

Lisa

I could not believe what unfolded in front of my eyes. "I hate you! I hate everybody! I hate this whole school," Emma screamed as she attacked her headmaster and ripped her smartphone out of his hands. I had known Emma as a kind, amiable, and outgoing 13-year-old teenager. She was an outspoken, feisty brunette who was well-liked among her peers. Ten minutes prior, Emma had received a phone call during art class and could not resist answering, despite calls being strictly forbidden. In accordance with school policy, the phone was to be turned over to the secretary and retrieved after the school day was over. If the rule was broken three consecutive times, a parent or guardian would have to pick it up from the office. This was exactly what happened to Emma. She knew her parents would not have time to pick up the phone that afternoon, and she would have to wait until the next day to get it back. The scene ended with Emma ripping her sim card out of her phone while taunting the headmaster that she had two backup phones at home, and he couldn't keep her from using those.

What took place that day is a phenomenon known as *nomophobia* that many teachers, social workers, and parents around the world witness daily. Nomophobia is an emerging field of study which revolves around feelings of anxiety and distress when not having access to a smartphone. It had caused Emma to panic and behave in ways that were completely out of character. Emma could not imagine spending half a day without her smartphone, inciting her to behave inappropriately. According to *Common Sense Media*, fifty percent of Generation Zers describe themselves as "self-identified digital device addicts."[32]

RUMB Challenge

Leave your phone in a drawer for five hours. Was this challenging? Why or why not? How did you spend your time without your phone?

Experts working in the field of technology found that the environment and circumstances of the present digital age "are far more conducive to addiction than anything humans ever discovered in history."[33] Adolescents are especially prone to developing a tech dependency, or even an addiction.

Nothing Is Off Limits

The internet and the ubiquitous smartphone have flung the gates to the adult world wide open. Nothing is off limits. Young, curious minds who believe they are ready to discover the world can now learn about relationships and sex, try out online personas, and connect with whomever they want to, including friends, friends of friends, or strangers. In the midst of an age that is all about discovering who you truly are and where you fit, with emotions surging, there are virtually no limits to what they can get their hands on. This urge is especially compelling for teenagers who strive for independence, because this world is theirs, secretly tucked away from adult supervision, and likely their only source of true privacy. What once was a battle that sounded like, *"Mom, can I please go . . . ?"* is now a readily available world that unfolds behind the closed doors of a child's bedroom. Teenagers use phrases such as, *"I just need to de-stress," "I'm just gonna check something real quick," or "I need this for homework"* as excuses to never put their phone away. Whereas a TV appears to be very dominant in the room, an obvious distraction, a smartphone in your hand has a different feel to it. While just ten years ago, parents would set limits on watching TV, the smartphone is often perceived as less invasive; an educational tool that is connecting us to the world and *real* people. Megan Moreno, leader of social media and adolescent health research at Seattle Children's Hospital, comments on the present dynamics, "In the olden days, your mom told you to get off the family phone or turn off the TV, and you did it. This time, kids are in the driver's seat."[34]

The Death of Empathy?

On July 9, 2017, a tragic story hit the global press. A man drowned in Cocoa, Florida, as five teenage boys watched and recorded the scene, laughing and mocking him as he screamed for help. The video surfaced on a social media site. Nobody stepped in, nobody called for help, nobody even acknowledged the severity of the situation.[35] It was as if it wasn't real because it happened behind a screen. This cruel scenario left many wondering: Was this just a terrible one-time incident, or did it reveal something deeper about a crippled culture? A meta-analysis of seventy-two studies involving 13,737 participants found that empathy declined dramatically among college students between 1979 and 2009, with the biggest drop occurring after the year 2000.[36] It is scientifically proven that there is a link between a lack of empathy and time spent in front of screens.[37] Children learn empathy by seeing how their words and actions affect the person in front of them.

Lisa

"My son's playmate had the habit of throwing sand in other kids' faces. She would see her victims cry when the sand got in their eyes. The tears and discomfort of her playmates were important indicators of inappropriate behavior. Her mom addressed the hurtful behavior, and the daughter soon adjusted her actions. Empathy grows as children learn how selfish acts affect people around them. Hitting someone or bullying typically results in direct negative consequences, often through an adult watching; yet, indirect communication through a screen does not provide the same type of feedback. The distance and control allow teens to lash out or attack others through indirect channels of communication. The safety felt behind the glass of the screen paves the way for cyberbullying, online harassment, and cruelty. An investigative journalism team in Germany wanted to know what students exchanged in their school messaging chats. They were shocked to discover aggressive violence (one clip showed a dog that was brutally beaten and kicked), deeply offensive and even illegal images inspired by the Nazi regime, racist imagery, and even child abuse images. No adult seemed to notice or step in while the deeply degrading images were forwarded to hundreds of classmates, with students being incredibly numb to the content they received. Nobody even realized that the possession of these images was a violation of the law.[38] If you believe this type of behavior is unique to Germany, you are wrong. If your child uses any social media app like TikTok, know that they will not only engage in an innocent lip-syncing app, but they will also be exposed to extremely racist, anti-Semitic, xenophobic, and homophobic content. Objectification, hyper-sexualization, and pornification of girls are the norm because users know the more sexual, shocking, and entertaining the uploaded content is, the faster the audience grows. ”

Sex Education 2.0

The complex mixture of closeness and distance, immediacy and control, and vulnerability and anonymity has fundamentally changed social interaction among the present generation. Perhaps the greatest impact the internet has had on the social development and sexual expression of young people is their early introduction to sex through online pornography. For Generation Z, the internet has become the primary source for sex education. According to *CyberPsychology and Behaviour*, by the age of eighteen, ninety-three percent of boys and sixty-two percent of girls have consumed online pornography.[39] They get used to the thrill of sexualized images early on. By the time they hit puberty, most teenagers are so accustomed to expressing their sexuality by masturbating to porn that nine out of ten teenagers encourage or accept porn.[40] Youth ages thirteen to twenty-four believe that not recycling is worse than viewing pornography.[41] The average age of first encountering pornography is eleven, implying that many are much younger when they stumble upon it.[42] I've witnessed the disturbing effects of this first hand during my teaching career. One Tuesday morning, I saw two of my students, both eleven-year-old boys who were known for being hyperactive, stand in the middle of the classroom after recess and reenact a full-blown porno while the other kids stood around them, laughing.

Kids and teens are naturally curious about sex. Boys that type in *sex* or *boobs* into the search engine will find the most extreme, violent, and degrading content within seconds. Most teens hide their internet habits from their parents, and consuming porn is likely among them. Even before they hit puberty, many kids have seen it all. Just sit in any sex-ed class, and you will be dumbfounded by the things thirteen-year-olds discuss, such as women drinking sperm, gang bang, and bestiality. Clay Olson, founder of *Fight the New Drug*, talked about pornography in a student forum: "This material is more aggressive, more harmful, more violent, more degrading and damaging than any other time in the history of the world. And this generation growing up is dealing with it at an intensity and scale no other generation in the history of the world has ever had to."[43] Instead of understanding sex as the most intimate form of communication, youth learn that sex is a purely physical act, where care and affection are completely absent. Boys and girls alike are lured into a world where personal sexual pleasure and the well-being of others are separated by a glass screen. The degradation portrayed by mainstream porn, such as violence and humiliation, is watched behind a barrier, which allows users to focus on their own sexual gratification without having any feelings for those involved. Anyone watching would hopefully be jolted into vigilantism if they saw a woman who was sexually assaulted on the street; however, as a video on a mainstream porn site, this act is considered entertainment.

Unlike the popular assumption that porn inspires amazing sex, the opposite has been proven to be true. Perhaps that is the reason why the best sex is experienced among people ages sixty-four and older. In comparison, Generation Z is the least satisfied generation.[44] Could it be that the older generation is the most sexually satisfied because they grew up with less graphic sex? They had to use their imagination and tune into their partner to please each other. I am not advocating for teens to have more sex, but we need to ask ourselves why the upcoming generation is growing up sexually unsatisfied. As teachers, parents, and respected adults in our teens' lives, many of us have not yet learned how to address topics of sexuality and graphic sex. The mystery around sex has created a vacuum that makes pornography consumption even more intriguing to young, inquisitive minds. Porn sends confusing and often morbid messages about gender, as well as how to love and show affection. The stay-at-home order during Covid-19 only intensified the tension of virtual sexual expression. Revenge porn has been soaring during the coronavirus lockdown.[45] The present generation is so accustomed to sex without the context of intimacy that it is starting to be less about human expression and increasingly about the interaction with devices and machines. One study on single people in America found that twenty-five percent of all adult participants are open to sex with sex robots.[46]

Digital Dating

Without a doubt, the internet has turned the dating world upside down. Justin Garcia, who works at *Indiana University's Kinsey Institute for Research in Sex, Gender and Reproduction*, says, "Suddenly, instead of meeting through proximity, community connections, and family and friends, people could meet each other virtually and engage in any amorous activity with the click of a button."[47]

Jason

"James was a young man in his twenties when I first met him. He was gregarlous, and seemed to be well-respected in his community. Despite this fact, James devoted his existence to online gaming. He had essentially rejected the tangible world and replaced it with a much more exciting fantasy life. His place was a complete dump in every sense of the word. I was a social integration specialist with a tough assignment. I was asked to more or less save James' life by pulling him back into reality. He had neglected every standard of healthy living to the point where his diet and lifestyle left him looking like someone living in an internment camp. His apartment was covered in garbage and thousands of flies had infested every square inch of living space. During our meetings, he constantly talked about his girlfriend, Harper. It turned out that she was one of his online friends he had met on *World of Warcraft*. James and Harper played day and night. They conquered the online world together, which led to deeper feelings. Harper lived on the other side of the country, making it difficult to meet in person. A couple of months later, overcome by romantic feelings, James embarked on a long cross-country road trip to meet her. Unfortunately, their romantic flame didn't last long. She wasn't the woman he had met online. Brokenhearted, James drove back home. His *dragon princess warrior* was, in reality, a woman he had never truly known.

One of the fascinating aspects of life online is that you can be whoever you want to be; the strong hero defending a guild, the sexy, photoshopped *Insta-queen*, or a player messaging dozens of girls on a dating site. In reality, this is a pixelated, carefully crafted, and often distorted version of our true selves.

Today's teens are following James' and Harper's example of searching for a romantic spark online. *Yubo* (formerly *Yellow*), the so-called *Tinder for Teens*, is used by more than twenty million teenagers worldwide.[48] By the time teenagers enter college, the dating world largely migrates to *Tinder* and other dating or hookup sites. Image and looks are more important than ever as people first stumble upon our online personas before ever hearing our voices, seeing the way we interact with others, or learning about our interests and perspectives. Teenage girls get nostalgic when thinking back to a time when a boy would be expected to ask them out on a *real* date. ”

Digital Media and Well-Being

Culture is always evolving. Could it be that today's Generation Zers have found new ways to express friendship, romance, and sex? Do they represent an evolution in social and relational development? We live in a hyperconnected world where people are only a few introductions away from knowing one another. According to Facebook research, "[e]ach person in the world is connected to every other person by an average of three and a half other people,"[49] yet feelings of loneliness are skyrocketing among youth. Loneliness rarely travels alone. Generation Z is at the brink of the worst mental health crisis in decades.[50] The links between feelings of loneliness, depression, anxiety, and screen time are shockingly evident.[51] Apart from obesity, which has tripled since 1971 (a factor that can largely be attributed to sitting in front of screens), depression, suicide, anxiety, and sleep deprivation have been off the charts ever since the smartphone was introduced.[52] College campus counselors are completely overwhelmed, as they simply cannot respond to the present demand of students seeking advice on mental health issues.[53]

Johns Hopkins Health Review reported that the probability that youth under the age of twenty-five will fall into clinical depression increased by thirty-seven percent from 2005 to 2014.[54] While we have to be careful to claim causality, there is scientific evidence that the introduction of smartphones, the rise of social media, and unlimited hours spent in front of screens correlate with depression.[55] Young people are especially prone to develop depression as a consequence of technology overuse.[56] According to Dr. Laurel Williams, Chief of Psychiatry at Texas Children's Hospital, "There's a lack of community. There's the amount of time that we spend in front of screens and not in front of other people. If you don't have a community to reach out to, then your hopelessness doesn't have any place to go."[57]

In 2011, fifty percent of adolescents admitted that they were overwhelmed by anxiety in the past year. That number rose to sixty percent by 2016.[58] Teenagers constantly compare their online appearance and are anxious when it comes to public approval.[59] Girls are growing up in a world that rewards them for their appearance above everything else. Chief Executive of the *Royal Society of Public Health,* Shirley Cramer, states, "Social media has been described as more addictive than cigarettes and alcohol and is now so entrenched in the lives of young people that it is no longer possible to ignore it when talking about young people's mental health issues [. . .]."[60]

What unfolds on the wild plains of the digital frontier often occurs without any adult ever noticing or stepping in. Think about Kerry's short-sighted choice to share intimate photos over social media. These photos will never go away. Kerry will grow up one day to be a wiser, more mature adult, but the naked images could follow her for the rest of her life. These photos are perfect ammunition for online bullies or invitations to unwanted solicitations from sexual predators. This is a harsh reality for tweens and teens who feel pressured or coerced into making poor choices online. Kerry's concerning behavior and suicidal thoughts are not just unique to her story. While the homicide rate among teenagers has gradually gone down, the suicide rate has reached an all-time high. According to the CDC, it rose 56 percent between 2007 and 2017 among youth between the ages of ten and twenty-four.[61] Teenage girls are especially vulnerable to self-harm because of negative internet experiences. The suicide rate for girls between the ages of ten and fourteen has tripled between 1999 and 2014.[62] Admissions to children's hospitals due to suicidal thoughts and self-harming actions have doubled in the past decade, making up the second leading cause of death among youth.[63] Roughly half of teenagers who spend more than five hours a day on an electronic device report at least one suicide-related emotion or thought.[64]

It is challenging to prove whether technology causes mental illness, but it certainly intensifies the struggles that are already present in a teenager's life. However, there is increasing evidence that compulsive internet use negatively affects emotional regulation. A recent four-year-longitudinal study in Australia found that compulsive internet use causes emotional dysregulation, such as struggling to make sense of one's emotions or the ability to set and pursue life goals.[65]

We live in a day and age where image trumps intimacy, quantity is valued over quality, and emojis replace physically laughing and crying together.

We live in a day and age where image trumps intimacy, quantity is valued over quality, and emojis replace physically laughing and crying together. Technology will never fulfill the relational void. Young people feel hyper-connected, but oddly alone. Countless youth learn early to turn to screens rather than a friend or a family member when feeling stressed, bored, lonely, or needing advice. Indirect communication is favored over face-to-face encounters, which results in a lack of focus on social awareness and conversational skills that pave the way to a successful life. For teenagers, screens are a source of inspiration and an escape from the inevitable frustrations of life. With technology and all its appealing benefits, kids and teens have not yet learned how to intentionally interact with it, but rather react to it. As Melinda Gates said, "Phones and apps aren't good or bad by themselves, but for adolescents who don't yet have the emotional tools to navigate life's complications and confusions, they can exacerbate the difficulties of growing up: learning how to be kind, coping with feelings of exclusion, taking advantage of freedom while exercising self-control."[66]

The rising generation does not need adults to frenzy in a moral panic or ignore the rapid changes of the technological world. They need advocates who help them navigate the problems they face online. It is up to us to step in and become the trail guides this rising youth so desperately need. The discussion surrounding digital media needs to be centered around the goals and values that can lead a teenager towards physical, mental, and relational well-being. The current trend towards unchecked digital indulgence requires all of us to enter a wider public debate about the keys to a prosperous life and healthy media choices.

Discussion Guide:

1. In your opinion, why is Gen Z considered the loneliest of all generations?
2. What are some screen habits that propel you forward in life?
3. What are screen habits that limit your potential to live life to its fullest?
4. What would life look like for you if you took a week-long break from screens? Would you be motivated to try new things?
5. Why has empathy declined drastically since high-speed internet was first introduced? Are people crueler online? Why? Why not?
6. Have you ever consumed something online that has negatively affected your mental health? How?

Chapter 2: Wired for People, not Pixels

The teenage idol and DJ Tim Bergling, also known as *Avicii,* was no stranger to success. His lead single, *Wake Me Up*, has accumulated more than one billion plays on Spotify. On April 25th, 2018, while vacationing in Oman, the twenty-eight-year-old took his own life. *Avicii* seemingly had everything, yet to him, it felt like nothing. In the end, it didn't matter that he was a social media icon adored by millions of fans, worshipped as one of the greatest talents in the industry, and sought after by beautiful women around the globe.[67] When the sum of our lives is laid out before us, our accomplishments are not nearly as important as the answers to these three questions: Have I been loved? Was I able to love? Did my life have meaning and purpose? It all starts with an honest evaluation of the values that have our fervent yes.

Values Online

Core values should be central to a teenager's interactions with digital media because they protect the things that matter most in life, such as friends, family, or significant others. As Brené Brown, leading expert in the field of vulnerability and empathy, put it:

> Living into our values means that we do more than profess our values, we practice them. We walk our talk—we are clear about what we believe and hold important, and

RUMB Challenge

Choose three core values you live by:

Authenticity – Honesty – Hope
Courage – Commitment
Faithfulness – Follow-Through
Grace – Truth – Integrity
Willingness – Humility – Love
Respect – Discipline
Perseverance – Service
Kindness – Justice – Consistency
External Focus – Mindfulness
____________?

How do these values impact your online choices?

For a more extended list of values, visit wiredhuman.org

we take care that our intentions, words, thoughts, and behaviors align with those beliefs.[68]

It takes courage and compassion to intervene in a cyberbully situation. It requires love and respect to say no to porn and yes to our current or future partner. A value for humility keeps us accountable for admitting when we are wrong, even when separated by a glass screen. There is a major disconnect between the values teenagers practice online and the ones they hold dear in their offline lives. The tragedy is that many of the negative practices lived out online gradually sift into real-life interactions.

Capitol Hill

Most of us are not fully aware of the impact that culture, power, and desires have on influencing the personal values that shape our lives. You need thick skin to survive on Capitol Hill, but not always for the reasons you might imagine. For many, proximity to power means everything. Despite the fact that there are great leaders on Capitol Hill who commit their lives to making the world and our country a better place, there are those who seem to be locked in a desperate race to feel significant and to be known by what they do. The rules of the Hill demand that you quickly divulge your occupational ranking so people can gauge if the interaction is worth their time. The influence you attain through your career can easily become the defining aspect of your identity. If you aren't careful, proximity to power and influence will become the most important thing in your life. If we are

RUMB Challenge

Examine your most valued asset: time.

Use the media time calculator:

https://www.healthychildren.org/English/media/Pages/default.aspx#calculator

How many hours are dedicated to what you love? How many hours a day propel you forward in life? How many hours do you spend using technology?

reduced to what we do Monday through Friday, our career becomes the center of our lives. The fruit of such a life is to have your identity wrapped up in who you know and what your job title says about you. The core values from which we live our lives can unwittingly become aligned with a very different vision and purpose than we once had. In a similar way, digital media comes with its own set of values that can interfere with what is actually important to us. Instant gratification, anonymity, and unhinged freedom present an entirely new set of opportunities for self-indulgence, which has the potential to override our core values. If teens are not empowered with a values-first attitude, their online choices are anchored to nothing, making them vulnerable to the aimless will of the wild web. Pioneers know the destination they want to arrive at and approach the wilderness with intentionality to reach their goal. How many teens are pioneering the digital age rather than becoming lonely wanderers of the web? Are teens allowing devices to dictate their core values, or are we empowering them to align their technology usage with the life-giving values that have their *unwavering yes*?

Our most Valuable Asset

Our time is the most valuable asset we have. It is the one resource that we cannot earn back once it is spent. How we use this resource is largely dictated by what we feed our mind and heart. What we store up in our internal world will eventually spill over into our public lives. What values are driving our teens' media choices, and in turn, what effects do their choices have on their internal development?

With the introduction of modern media that inundates them for most of their waking moments, technology often has a deeper connection with our teens than we do. It is competing for their most valuable assets: time and meaningful relationships; the very elements of life that our core values should be protecting. This rising generation is in a battle between relationships with people and pixels. The winner of this fight will dictate the course of their lives and the fruit of their success in the seasons to come.

Farm of Brothers

Jason

"Lucas was fresh out of high school. Full of youthful charisma, he greeted me with direct eye contact and a firm handshake, something I rarely experience from teenagers. He was the perfect fit for his internship as a teaching assistant in a local school. He loved the challenge of taking on troubled youth and making a difference in their lives. There was something about Lucas that encapsulated the essence of youthfulness. When it came to technological consumption, he defied the status quo of his generation with confidence and passion. I asked Lucas how the teens he worked with reacted to him not using a smartphone; "Did this build a barrier between you and the kids?" Lucas laughed as he recalled their amazement and confusion that he still used an old *Nokia dumb phone* to stay in touch. "They thought I was crazy! They thought I was antisocial," he replied. The idea of doing life without social media was unthinkable. "We were eating lunch together in the cafeteria, and I asked the students to look around the room and tell me what they saw." Sure enough, all the teachers, social workers, and other assistants were glued to their smartphones, not even looking up to talk to one another. He recalled, "I was the only leader in the room who was sitting and talking with students." His point was simple and clear: people are more important than pixels.

I met Lucas in a little community in the far east of Germany called *the Bruderhof*, which translates roughly to *Farm of Brothers*. My family and I had arrived in the Holzland region in the far east of Germany, about an hour and a half away from the Czech Republic. It was as if we had been transported to a different time period. Many of the surrounding houses and farms told an ancient story from a simpler time, and the backdrop of rolling meadows and flowing fields was nothing short of picturesque. One of the brothers from Lucas' community had been patiently waiting to pick us up. He warmly greeted us and relieved us of our heavy bags. Our quest to discover a place where people lived in a community without digital distraction led us to join their world for a few days. *The Bruderhof* was birthed out of a small group of Christian pacifists who refused to serve the Nazi regime in the Second World War. It has since grown to roughly 3000 members, divided up into communities around the world. Members refer to one another as brothers and sisters because they see everyone in their community as belonging to the same family. They live together, eat together, sleep under the same roof, and even share their finances with one another. No one owns personal possessions. Their clothes are simple yet functional, and their living spaces are absent of laptops, tablets, or Wi-Fi. Instead of technological distractions, thousands of books line the walls of their in-house library. There is a refreshing sense of people being fully present in their conversations, daily tasks, or leisurely activities. There are no TVs running in the background or smartphones buzzing on tables. People are truly focused on other people. Technology use is productivity-driven, with internet access being allocated to their local office so as not to compete for people's attention.

After spending a few nights at *the Bruderhof*, I got the impression that members were genuinely content. However, there is a big difference between visiting *the Bruderhof* and becoming a full-fledged member. The members I spoke to acknowledged the challenges of community life, and even voiced that their greatest struggle was learning to get along with one another. Freedom is the price for unity and community. Personal gratification and goals yield to the interests of the group. This mentality to serve others and the overarching needs of *the Bruderhof* transfers to every element of daily living. However, the sacrifice of personal liberty, autonomy, and individualism was a price that they were willing to pay for the opportunity to be intimately known by each other; to belong to a group of people who deeply and sincerely cared for one another. Their focus on being available to one another sustained them. They had tapped into a highly valuable resource that can lead to a flourishing life: social capital.[69] Their riches weren't found in financial success or personal accomplishments, but rather in the people they called brother and sister.

Being at the *Bruderhof* reminded me of an era where community seemed simpler. People worked in smaller towns and knew their neighbors. Today, we are living in an age of growing individualism, unlimited consumerism, instant gratification, transience, neighborly isolation, distrust, and division. In many ways, we have become digital nomads; we are more connected to people behind the glass of a screen than the ones outside our doorstep. Today, values that support and strengthen the relationships with those dearest to us are often compromised for the sake of success and productivity.

The Bubble-Wrapped Generation

Childhood in the United States has drastically changed in the last few decades. We are raising a *bubble-wrapped* generation. There used to be a time where it was normal for kids to walk to school or play in a park. Now, letting our kids walk around the neighborhood seems careless. With terrible news all around, our culture has taught us to keep a constant eye on our kids and teens. Helicopter parenting is the norm in a world where a perceived danger is lurking around every corner, even though many of our neighborhoods are much safer than they were decades ago. According to the FBI, the violent crime rate decreased by 51 percent between 1993 and 2018.[70]

Teenagers are growing up in highly regulated, supervised, and scheduled environments. Access to friends is limited due to their overly structured lives and limited geographic freedom. This generation is used to boundless electronic entertainment, yet failing to launch into a life of their own where self-reliance, forged through diverse real-life encounters, is fundamental.[71]. Nebraskan senator and best-selling author, Ben Sasse, reflects, "[There is a] societal affluence that allows us to 'entertain ourselves to death' [...]. How do we awaken an aspiration to self-disciplined independence when the neighbors' kids are almost all suffering from the same affluenza?"[72]

The Essence of Human Flourishing

Many have lost what the people of *the Bruderhof* community modeled so beautifully; "[...] relations are the essence of human flourishing."[73] Despite the growing distance, people are largely unaware of how crucial their ties to each other are for their mental and physical health. Do teenagers' core values protect and cherish relationships in the digital age? Social media, gaming, and pornography are transforming how young people experience, practice, and value vulnerability, intimacy, and trust, which has a direct impact on the inward development of their hearts and minds. Screens are a proxy through which people can represent themselves, but they are not the essence of a heart-to-heart interaction.

After week three of the stay-at-home order, I got hit by a severe "Zoom fatigue." I was tired of staring at myself instead of truly locking eyes with someone. I was tired of the awkward silence after sharing a vulnerable thought. I was tired of not being able to pick up on nonverbal cues the way I used to. I was tired of conversation being the only piece that fueled my connection with others. If anything, the pandemic revealed that the health of our friendships needs more than pixels on a device; they require the entirety of our personhood. Too often, friendships in the digital age are driven by *likes*, *Gifs*, and *emojis*. If our core values are not protecting the sanctity of relationships, mental and physical health deteriorate.

A lack of meaningful relationships severely harms mental and physical health, rivaling the dangers of well-documented health risks such as high blood pressure, obesity, cigarette smoking, and lack of regular exercise.[74,75] People who have weak or limited social ties are statistically more likely to be diagnosed with cardiovascular disease, cancer, and report slower recovery from injuries.[76] A meta-analytic review of 148 independent studies consisting of more than 300,000 participants revealed that social ties are a key predictor of mortality, indicating that those who steward healthy relationships well are fifty percent more likely to live to their golden years than those who lack intimacy with others.[77]

Despite the fact that we live in the most technologically advanced age, our life expectancy has decreased three years in a row, from 2014 to 2017.[78] Kathryn McHugh of Harvard Medical School concluded, "We're seeing the drop in life expectancy not because we're hitting a cap [for lifespans of] people in their eighties, [but] because people are dying in their twenties [and] thirties."[79] The main contributors are rising suicides rates and opioid-related deaths; both signs of a lack of community, support, and failed mental health care at a societal level.

If we are not encouraging teens to grab on to fundamental truths that will shape their healthy internal development, then we are setting an entire generation up for disaster. What we consume through smartphones has a direct impact on our internal being, and this will always seep its way into how we live and manage our lives. This is why digital media is such a crucial topic to tackle during adolescent years. The media our teens devour is a portal to their hearts and minds. Our lives are lived from the inside out, not from the outside in.

The Harvard Study of Adult Development, enduringly known as *The Grant Study*[80], is one of the world's longest ongoing longitudinal studies, with close to eighty years of data collected. In the midst of the Great Depression, scientists chose 268 Harvard sophomores to follow throughout the entire course of their adult lives. Notable subjects of the study included former president John F. Kennedy and well-known former editor of *The Washington Post* Ben Bradlee. The study revealed that close social connections are far greater determinants of one's physical-mental health and overall happiness throughout life. Relationships outranked wealth, fame, IQ, social class, and genetics. Robert Waldinger, a psychiatrist serving as the current director of the Harvard Study of Adult Development, found that a lack of social ties or loneliness is a more dangerous killer than smoking or alcoholism.[81] Harvard News reported Waldinger stating, "'Good relationships don't just protect our bodies; they protect our brain.'"[82] He went on to clarify that the relationships observed throughout the study were far from perfect. For example, couples who frequently bickered were still beneficial to each other's mental health and physical longevity, "as long as they felt that they could count on the other when the going got tough."[83] A meta-analytic review of nineteen studies found that a lack of social interactions increased the risk of dementia by fifty-seven percent.[84] In a 2009 interview with *The Atlantic*, George Vaillant, who was the longest-serving director of the Grant Study (1972-2004), was asked to identify the most important findings. He responded, "The only thing that really matters in life are your relations to other people."[85] He stated, "I was finding hard data to support the fact that your relationships are the most important single thing in your well-being."[86] From an economic standpoint, the men of the Grant Study who were rated highest for having warm relationships earned an incredible $141,000 more per year than those who were rated poorly for their lack of social connections.[87] We are not often taught that neglecting relationships can be more destructive to our health than choking down cigarettes, dieting on junk food, or taking up couch-surfing as a sport. Today's teenagers belong to the loneliest generation ever

The media our teens devour is a portal to their hearts and minds.

recorded in comparison to any other previous generation at the same age.[88] We are raising up a generation that has been taught to have it all together for their college applications, but their social development and the role that relationships play in their mental and physical health are widely overlooked.

Do We Consume Technology, or Does it Consume Us?

The average American spends an equivalent of forty-nine days a year in front of their mobile devices and tablets.[89] This equates to ten and a half years of their average lifespan devoted to screens. Replace *average American* with *teenager*, and the results are sobering. Teens give up over thirty-seven percent of their life to screens.[90] Long gone are the days of indulging in a few hours of Saturday morning cartoons before mom threw us out of the house. We consume technology as voraciously as it consumes us. A friend and leader in the field of internet communication systems told me, "The first four decades surrounding the development of the tech industry was about maximizing productivity, while the last decade of tech development has been the sheer opposite."

Perhaps the biggest downfall of our tech-savvy teens is their inability to engage with the people right in front of them and experience the fullness of relationships in their lives. A seventeen-year-old junior shared with me during our interview:

> I wish I lived in my grandparents' time. Just go out and run around the neighborhood. It probably wasn't really like that, but this is how I see it, and I see myself wasting a lot of time on social media. Now that I have only one year of high school left, I think it is so stupid, wasting all this time on a screen.

Jason

"It isn't hard to notice that we are frequently absorbed in our devices. While I was waiting to meet a friend at the Metro Center in Washington D.C., I took a moment to look around. Everyone was glued to their phone. I was surrounded by hundreds of people but felt completely disconnected. It only got worse when I boarded the metro. No small talk, no eye contact, no interaction. Everyone was in a different world, present in body, but completely checked out. Today, teenagers' social encounters are predominantly established by interacting through a device. Even when teens are physically together, many struggle to find ways to connect and entertain themselves without the involvement of a screen. They share the same space, but are essentially in their own world. Michelle, a junior in high school, recalled connecting with her peers at school:

> [E]veryone is just on their phones. So, I think if we didn't have our phones so much, we would have different relationships. [. . .] Sometimes when we are all on our phones, we all see something and then interact on some level, but we do not have real profound conversations.

Social media developers have done a brilliant job selling us the narrative that technology brings people closer together. It isn't a coincidence that Facebook creates ad campaigns that promise to provide a superior relational experience, where the depth of friendships is discovered. One campaign talks about the beauty of friendship, where friends "make us heroes in their *stories*, so we make their *likes* our *likes* and the things they *share* we share [so] we trust them just enough to *follow* [. . .], each shifts the trajectory of our lives simply by being our *friend*."[91] The campaign ends with sentimental music and the Facebook *friended* logo appearing on the screen, as if to say, this is what Facebook makes possible. Social media platforms such as Facebook, Instagram, and Snapchat are indeed effective tools for building initial connections, keeping in touch, and documenting the moments we share with others; however, they can only represent a fraction of a full, living friendship. No amount of *followers* on Instagram, retweets on Twitter, likes on Facebook, or subscribers on YouTube can fill the void that friendship, romantic love, and faithfulness can. Matthew Lieberman, a neuroscience professor at the University of California, Los Angeles (UCLA), argues that the human desire to belong, be in relationships, and commune with others is a fundamental basic human need that is just as relevant to our health as food, water, and shelter.[92] Herein lies the most profound reason internet media, such as social media, gaming, and pornography, are so enticing. Digital media preys on our teens' most fundamental longings and desires: to belong, to be known, and to be affirmed in who they are. It bombards them with surface-level connection and feigned feelings of conquest, but to no sustainable end. It provides no guidance for sustaining healthy relationships. Most relationships formed online never blossom in the real world.[93] Perhaps it is the lack of life-giving relationships that drives so many seemingly successful people to the black hole of substance abuse. Euro-American countries place career, notoriety, and academic success on a pedestal, creating the illusion that achievement will fill our deepest longings and desires. People are praised for who they present themselves to be, but feel insecure about who they are in their private lives."

Socially Bankrupt

No one is immune to the hardships of life, feelings of loneliness, or the struggle to find meaning in this world. News headlines are a constant reminder that the only perfect statistics are birth and death; money, success, and fame will not exempt a human being from this fact. We aren't designed to do life alone. As Waldinger concluded, loneliness is a lurking killer. We should evaluate whether our relationships are grounded in mutual care for each other's well-being. Which of our friends would go out of their way to look after us when we're sick? Who texts, calls, or visits us if we're unexpectedly absent from school or work?

Teens should consider what values and priorities dictate their online habits. Having a thousand-plus Instagram followers, a close network of gaming buddies, or a harem of online sexual fantasy partners means nothing if none of them would be there for them in their moment of need. This is overwhelmingly the story of teenagers growing up in the new digital frontier. They are hyper-connected, but socially bankrupt.

Without a doubt, there are countless prosocial ways to use digital technology. We can check in, write encouraging messages, inspire, and document time spent together. However, loneliness is a festering crisis on the verge of becoming a global pandemic. It is not the media content or platforms themselves that cause dysfunctional media consumption, but rather, the gaping void that no amount of *likes*, *friend requests*, gaming rankings, or pornography can fill. Digital media too often draws us away from true connection by blasting us with instant reward in exchange for our most valuable assets: our time and ability to be present with the people around us.

Pixels and Presence

In a special *ABC News* report, Diane Sawyer and her team traveled across the United States to answer the question of how all this screen time is affecting American families and their relationships. A family from the Midwest allowed *ABC News* to install six cameras in their home to track their screen time and online media habits over the course of thirty hours. The parents were well-educated and successful in their career fields. As soon as their three teenagers would come home from school, they would immediately find their devices. The mom said they used to enforce family screen time rules, but those boundaries were slowly worn down over time. Her only remaining wish was for them to share the evenings together. At night, the family would gather in the living room, present in body but absent in mind. The gestures of kindness and affirmation she poured into her kids went completely unnoticed. No conversation, no eye contact, no laughter or discussion of the day's events. It was surreal to see how the teens could spend up to five hours at a time plopped on a sofa and glued to their screens without physically moving or even acknowledging what was happening in the house. Even when their grandfather came to visit, the devices took priority. Throughout the documented time, the youngest son spent nearly twelve hours on his device, playing *Fortnite* most of that time. The oldest son spent fourteen hours behind screens, even sneaking out of bed to get a few more hours of gaming time in before sunrise. The daughter logged twelve and a half hours mostly using Instagram and Snapchat. The parents each spent five and a half hours on social media.[94] As overwhelming as these numbers might sound, this family's battle with technology is no exception. Their situation strikes a similar chord with what most American families are going through. I know I have often been the one in my family lying on our sofa, fixated on a device as the world passes me by. My two-year-old son is bent on destroying my laptop, always ready to take a swing at it if he is close enough. He knows these devices are his main competition for my attention.

When digital connection hijacks real-life encounters where people are fully engaged, society loses. Digital media tells us that connection is the same as relationship. Teenagers see the thousands of "friends" they have amassed online. Users can track the "likes" and feedback they get for their photo uploads in real time. They collect "followers", and even masturbate to a never-ending entourage of sex workers performing whatever their lust desires. However, the craving for being known remains unfulfilled.

Relationships Unpacked

Building relationships is hard work. It requires us to invest our time and to be vulnerable by trusting others to lovingly receive who we truly are. If we don't think critically about our values, relationships will never take the front seat. There is a widely known Chinese fable that refers to friends as, "Those I have sat down with and consumed an entire sack of salt." The moral is clear. It takes time and investment to get to know the depth of the person you call a friend. Internet media offers instant connection with little risk. Young people temporarily numb their anxieties and trade them for pixels, but the investment of their time and attention has little substantive return. Digital media is a consumable product, and therefore, engineered to be relentlessly appealing. Social media sites, gaming platforms, and especially pornography all function with the purpose of providing instant gratification to make its users addicted. The longer youth are online, the more money the industry makes, and the less youth learn that stewarding meaningful relationships, not connection bombardment, is a better way to cope with the inevitable struggles of life.

Teens learn to compensate for this lack of offline interaction with exaggerated punctuation and *emojis*, while the nuances of in-person communication, such as facial expressions, tone of voice, and body language are rapidly becoming a lost art. When I met seventeen-year-old Kathy at a coffee shop, she reflected on her generation's interaction through devices, "You don't have that same emotional connection with someone that you have been talking with through a screen instead of hanging out with them."

Most communication is expressed without words. Based on two studies conducted by Albert Mehrabian, some scholars argue that more than ninety percent of communication is nonverbal.[95] True communication requires a combination of tone, body posture, melodic rhythm, social setting, and facial expressions for the words to come alive. A person's eyes are the windows to their soul. They reveal one's true emotional state of being. When a person is romantically interested in someone, their pupils dilate in response to the excitement they feel.[96] The eyes also reveal when one is faking their emotions. You can smile all you want, but your eyes usually tip the other person off if your emotions are not authentic.

Jason

"My Chinese language professor was in her late 60s. We were tackling the theme of romantic love in the Mandarin dialect. She taught our class that the word *love* is rarely used among those belonging to her generation. She proudly claimed that throughout their forty-five years of marriage, her husband has never said that he loves her. Rather, he shows her his love through his actions, choices, and commitment to their relationship. She explained that words are cheap. She would rather see love in their relationship than hear the words, "I love you." This example is a bit extreme, but illuminates the importance of action in relationships; written texts and spoken words can only represent what is already present in a relational dynamic. They need to be supported by action; otherwise, they are meaningless.

I once worked a part-time job at a restaurant to pay my school tuition and make ends meet. One of my coworkers and fellow classmates went out of her way to gain my attention. She would text me dozens of times a day, and even skipped some of her classes to come sit with me in my own lectures. I interpreted her endless texting as a flattering expression of being interested in me. After a while, I sent her a bold message to meet up for coffee, on a live date. My goal was to have a real conversation and get to know her better. Unfortunately, I had misinterpreted her intentions. It seemed she was not interested in pursuing an actual relationship, but only a virtual *flirtationship*. My attempt to escalate things to real life was rejected, via text message, of course. I was confused. I reviewed the hundreds of texts she sent me, and could not make heads or tails of what went wrong. Looking back, the flirty texting was probably, in her mind, a fun game or perhaps an ego boost that she did with many other guys on a regular basis. One thing I did learn, like my Chinese professor told me: words, and in this case texts, are *cheap*."

The Communication Maze

Indirect communication by way of technology allows for maximum control over the conversation. As the internationally recognized psychologist Catherine Steiner-Adair put it, "The worst thing about teen texting culture is that it is unacceptable to call or ask a direct question."[97] Roughly a third of teenagers between twelve and seventeen have broken up or have been broken up with via text message, despite the fact that it is largely looked down upon among peers.[98] When asked about breaking up over a device, one middle schooler commented:

> I think it's easier to break up with them [this way] because you don't have to see them if they get sad. If you see them getting emotional, then you'll feel bad and be harder on yourself to break up with them.[99]

I met Bella in a local restaurant to ask her about the effects digital media had on her generation. Bella was outgoing, talkative, and conversed well. She was deeply concerned about her generation communicating mostly through screens. She admitted that so often she writes "*LOL*" in a text message or sends a laughing smiley emoticon when in reality she sits alone, feeling numb to her emotions.

Lisa

"One afternoon, a mother of one of my students had scheduled a meeting with me. As we sat down in the empty classroom, she looked deeply troubled. She could not believe what she had found on her son's phone. Luke, a fifteen-year-old, strong-willed boy with a skilled business mind, had been pulling his classmates into his latest money-making scheme. His temper would occasionally get out of control when his classmates couldn't pay up. While he knew he couldn't get away with mocking kids in school, he would use the voice recording function on his phone to leave hateful messages for fellow students. It took months before the mom of a threatened student finally found out what was going on and sat down with me to seek help. Digital avenues allow for things to be said that nobody would ever have the guts to say in person. Cruelty, shaming, mocking, cyberbullying, and revenge are omnipresent in our kids' online universe.

Sauder School of Business at the *University of British Columbia* found that texting made it significantly more tempting to disappoint someone or back out of a promise to preserve one's own interests. During an experiment, the instructors challenged students to unload fictional stocks with their classmates, knowing that they were about to go bust. Some deals were made in person, while others through text messages. Deals done via text message were thirty-one percent more likely to contain lies. Digital media makes misunderstandings, excuses, and in some cases, lying easier. I have observed a dramatic shift in follow-through and commitment while working with teens and young adults. It has become common to cancel last minute via text. Removing the face-to-face encounter makes it easy to opt out without fully acknowledging the consequences of their decision.

When teenagers don't learn to prioritize values and protect their relationships, their emotional development will be stunted. If everything is solved through a text message, it will be significantly harder for them to learn healthy conflict resolution skills. Is it possible that the state of their internal being is relationally malnourished? How will this impact them in their public lives? What are the implications of a relationally starving generation rising into the ranks of our society? The spoken word music video by Prince Ea, *Can we auto-correct humanity?* received over twenty million views on YouTube. One teenager left a riveting comment:

RUMB Challenge:

It takes at least seven uninterrupted minutes for a conversation to go past superficial. Try to put your phone away for ten minutes and ask your conversation partner to do the same. Did you notice a difference in the quality of your time spent together?

> I started crying. I am fourteen years old and my family raised me around technology my whole life. When I was six, I was addicted to the computer and already had my own phone. I was always the shy girl and the kid who didn't talk at family parties. Fast forward four years and my whole life is a mess. I forgot how to communicate like everyone else, I just don't know how to. I look at other people and how they talk their butts off, and wonder, 'How do they do that?[100]

Research shows that it takes at least seven uninterrupted minutes for a conversation to go past superficial.[101] If the average teenager checks their device every three minutes, what chances, if any, do they have of reaching a place of intimacy, vulnerability, and trust?

A mass-migration of kids and teens have retreated to the online world to carry out most of their social and sexual communication. So much of our human expression is delivered in a moment when we are fully present in mind, body, and spirit. We shake each other's hands. We hug and embrace one another. We can sense how our friends are doing when they walk in the room. We can see their body posture, their facial expressions, and hear the tone of their voice. A high school junior told me that she can always tell which families have created a healthy media culture. Teens who grew up in families with a high value for authentic social interactions are open and excited about engaging in a conversation. If not, they seem disinterested from the start, barely looking up to make eye contact, don't really ask questions, and quickly retreat back to their screens. Throughout my interviews and casual encounters with teachers, I have had the opportunity to ask them about what they believed was the greatest challenge facing this rising generation. Their answers were strikingly similar: "Kids and teens don't know how to do friendship or social engagement in real life."

Vulnerability Matters

Digital media allows anyone to spill their guts online. Youth pour out their hearts in forums, on social media, and through messaging apps. However, their relational vulnerability lacks risk, and therefore, depth. They are attempting to share intimacy from the safety of their bedrooms while sitting alone behind the protective barrier of a screen. Something is missing. Teenagers can date online and tell their crush everything about them, or even send nude photos to feign a level of intimacy, but inevitably, everyone feels the distance. The screen becomes a wall. They share their feelings, but they never know the raw and unfiltered response of the person with whom they are interacting. By controlling vulnerability from behind a screen, they don't develop the same level of intimacy as they would if risking vulnerability in the physical presence of another who sees them in their entirety. Being accepted in their unfiltered realness builds far deeper bonds than finding acceptance through the curated lives they present online.

The Netflix original series *Stranger Things* pulls us into a world where close relationships are fostered without the aid of a smartphone. The show takes place in the early 1980s in the small fictional town of Hawkins, Indiana. The lives of the characters are set in a pre-internet age where the humble walkie talkie was the closest form of digital connectivity available. The depictions of community and acceptance are enthralling as the adolescents forge their friendships, battling the challenges of pubescence the same way they combat a mysterious otherworldly monster: together. When the show first introduces the four male protagonists, they're playing the board game *Dungeons and Dragons*, a fantasy role-playing game. Even though they're just rolling dice and reading cards, there is something special happening. Where video games do the imagining for you, the boys are at liberty to use their imagination and get lost in a world of their own making. After playing the game for ten hours straight, they ride their bikes home and make plans to meet up the next day. The scene evokes a sense of wonder and nostalgia.

Jason

"I also grew up in a small town in the middle of nowhere. I had friends who played board games with me until our parents forced us to go to bed. As boys, we camped out alone in the woods. We imagined we were explorers claiming the land as our own. The only thing missing was a nifty theme song to hallmark a day in the life of a 90s kid. There was something authentic about growing up without digital distractions or pressure to photo-document every moment. There was a sense of innocence in our interactions. We had no access to the internet, so gaming wasn't much of a distraction either. Boredom drove us to explore abandoned farms and motivated us to get lost in over eighty acres of unclaimed land. The experiences of exploring uncharted territory bonded us. We didn't know it, but we belonged to a dying breed of teenager: a kind of teen that is now marketed on a modern hit TV series as novel. For us, vulnerability and acceptance unfolded in wild nature, rural forests, and abandoned barns. It was not just the words we shared, but the experiences we lived. We trusted each other when getting lost in the woods. We were able to show our true selves, even when getting just a little creeped out camping outside on our own. We were a generation whose lifestyle was soon to go extinct. A generation that has tasted and seen what it means to be human with all of our senses, without the buzzing of notifications in our pockets.

When it comes to nourishing a teenager's internal world, the stewarding of values such as vulnerability, intimacy, and trust is essential for developing meaningful relationships. John Joseph Powell, Author of *The Secret to Staying in Love*, said it best: "It is an absolute human certainty that no one can know his own beauty or perceive a sense of his own worth until it has been reflected back to him in the mirror of another loving, caring human being."[102]

Teens can formulate the right response, word the funniest status update, or post the perfect photo, but this curated version of themselves prevents others from seeing and accepting them for who they really are. Pursuing intimacy is not an easy undertaking, especially for teenagers who are in the process of developing their social skills. When teenagers feel safe and understood, they are more likely to become vulnerable, allowing others they trust to see a more intimate and unprotected version of themselves: *in-to-me-you-see*. Intimacy can be understood as the destination the relationship is heading towards, while vulnerability is the vehicle that drives them towards this destination. However, the very nature of becoming vulnerable is to permit the risk of getting hurt.

When intimacy and vulnerability go online, things can get messy. Being absent in body creates the illusion of being safe and in control. In reality, digital media enables exploitation and abuse. Consider Candace, a sixteen-year-old whose fleeting relationship was terminated with a text. One night, her boyfriend texted her that he was pursuing other women, simply because he thought Candace was not as attractive as other women he had met online. Candace broke down and fell to the ground, reeling from emotional pain. The following night, her ex-boyfriend posted pictures of himself on social media with a new girl he had gone out with. Candace felt broken inside. The pain was so unbearable that she felt it was easier to die than to keep on living, so she overdosed on antidepressants. Miraculously, her parents found her and took her to the hospital before it was too late.

Relationships that develop through face-to-face encounters come with a natural degree of accountability. Interactions are often public and observable by peers and adults. If someone exploits a relationship, there will hopefully be naturally occurring consequences. The design of empathy makes it harder for someone to verbally abuse a person who is standing right in front of them, because they will have to endure the fullness of that person's response. With the vast majority of interactions unfolding online, those safety rails vanish. Being physically removed from the situation allows for words to get out of control. Candace's boyfriend never saw how his actions broke her spirit. He never saw her fall to the ground; he never witnessed her sobbing, and he never watched her try to take her own life.

Vulnerability in a relationship can strengthen our bonds with one another, but it also has the potential to create excruciating pain if we are mistreated after exposing our most private selves. The latest research in the field of psychology reveals that being rejected by a romantic partner activates the pain center of the brain, giving a whole new meaning to the phrase "love hurts."[103] When teenagers stop performing and allow trustworthy people to see them for who they truly are, an incredible experience follows: acceptance. They discover an inner circle of people with whom they can share their lives.

Overcoming the Prison of Aloneness

Nothing can have a more positive impact on their overall well-being than friends and family who accept them for who they are and not who they strive to be. The deepest need of man, as the philosopher Erich Fromm wrote, "is the need to overcome his separateness, to leave the prison of his aloneness."[104] Intimacy and acceptance are the cornerstones of deep relationships, where we feel known and develop our sense of belonging. If loneliness is a prison, then vulnerability, intimacy, and acceptance are the keys to set us free.

Today, our teens don't have the luxury of growing up in an unfiltered environment, free from technology. In many ways, their relational interactions have grown more complex. They are often left with two choices: indirect engagement through a digital device, or isolation from the world of their peers. If values and priorities that favor the raw emotions aren't clearly instilled in them, the digital vortex will suck them in. The tech industry has made millions of dollars by capitalizing on our

> **If loneliness is a prison, then vulnerability, intimacy, and acceptance are the keys to set us free.**

deepest desire for connection to deceive us into thinking devices can cultivate true intimacy.

If we want to mentor this generation in the digital age, we need to prioritize the value for relationships. Rules regarding their online activity will not speak to the hearts and minds of our teens. We must first establish that our value for relationships with our kids is above other competing factors, like career, income, or self-actualization.

Discussion Guide:

1. If you could describe the relationships in your life with one word, what would it be?
2. What are some of the core values that mark your interactions with others (e.g. courage, kindness, honesty, trust)?
3. How do these values guide your online interactions?
4. What are some of the differences between "connection bombardment" and "real relationships"?
5. How do conversations with anonymous people you meet online differ from offline friendships?
6. What ingredients do relationships need to blossom in the digital world?
7. Do your tech habits strengthen the closest relationships in your life? Why? Why not?

Chapter 3: Hijacked

Jason

"Thump . . . Thump . . . Thump . . ." blasted the sound of a heartbeat through our television speakers. It was an all-too-familiar sound that my father, brothers, and I hated. It meant our treasured weekly show, *24*, had come to an end. The room would explode with excitement and frustration. I remember wondering how I was expected to go about my life for the next week without knowing if Jack Bauer, the show's hero, would be able to ditch a small plane before being obliterated by the nuclear bomb inside. Jack had volunteered to fly the bomb into the desert, sacrificing himself to avoid turning Los Angeles into a crater. The sheer bravery and patriotism that Jack displayed were exhilarating. The professionals at 20th Century Fox had us hooked. *Come hell or high water,* we would tune in to next week's episode to see how Agent Bauer would rescue the world from global terrorists bent on destroying our beloved country.

I can't think of a better series than *24*, where the writers understood the art of implementing the perfect mind-blowing cliffhanger after every episode. The show loaded their endings with unexpected betrayals and outrageous plot twists. The writers had no problem killing off our favorite co-stars, only to bring them back as double or triple agents later. It was a grueling 24-week-series that constantly left you hanging on the edge of your seat, only to reveal the outcome when the next show aired, which of course ended the exact same way every week. It literally felt like one could not go on living until the mystery was revealed. However, after 10 to 15 minutes, the adrenaline would wear off and the dopamine rush would settle down. We slowly pulled ourselves off the sofa as our sanity returned, until next week, when we would all head down to the basement and get ready for the next adrenaline-filled, terrorist-butt-kicking adventure.

Hook, Line, and Sinker

Companies that produce entertainment media have sunk billions of dollars in research to make their products as addictive as possible. We get to experience intense adrenaline rushes and dopamine kicks while sitting in a comfortable seat, sipping cola and munching popcorn. Many of us can relate to the intoxicating buzz of a gripping action flick or the dopamine high of a romantic drama that pulled all the right heartstrings. Like skilled fishermen, the industry producing modern-day media entertainment knows just how to lure us in, *hook, line, and sinker.* However, since *24* first aired in 2001, the barriers to consuming media have become virtually nonexistent. Media is accessible all the time; the only blockade standing between us and binge-watching whatever our heart desires is ourselves. Adolescents are trapped in a loop of consumption when Netflix automatically starts playing the next episode post-mind-blowing cliffhanger, and YouTube auto-plays their favorite content without them even selecting it.

The Business of Personal Data

Mark Zuckerberg, the 35-year-old billionaire and owner of Facebook, stood in front of a packed Congress on April 12th, 2018 to justify the outrage his company had stirred. Facebook's lack of incentive to protect users' personal data had forced Zuckerberg to appear in a public hearing after the Cambridge Analytica Scandal made world news.[105] It was the straw that broke the camel's back. Nearly 87 million Facebook users' personal information had been passed on to the third-party app developer under the guise of "academic research."[106] Cambridge Analytica was accused of influencing the presidential election in 2016, as well as Brexit in 2017, through the data collected by Facebook. After the company's alleged tampering made headlines, Facebook's stock value dropped $50 billion within two days.[107] You would think that Facebook would have radically changed their business model to prioritize the security and privacy of their billions of users. However, a few months after the public outcry, it seemed like the storm had blown over. Facebook managed to temporarily silence the masses through empty promises to protect their data. Despite losing a couple of lawsuits,[108] the company has largely kept their business model, and remains one of the largest global tech companies. In their 2018 quarter, Facebook managed to make more money than ever before, earning 16.9 billion dollars in profits.[109]

The *Cambridge Analytica* scandal did not only reveal Facebook's failed attempts to protect personal data, but also gave us a taste of how the attention economy works. We must understand the ways in which social media, gaming, and pornography industries have manipulated their products in order to fully grasp the influence they can have on a teenager's social development. The larger aim of the technology industry is to create a product that responds to our most fundamental human needs and desires, keeping us locked to our screens as long as possible. Their model for making profit parallels a con artist's scheme; they tantalize us with the hope of fulfilling our deepest desires through a screen—finding the perfect relationship, thousands of approving followers, or sexual satisfaction. This fixates our attention on something dazzling, while the pickpocket fleeces us for as much time and data as they can get. The industry views us as a confident conman sees his mark. All we observe is the curated interface of digital media portraying a seductive commentary on the world around us, while algorithms analyze our personal data and predict what will evoke the strongest responses. The more time we spend on a specific internet platform, the better our habits can be studied. Sean Parker, co-founder of Facebook, explained in an interview with *Axios* that the founders were driven by one question: "How do we consume as much of your time and conscious attention as possible?"[110] We unknowingly reveal unfathomable amounts of personal data that is used to customize specific advertisements geared to our interests, needs, and desires. For digital media innovators, attention equates to profit.

RUMB Challenge

Analyze five of the top addictive aspects of the media you consume.

What characteristics make it so difficult to stop consuming?

Tech giants such as Facebook, Google, Amazon, and Apple are the wealthiest companies in the world with a combined stock worth more than $2.3 trillion.[111] Facebook alone is worth $420 billion, and is crowned as the world's biggest display marketing firm. It promotes ads from five million different advertisers every month.[112] In an attempt to remain the dominant social media platform, Facebook used its seemingly infinite resources to purchase Instagram in 2012 for 715 million dollars.[113] Zuckerberg could foresee that Generation Z would gravitate towards more visual-based platforms of communication. His decision paid off. To date, Instagram is worth more than $100 billion.[114] Instagram is expected to amass two billion users within the next five years.[115]

The entertainment industry floods the market with products that are designed to reward us with euphoric adrenaline rushes for essentially doing nothing. The lack of actual effort it takes to receive such a reward is likely what makes media consumption so enjoyable. Humans are wired to take shortcuts whenever possible. This programming can make us highly efficient people when channeled in healthy ways. A teenager will most likely find the path of least resistance to get a good grade. The desire to accomplish tasks quickly can help streamline their study habits, which improves productivity. However, being pre-programmed to favor shortcuts can also lead to less desirable behavior, especially among maturing adolescents.

Hooked

Cam Adair, a Canadian national, was fifteen years old when his online gaming obsession led him to drop out of high school. He even pretended to have a job so no one would hold him accountable. When his parents would drop him off at a restaurant where he was supposedly training as a prep cook, he would catch the bus back home to game. Cam, once a successful hockey player in his early teen years, was bullied throughout high school and found solace in online gaming. In the digital world, he mattered; he was somebody; he had friends. This world didn't judge or ridicule him. In the virtual world, he had a safe place to escape his real-world problems.[116] Cam had learned that this technology could grant him what he was deeply lacking in real-life: acceptance, purpose, and community.

Human behavior is largely influenced by our brain's reward center. Cravings and pleasure are experienced in the reward circuitry, for the purposes of self-preservation and procreation, by creating a desire and reward for natural reinforcers such as food, love, friendship, sex, and novelty.[117] The brain releases varying amounts of dopamine (the so-called "happiness chemical") based on the anticipated value of what a person is expecting to experience. What we experience as enticing, our brain sees as an opportunity to fulfill our primitive needs. For example, seeing attractive women or men triggers a dopamine release as a biological response to finding a potential mate. Junk food equates to valuable calories once crucial for survival. Novel experiences such as exploration and learning evoke high doses of dopamine, which increases our desire to discover the world around us.[118] Dopamine solidifies these experiences by signaling the brain to strengthen neural connections, so the activity that released dopamine can be remembered and repeated. Neurons that fire together, wire together.[119] Thus, the brain begins to make physical alterations by strengthening the connections in the reward circuitry and pruning unused connections to make the brain more efficient.[120] This phenomenon largely dictates how teenagers interact with digital media.

Lisa

"I met Hanna at a coffee shop. The tall, seventeen-year-old brunette was sipping on her latte. Hanna looked deeply grieved when I asked her about social media. She expressed her experience of uncontrollable interaction with social media:

> I share a lot on social media. [. . .] I have mixed feelings about that. I want to stop doing that, because I think that it prevents me from living in the moment, because I am posting literally everything I am doing on my private story and videos where I share, "Oh my gosh, this just happened" and so I don't like that I do that, but it has now become an outlet for me, kind of like therapeutic [. . .] but even though it has helped, it has also done damage and is something I want to stop doing [. . .]. You can just sit there for hours responding to Snapchat, back and forth.

Our brains are highly sophisticated miracles, but they tend to respond very primitively to external input.[121] The content we choose to consume online is often based on how it makes us feel, rather than its objective quality. This can help explain why we are so captivated by digital media. Emotions, impulses, drives, and subconscious decision-making are controlled by the primitive circuits of the brain.[122] Digital media, whether it be a gripping mystery series, a compelling gaming universe, or seductive sex videos, is designed to harness the raw power of these internal survival instincts, which then control our behavior by keeping us glued to the screen. The more often the behavior is repeated, the stronger these connections become.[123] The strongest natural achievable release of dopamine is through the anticipation of sexual stimulation and orgasm,[124] hence the saying, "sex sells."

Jason

I met Alice Taylor at the 2018 Coalition to End Sexual Exploitation Global Summit in Washington D.C. Now a passionate anti-porn activist and successful author, she runs a non-profit called *The Grace Spot* that helps young women overcome addiction to pornography. Alice became acquainted with pornography at the age of twelve and battled porn dependency as a coping mechanism for years. She talks openly about using porn to numb feelings of depression, anxiety, and shame. She told me, "You feel, 'I need comfort.' The quickest way to do it is to get the dopamine rushing and the quickest way to do it is an orgasm. I know porn can do it. It's anonymous. It's quick. It's easy. It's free. I can do it in my room. Nobody will even know. There is absolutely no risk." Many teenagers share Alice's story; they too use porn as a coping mechanism to escape feelings of stress and anxiety.

Dating is Dead

One doesn't have to look far to observe how digital media has influenced the relational fluency of Gen Z and Millennials. Type the terms "Millennials" and "dating" into your search engine, and you will find trending headlines like "Dating's Dead," "Commitment Phobia," or "Why Dating as A Millennial is so Screwed Up." As a blogger writing for *Glamour Magazine* put it, "I belong to a generation that downloads their love lives via the App Store and considers liking one another's Instagram selfies 'flirting.' The concept of actually meeting someone IRL (in real life) has become alien to us, so much so that we genuinely believe technology is the only way to find love."[125] In the present age, many find it easier to choose solace behind a screen than to work through the ups and downs of a real relationship. Sexual frustration can wreak havoc on our relationships when instant porn-induced orgasm becomes the brain's shortcut to the reward system, rather than wooing or pursuing a significant other for a well-earned dopamine kick. Hanna reflected on dating in her generation:

> It is all about sex [. . .] It is all sexual relationships. I don't see anything further than a sexual relationship there [. . .]. I wasn't alive in my parents' time, but when I see movies, I just don't see that type of romance anymore. I don't see a guy just randomly telling a girl she is beautiful. I just always see an ulterior motive [. . .] I think that people want that romantic relationship, but it is not how our generation approaches it.

Unlimited online sexual content creates a dopamine highway between the reward and the behavior of watching online sex, which makes sharing nudes through a screen appear normal, but can override or even cancel out the desire to risk becoming vulnerable and intimate with a real partner.

Friends of Dopamine

Our brains are hardwired to initiate behaviors that make us feel good. This survival instinct shapes our response to certain stimuli, which can improve our ability to effortlessly navigate the complexities of social interactions. It streamlines our relationship fluency. We learn how to be nice to others largely because the brain relishes the neural chemical bath of feel-good hormones produced by friendship. Thanks to our brain's reward circuitry, we learn early on how to naturally behave in ways that attract people to us rather than repelling them away. These behaviors are remembered and hardwired, and become our go-to responses when we are faced with similar situations.

The drive to belong and be known is one of our most fundamental human needs. The power of friendship, the comradery felt when we are accepted by others, or the ability to be vulnerable with someone we love creates strong neural rewards that promote positive social behavior.

We work assiduously to steward our relationships to produce a healthy social network that strengthens our sense of well-being. In moments of relational tension, we learn to exercise conflict management by keeping our cool to avoid damaging the relationship. The reward system in our brain reminds us through the release of dopamine that people are worth our effort, time, and attention. Thus, we take on behavioral adaptations that represent our desire for intimacy, vulnerability, and companionship.

Hijacked

Online media hijacks teenagers' reward circuitry by creating illusions of reality that trigger very real responses in the depths of their brain. Media is not their friend or their lover, but teens engage with online content that portrays powerful emulations of friendship or sexual intimacy. In many ways, media is an artistic expression; it is designed to evoke powerful emotions. However, the media industry is well-aware of the effects their products have on human behavior. Digital media is a great tool when used in accordance with our values; but when entertainment media becomes a hardwired coping strategy, it creates relational dysfunction. Rather than drawing upon their friendships or families, teenagers turn to digital media for comfort. Their brain's reward center has the capacity to forge new pathways based on specific media habits, which can override their ability to prioritize long-term goals over short-term rewards.

Online media, especially novel sexual content, is designed to hack the reward system of the brain by creating instant gratification with little investment. However, such media presents powerful neural rewards with no sustainable solution to the tension we feel. If teenagers don't develop healthy coping strategies, their brains will follow the path of least resistance when confronted with a situation that evokes negative feelings. When they are bored, do they feel the urge to meet up with friends or stream another episode on Amazon Prime? Essentially, any discomfort in life can become a trigger to get caught up in online media. When I spoke to Hannah, she put it this way: "The people that I know with the most followers on Instagram usually have the most problems going on [so] they start to lean on social media more, but once they are on social media, it heightens their problems."

Quality Control Function?

Our biology is adapted to life before the internet. Tweens and Teens are simply not wired to respond wisely to the never-ending smorgasbord of digital entertainment. They find it difficult to put off instant gratification and ponder on the consequences of their actions. The reward circuitry does not objectively process the content consumed, but rather the amount of dopamine released. There is no quality control function. This job is left to their higher-thinking brain, known as the prefrontal cortex, which is central to crucial executive brain functions. This can be very confusing for a child or adolescent who is exposed to degrading content, such as hardcore pornography or excessively violent games. Their higher thinking or logic may process the acts of violence and degradation as unacceptable; however, their association with sex and novelty create arousal and excitement. This could prove to be a toxic combination when they stumble across online content they know is inherently wrong, but feels really good. The reward circuitry of the brain is a tough competitor when it comes to decision making. This part of our brain has an all-access pass to our body's feel-good pharmacy. It releases an instant, intoxicating dopamine buzz with the cost of only the click of a mouse or a tap of a finger. Suddenly, putting in the time and effort to achieve relational rewards the old-fashioned way—by meeting up with friends, or pursuing a crush—sounds like a lot of unnecessary work. I met Julie, a sixteen-year-old, over a cup of tea. She talked about her friend, who became popular on social media when she started portraying herself as the party girl:

> Then I saw her again this summer and realized how much social media had changed her. Of course, it is not just social media, but for her, her identity is so attached to social media [...]. If one day Instagram was gone, that would have a huge impact on her life, because she is so dependent on that to get attention from so many people [. . .]. When you start getting more attention, you start craving it even more.

She went on to say that her friend eventually took on the new social media personality in real life. She had slowly become the superficial party girl she had portrayed online.

The Digital Universe, Broccoli, Sweets, and Poison

Enjoying a good movie, socializing through media, or playing video games online can be great entertainment if we have a balanced approach to consumption. We refer to such media as digital sweets. They are designed to taste great. They are coded to make us feel good and can temporarily improve our mood. Using the internet as a tool to support a friend or plan fun get-togethers is like a healthy serving of broccoli. This doesn't always equate to a heavy hit of dopamine in our reward circuitry, but it does build a healthier lifestyle. When COVID-19 hit, we all benefited from the ways the internet connected us with each other. Most of us were still able to continue schooling, get the essentials we needed, and converse with co-workers and loved ones. Using web-based functions can never measure up to real-life encounters, but it can promote a lifestyle that connects us in meaningful ways, which improves our overall sense of well-being. On the other end of the media nutrition scale is what we refer to as poison. Harmful media, such as violent, humiliating, sadistic sex videos and racist or degrading comedy acts, have the potential to harm impressionable minds and hijack an adolescent's healthy development. Too often, teenagers are completely unaware of the imprint the often-subconscious consumption of such media leaves on their internal selves.

Neural Highways

It is important that teens take control of their neural highways, because what they feed their brains shapes their thinking. Their choices of how often, how much, and what kind of content they consume carries over into their adult lifestyles, and will majorly affect their health and well-being over the course of the rest of their lives. Kids who grow up eating excessive amounts of junk food are less likely to crave healthy nutrition choices later. The same is true for kids who develop largely behind a screen and receive little guidance or accountability regarding their media choices. Their social development may be stunted if they don't learn to cope with life's highs and lows by making healthy choices, or to draw near to friends and family rather than a screen.

Lexy was straight out of the heart of Georgetown, D.C. She was a homegrown third-generation Washingtonian. We sat down on the rooftop garden of one of the city's finest cafés. This seventeen-year-old senior had a strong sense of who she was and where she had come from. I was intrigued when she accepted my request for an interview. She shared with me, "Our generation will definitely have more singles throughout adulthood. By only using the internet and social media, we avoid learning and practicing key skills one needs in a lasting relationship."

RUMB Challenge

Common Sense Media is the leading source of entertainment and technology reviews for families and schools. It rates online games, movies, and TV shows and gives age-appropriate recommendations.

Check out Common Sense Media:

https://www.commonsensemedia.org

and examine some of the digital media your teens engage with.

When we talk about internet media and youth, we must be aware of the uniquely vulnerable state of developing adolescents. Based on their status as children, youth are given special privileges and protections to have the space and time to develop into responsible, self-sustaining, and productive members of society. Youth are pre-programmed to absorb and learn about the world around them. Their brains are far more flexible and plastic than adults. The adolescent brain is loaded with an excess of billions of neural connections, giving them a wide canvas of learning potential. However, their brains are undergoing incredible changes in preparation for adulthood. After the age of twelve, a natural shrinking process of their brain takes place, where billions of neural connections are pruned or hardwired.[126] This is also known as the "use it or lose it principle,"[127] which translates to behavior adaptations as teens act upon what they observe and learn. In other words, the very nature of being young is to be impressionable.

Adults tend to perceive internet media consumption and smartphone use from their own individual perspectives. It is easy to visualize adolescent struggles and imagine what we would do. However, adolescents don't share our state of mental maturity or developed identities. They are in a mind-bending stage of physical and mental development. They are rapidly becoming intellectually, hormonally, physically, and socially mature. Adolescents are raging with a potent cocktail of sex hormones: estrogen, progesterone, and testosterone. Their current state of brain development "remains structurally and functionally vulnerable to impulsive"[128] behaviors related to natural reinforcers, such as sex, sleep, and eating habits. They are significantly more vulnerable to the allure of risk-taking and novelty-seeking behaviors. The adolescent brain is undergoing a massive rewiring process that does not reach full maturity until roughly twenty-five years of age. In comparison to adults' fully developed brains, adolescents are prone to being seduced by the foreseeable positive reward of a decision or behavior, and are less likely to be swayed by the possible negative outcomes of their choices. Consequently, most addictions develop during adolescence.[129] Teens are more likely to follow their emotions, doing what feels right in social interactions or when making important decisions. During my teen years, I would often hear the words, "What were you thinking?" Scientifically speaking, I wasn't thinking. I was feeling. More than at any other stage in life, teens are influenced by their emotions. Digital media is tailored to acquire swipes, clicks, and views from youth who engage with its highly sensual content.

Emotional vulnerability is just the tip of the iceberg when it comes to understanding how teens engage with online media. The prefrontal cortex is the last area of the brain to reach full maturity. This can help explain the familiar and less-than-desirable adolescent behavior that drives parents, teachers, and youth workers crazy. The prefrontal cortex processes feedback from all senses and coordinates thoughts and actions to accomplish distinct goals. It is responsible for a vast diversity of higher thinking processes, such as: the capacity to balance short-term rewards with long term goals, impulse control, delaying gratification, assessing consequences of behavior, predicting future outcomes of decisions, and avoiding and correcting inappropriate behavior. Such deficiency in crucial thought processes can help explain why teens are known to make decisions that make no logical sense to their adult counterparts. In fact, due to the underdeveloped prefrontal cortex, adolescents who are well-aware of the potential danger of certain behaviors are predisposed to override logical thinking to participate in risky activities.[130]

The adolescent brain is a biological construction site. Adolescence is largely about learning, gaining experiences, and being motivated to try something new. If teens skipped this developmental process, they might never come to realize their boundaries, uncover their passions, or embark on the fundamental journey of self-discovery. This is not to say that anything goes. Digital youth are especially vulnerable and need boundaries and guidance. Sadly, the mortality rate among fifteen- to twenty-four-year-olds is three times higher than middle-school-aged children.[131] Teens are capable of complex thought, such as assessing hypothetical situations and considering appropriate choices. However, such thought processes are significantly influenced by emotional or high-intensity situations. This is referred to as *hot cognition* (high arousal and intense emotion) and *cold cognition* (critical and over-analyzing).[132] A thirteen-year-old using the family computer in the kitchen is most likely going to make better choices with their parents around (cold cognition) than the same adolescent who is being coaxed by their peers to make fun of somebody online (hot cognition). The same goes for teens who send sexts. A girl who is being wooed by the attractive football star at school is in a state of hot cognition when weighing the consequences of sending him an intimate photo. Teens' predisposition to novelty and sex places them in a state of high arousal, making it incredibly difficult for them to assess the consequences of their online media choices. The reward circuitry of the adolescent brain is very sensitive during their development. It sends out impulses to act upon something desirable, which can be as simple as *likes* on Instagram, another gaming level, Snapchat followers, or porn-induced orgasm.[133] It's hard enough for adults to resist such primitive pleasures. How can we expect youth, whose ability to judge and make decisions is still developing, to manage this on their own?

When Pixels Win

Gabe started consuming porn at the age of twelve. At the age of twenty-three, he knew it was time to quit when he was no longer able to get an erection without internet pornography. He explained that his brain was so conditioned to online sex that he could not "get it up" with his girlfriend, even though she was someone he was very attracted to. He first thought it could be an early onset of erectile dysfunction, but there was something very odd about the way his body was responding to sex. Gabe reflected:

> I literally had porn every time I tried to masturbate for a decade. [. . .] to be really explicit, no matter how hard I stroked myself, no matter what I fantasized about, nothing could give me the slightest of an erection, but just typing in the [porn]site gave my body this rush and I got a full erection in anticipation. It was obvious to me in that moment. It could not have been clearer that I was dependent on porn for arousal. I had this big epiphany, porn screwed me up, and I broke down crying. I could not believe that I did not see this coming!

Upon researching his condition further, Gabe found that he was not alone. "I was reading [the posts of] thousands and thousands of guys that were going through the same thing." Today, Gabe Deem is one of the most inspiring and courageous anti-porn activists I have ever met. He runs an organization called *Reboot Nation* that informs youth about porn's true destructive nature.

The Plastic Brain

Nicholas Carr, author of *The Shallows*, provides an explorative journey through the internet's intellectual and cultural consequences. In his book, he recollects how the web began to shape his way of thinking: "The very way my brain worked seemed to be changing. It was then that I began worrying about my inability to pay attention to one thing for more than a couple of minutes." According to a Microsoft study from 2015, the average attention span has decreased from twelve seconds in 2000 to only eight seconds in 2013, which is one second shorter than that of a goldfish.[134] Carr described what was happening to his brain: "At first I'd figured that the problem was a symptom of middle-age rot. But my brain, I realized, wasn't just drifting. It was hungry. It was demanding to be fed the way the Net fed it and the more it was fed, the hungrier it became."[135] The neuroplasticity of our brain allows us to adapt to new situations and circumstances. We learn how to deal with life's twists and turns and adjust our thinking accordingly. Just like remodeling your house to make way for another child or moving furniture around for maximum room efficiency, the brain can also initiate its own renovation projects when exposed to new situations that require a different set of skills. However, as liberating as the plastic brain may be, it also has the potential to trap us in unhealthy behavioral cycles.

Once the brain goes to all the effort to solidify and strengthen specific neural pathways, it favors using these synaptic highways over blazing new trails.[136] Therefore, we can fall back into certain habits and ways of behaving when triggered by boredom, stress, anxiety, loneliness, or depression. As Carr put it, "[p]lastic does not mean elastic [. . .]. Our neural loops don't snap back to their former state the way a rubber band does[. . .]."[137] Our brains don't always wire themselves to desirable behavior. When the teenagers in our lives feel bored, lonely, or anxious, it's only natural that they respond to the draw of technology. The most popular times to stream porn are between 10 p.m. and 1 a.m.[138] When our kids are alone with their smartphones, how have they conditioned their brains to respond to the pull of sexual content? What values drive their online habits? Do they immediately get the urge to watch deviant videos because their brains are conditioned to get dopamine rewards when people aren't watching? We need to teach the next generation that they are responsible to be the gatekeepers of their minds and the masters of their choices. Circumstances should never dictate mindsets and behavior.

From Trauma to Triumph

Jason

"Perhaps one of the most dramatic personal examples in my own life of the brain's ability to rewire its circuitry was when I almost lost my life. I used to play college basketball during a season of my life when the pressure to perform burdened me everywhere I went. If I wanted good grades, I had to learn to balance approximately forty hours of basketball alongside forty hours of lectures and homework a week. When I hit my limit of screaming coaches and a never-ending pile of deadlines, I would find my solace in skateboarding. I was certainly no Tony Hawk, but more of an asphalt surfer. Sometimes, I would cruise for hours on the midnight streets of LA's suburbs. I relished the adrenaline rush of screaming down hills and sliding through corners. It was only a matter of time before the adrenaline caught up to me. The weekend had finally arrived. I went to visit my little brother, who was finishing his senior year at a nearby prep school. I threw my skateboard in my trunk. After a 45-minute drive, I arrived at his house. We took off to catch the last rays of sunlight before dark. The rest of the story is a bit fuzzy. I know I landed on my back because of the holes in my t-shirt. My head whipped into the asphalt so hard that my brain bounced off the back of my skull, only to slam into my forehead. My brain hemorrhaged. After regaining consciousness, my mind was only half there. I couldn't even remember who my parents were. My brother, who was with me when the accident occurred, told me later that my memory was stuck in a five-minute loop.

I spent four agonizing days in the hospital and a few nights in the ICU before being released. The pain was all-consuming. I spent the next few days vomiting and experienced throbbing migraines at the slightest sound. It was about a two-year recovery process that was nothing short of a miracle. I moved back home to live with my parents. Everything I valued in life previously was gone. In a matter of moments, I had lost basketball, school, and my friends. I struggled with major depression and felt completely hopeless. My doctor told me that I should lower my expectations. "Don't expect to get the same grades you once had," he warned me. In one appointment, he showed me the MRI scans of my brain. It was peppered with black spots showing where all the damage had occurred. He shook his head. "I have another patient with the same injuries. Skateboarding accident. He is most likely not going to survive."

I no longer recognized my face in the mirror. I looked like a drug addict, and had dark circles around my eyes. I wore sunglasses and a hoodie to block out the world around me, because light exposure felt like a jackhammer drilling into my head. There came a point where I had to make an important decision. I could either spend the rest of my life crawling through my own grief, or I could take responsibility for getting healthy again. I rejected the rehab plan the doctor recommended and substituted my own. I got a job at a coffee shop and drove my colleagues crazy. I couldn't remember the drink orders to save my life. However, I knew that it was good for me. I practiced every day and eventually got the hang of things. I learned to process lots of information, respond to customers, take orders, time espresso shots, and synchronize the construction of multiple drink orders.

I amped up my rehab program and enrolled in a Chinese course at the local community college. It was grueling work. I memorized hundreds of characters and learned to pronounce the coinciding words with the proper tones. I could feel my brain regaining its strength. My doctor administered a test to gauge where I was in my recovery process. He found that, based on previous testing, I was smarter than I was before the accident. I went from sleeping twenty-three hours a day to completing my bachelor's in Organizational Leadership, a master's in International Human Rights and Humanitarian Law, and learning German at a professional proficiency. I intentionally chose to feed my brain what it needed to rewire itself and bypass the damaged regions of my neural network. I certainly can't take all the credit for my miraculous recovery, and could not have done it without supportive family and friends. However, my experience highlights the power of goals and choices as they influence our brain's neural structures. I'm sure that if I had simply chosen to be a victim instead of a fighter, I would be a very different type of person today.

We need to challenge teens to anchor their choices in their personal values and convictions to reach what they desire to become in life. When our values and goals chart the courses of our lives, the brain understands tech as a tool for the journey rather than the destination itself. ”

Discussion Guide:

1. What are some of the online habits you turn to if you need comfort?
2. If you compared online media to food on a nutrition scale, what kind of media would be healthy, unhealthy, or poisonous? Why?
3. Have you ever come across media content that felt good and wrong at the same time? How did this affect the way you saw yourself?
4. What does your generation need to learn about building healthy relationships in the digital age?
5. What are some of the goals you have for your life? How do your media habits support or hijack the pursuit of these goals?

Part Two:

Relationships: Digital media has a profound effect on our relationships. When social media, gaming, or pornography pull teens away from real-life connection, their mental health suffers.

Understanding: Teens are born into the world of social media, gaming, and porn. They don't know a time before smartphones and digital media. We need to take the time to develop an understanding of these worlds, so we can relate to our teens' fascination with digital media and replace shame by revealing the underlying currents that exploit their development.

Mentorship: Once we have established our own baseline of understanding, where our teens feel seen and known, we can speak into harmful habits that hijack their healthy development and well-being. We can help teens develop vision and purpose for what they would like to achieve in life and leverage these dreams as fuel for self-control and healthy choices. We need to empower our teens to establish their values as the driving forces behind what they choose to consume and produce online.

Boundaries: We need to challenge teens to own their media choices by setting boundaries that protect their long-term goals and desires. We have to teach teens that boundaries protect them from being exploited by the intoxicating draw of digital pleasure. Setting limits that protect their vision and purpose creates ownership over their online choices.

Chapter 4: Me, My Selfie, and I

Essena O'Neill had made it. With over 500,000 followers on Instagram, she had cracked the code to becoming an "influencer" by curating a picture-perfect life. The photographs on her profile looked effortless and sexy. The nineteen-year-old up-and-coming "insta-star" portrayed herself as living life from one exotic adventure to the next. Stunning dresses, glamorous makeup, exclusive locations, and steamy bikini shots dazzled her exploding fan base. Her fans expressed their envy and admiration for her amazing outfits, flawless smile, and perfectly toned body. Then came November of 2015; Essena quit. Despite the flood of modeling contracts, YouTube gigs, and advertising deals, she gave it all up. She was making more money than any teenager could dream of. She vanished from all social media platforms, leaving her fan base with a few comments. "Not real life," she proclaimed. Her last picture on Instagram was captioned:

> I've spent the majority of my teenage life being addicted to social media, social approval, social status, and my physical appearance. Social media is contrived images and edited clips ranked against each other. It's a system based on social approval, likes, validation in views, success in followers. It's perfectly orchestrated self-absorbed judgement.[139]

She took to YouTube to express her final thoughts; "Everything I did was for views, for likes, for followers. I did shoots for hours for photos for Instagram . . . I let myself be defined by numbers."[140] She talked about the reality of her career as an influencer. Even though she was collecting a massive following and portrayed the perfect life, she felt completely lonely and miserable inside. She admitted that her smiling in photos and vlogs did not convey any true emotions.[141]

Essena went on to share that she was portraying a bubbly façade while she struggled with body dysmorphia, depression, and anxiety. She acknowledged that she constantly thought that people were making fun of her and labeling her as stupid; "I realized how I am never present, I don't really talk to people . . . but more so how my days had morphed into constant shoots, constant planning to do things to make my life look good on a screen."[142] Instead of living a life that reflected her personal values, she realized social media had trapped her into monetizing her appearance. It was evident that she felt relationally malnourished, until she woke up one day and asked herself the inevitable question: what do I want my life to be about? It took her five years until she made a careful re-entry into social media. This time, her social media engagement was centered around asking life's deeper questions, sharing vulnerable thoughts, and connecting with others.

The Race to Retain Human Attention

Lisa

When the COVID-19 stay-at-home order was mandated, social media paved the way for us to stay connected, entertained, and inspired. In fact, most of us spent exponentially more time on social media while being constrained to our homes. Without it, there would have been nothing standing between us and the crushing effects of loneliness. I can't imagine how I would have survived life without Zoom, Instagram, Facebook, iMessage, and WhatsApp during quarantine life. Social media will certainly come out on top in the aftermath of the pandemic, with more people conditioned to find meaning on their platforms than ever before.

Despite this fact, Essena is not alone in her critiques of social media. In 2018, former Google and Facebook employees launched *The Center for Humane Technology* with the aim to promote people's well-being using technology. The leaders of the project included Justin Rosenstein (one of the inventors of the *like button*), Sean Parker (Facebook's first president), Tristan Harris (former Google design ethicist), and Roger McNamee (a business pioneer who invested 2 billion dollars when Facebook first launched). They joined to challenge tech developers to meet higher ethical standards. Harris, who has been referred to by *The Atlantic* as the closest thing there is to a moral conscience in Silicon Valley, commented on the current state of Big Tech: "They've created the attention economy and are now engaged in a full-blown arms race to capture and retain human attention, including the attention of kids."[143] Social media curates our online experiences. What looks like a random collage of photos and posts from friends is actually an algorithm working to maximize profit.[144] Roger McNamee concludes that today's Facebook "[. . .] reads like the plot of a sci-fi novel: a technology celebrated for bringing people together is exploited by a hostile power to drive people apart, undermine democracy, and create misery."[145] Smartphones have exacerbated privacy violations by capitalizing on the exploitative business of harvesting and selling their users' private data. Facebook's algorithms are used to target specific groups in limited geographic areas, making youth an impressionable audience for marketing.[146] It deliberately features stories that evoke strong emotions, such as fear or anger, to keep its users as actively engaged as possible.

Social media platforms make us feel like we are in control, yet we are easily seduced by the allure of just one more like, photo upload, or friend request. Sean Parker explained, "It's a social-validation feedback loop . . . exactly the kind of thing that a hacker like myself would come up with, because you're exploiting a vulnerability in human psychology."[147] In the movie, *Swiped: Hooking Up in the Digital Age,* Jonathan Badeen (founder of the dating app Tinder) explains that the swipe right function was largely inspired by a questionable pigeon experiment by behavioral psychologist B.F. Skinner. Skinner managed to turn pigeons into gamblers through intermittent reward. The pigeons peck, but don't receive food right away. In fact, they never fully know when they will get fed. After receiving their reward, they just keep pecking.[148] Similarly, the swipe right function allows the user to "keep pecking." The perfect match is just one more swipe away.

The tech industry has built its business using knowledge of human biological responses. Facebook, Twitter, and Instagram share the *like* button. Even the red-colored heart of the *like button* is intentional. The color "red" captures our attention and elicits excitement.[149] Tristan Harris rightfully concludes, "All of our minds can be hijacked. Our choices are not as free as we think they are." Youth are impressionable targets, as they are especially vulnerable when it comes to social approval. Twenty-four-year-old Canadian social media influencer Melina Roberge was so driven by *likes* and *followers* that she was willing to smuggle ninety-five kilos (209lb) of cocaine to afford a vacation worth $17,000 with the intention of posting about the vacation on Instagram.

She explained that *getting likes* was the currency she hungered for.[150] It is part of human nature to want to be seen, known, and affirmed. Adam Alter, author of *Irresistible: The Rise of Addictive Technology and the Business of Keeping Us Hooked* compares *likes* to slot machines. Alter observed that it is our human nature to doubt our self-worth, as it isn't measurable like weight or income. "Some people obsess over social feedback more than others do, but we're social beings who can't completely ignore what other people think of us. And more than anything, inconsistent feedback drives us nuts,"[151] he said. Apps are designed to control our attention; for us to pick up the phone as often as possible, check notifications, and stay tuned in.

A Tool for Connection

In this day and age, there is nothing that influences the relational fluency more than social media. Facebook alone has more than 2.7 billion users. Every sixth person on the planet uses Facebook daily.[152] It owns three of the five social media platforms that surpassed 100 million users: Facebook, WhatsApp, and Instagram. Perhaps the key question is not if social media is good or bad, but rather, does social media do what it promises: to create connections that bring us closer together and enrich our relationships?

There is no doubt that it is an effective tool to converse with friends and family. It helps us remember birthdays, update our social network about significant events, and informs us about major life milestones of people from all corners of our social network. Everyone shares a group with family members in some form of social media outlet. Social media responds to our desire for connection, approval, and belonging. Singles often "stalk" their crush on social media, vetting them before making the first move. In fact, many married couples expressed their initial interest via social media by sending their crush a *friend request, liking* their posts, or starting a conversation via iMessage. We feel seen and affirmed when people like and comment on our virtual diary.

Connection across Continents

Lisa

Between the ages of sixteen and twenty-six, I made a home on four different continents. It is social media that allows me to maintain a worldwide network and reconnect with friends across the globe. During my studies of bilingual education, I spent a semester abroad in Cape Town, South Africa, where I interned with a non-profit organization. It was Facebook that allowed me to keep up with my newfound friends after I left. Ten years later, I was sitting in my apartment outside of Washington D.C., scrolling through my newsfeed, when a post popped up. One of my good Zambian friends I had met during my internship was attending a conference just down the street. Thanks to Facebook, we didn't miss the rare chance to reconnect over a meatless burger and coke.

For many who grew up with snail mail, or at the very most, AOL Instant Messenger, social media is used as a tool to stay connected, but it is not at the core of their social lives. They are able to distinguish between digital and personal connection because their adolescent years unfolded largely offline. Today's Gen Zers experience a vastly different childhood. A twenty-nine-year-old uses social media in a completely different way than a thirteen-year-old who was born into the digital age.

Snapstreaks, Friendships, and Numbers

Lisa

Fifteen-year-old Ella gave me a glimpse of dating in the digital age when we sat down for an interview. She shared that the boy she was dating was rated *best friend* on Snapchat for two months straight, due to their unbroken *Snapstreak*. She bawled her eyes out when he failed to keep the *Snapstreak* going, forfeiting their status as *best friends*. The *Snapstreak* had become such a strong symbol of friendship that she was convinced their freshly kindled relationship was doomed to fail, for all to see. Looking back, she wondered how an app had gained so much power over her that she would sob for hours. She had become so dependent on engineered social feedback that she could no longer feel secure in their relationship without it. As of 2019, Snapchat has accumulated over 238 million daily users worldwide.[153] To teens, numbers matter. An insecure teenager feels affirmed if their stories are watched by the masses because social media makes value quantifiable.

Relationships of all kinds can be messy. Peer pressure, raging hormones, and the quest for independence all add to the drama, but now society is throwing another challenge into the mix. Social lives are measured in front of the public eye. Who hangs out at the most exclusive locations? Who has the coolest friends? Who scored the hottest boyfriend or girlfriend? So often this phenomenon hijacks intimacy and vulnerability for the sake of quantifiable approval. It pushes teenagers onto the sidelines, becoming mere observers of other peoples' ostensibly flawless lives. It leaves young teens in despair as they get bombarded with the collective social endeavors of their entire peer network. Teenagers have some awareness of the unhealthy emotional consequences social media has created. They frequently use the term "FOMO", meaning "fear of missing out", to explain why they succumb to social norms.[154] It's easy to feel miserable when you learn all about something you weren't invited to through social media. Moments of exclusion are on public display. FOMO is one of the motivating factors that inspire teens to check their phones constantly, leaving them in a perpetual state of anxiety.[155] No one wants to feel that they are on the outside, so they stay on high alert, attuned to their friends' social media developments. A recent study found that the more time people spend on social media, the more isolated and lonely they felt.[156] Eighth-graders who spend ten or more hours a week on social media are fifty-six percent more likely to say they're unhappy than those who devote less time to social media.[157] One of the teenage girls I interviewed shared about her classmate. In her mind, Jessica's life was pretty mundane. She was neither popular nor close to any of her peers. Yet, throughout the year, Jessica regularly posted bikini pictures on Instagram displaying a sexy life of adventure and travel. In reality, these photos stemmed from a single week of vacation with her family.

Social Media Fame and The People in Your Circle

There are few celebrities who have talked so openly about the struggle surrounding social media as Selena Gomez. With more than 195 million followers, she is referred to as the "queen of Instagram". Selena, a former Disney star, identified the lucrative business of becoming a social influencer early on. Her fan base blew up after she cultivated a persona on Instagram, Facebook, and Twitter, with a combined following of 254 million fans across the three platforms.[158] Her photo of her birthday celebration on a yacht in 2013 broke the record for collecting a million likes in a mere thirteen minutes. That's nearly 1,300 likes a second. With a following over the size of two-thirds of the U.S. population, Selena has the attention market by the tail. Just one of her social media posts is worth an average of $550,000.[159] Yet Selena stated, '"I think it's really hard to be a kid now, especially with social media. I can't imagine what it would be like to grow up with that. It's already difficult to get up every day and just feel good about yourself without seeing the highlights of everyone else's life."'[160] Selena Gomez demonstrates that notoriety and wealth are not the source of a flourishing happy life. Her success doesn't shield her from the harmful effects of social media. She admits openly that she has a complex relationship with Instagram, and that social media affected her mental and relational health. "I was an addict, and it felt like I was seeing things I didn't want to see, like it was putting things in my head that I didn't want to care about. I always end up feeling like sh*t when I look at Instagram."'[161]

Selena Gomez had to take breaks from social media, sometimes several months at a time, and received treatment for anxiety and depression. She has come to identify that relationships matter most, despite her unfathomable wealth and fame. "You have to figure out the people that are in your circle. I feel like I know everybody but have no friends," the singer confessed. "I have like three good friends that I can tell everything to, but I know everyone. [. . .] You have to have those few people that respect you, want the best for you and you want the best for them. It sounds cheesy, but it's hard. I see a disconnect from real-life connections to people, and that makes me a little worried. "'[162] The success of social media rises and falls with the stars who use it. When Kylie Jenner, who ranked among the top ten most-followed social influencers, criticized *Snapchat's* new app design, *Snap Inc's* stock fell by $1.3 billion.[163] The

2018 *Netflix* Original documentary, *American Meme*, exposes the price of exchanging one's private life for fans and turning a digital following into a business deal. It revealed that anxiety and depression are recurring mental health issues among social media influencers such as Paris Hilton and Brittany Furlan, who become the product themselves for the approval of the masses. They know that you have to increase your likes, which certainly does not equate to liking yourself.[164]

It is fair to say that the life of the common teen looks a little different than that of a superstar. Most adolescents don't try to make a living out of social media, yet many can relate to the struggles of social influencers. Driven by the desire to be seen, noticed, and affirmed, teens share private details about their lives on social media apps; from mood swings, to bikini shots, to drinking parties.

Selfie Sunday

Selfie culture is real. Taking thousands of photos of yourself in various outfits only to show to everyone would have been considered narcissistic in the past, but today, it functions as the formula for gaining followers and likes. This is only affirmed by the most popular social influencers being glorified for doing just that. Almost nine in ten teenagers believe that people overshare on social media.[165] Teenagers take hundreds of pictures before choosing the one that will most likely give them the amount of *likes* they so desire. While on vacation in Italy eating lunch by the water, we took in the breathtaking view of Lake Como while others saw it as the perfect *Insta-worthy* backdrop. I remember feeling sorry for a guy who had been roped into his girlfriend's endless photoshoot. The woman had the "look": push-up bra,

RUMB Challenge

Make a list of all social media accounts you have. Comment on each of them.

1. How does **(specific platform)** affect your self-image?
2. How does **(specific platform)** support close friendships?
3. Do you feel relaxed or stressed when you use **(specific platform)**? Explain why.

Make a commitment to take a break from all social media for one week and take note of how you feel afterwards.

skin-tight dress, and hair groomed to perfection. It was quite comical to watch the boyfriend scurrying back and forth, taking hundreds of photos and then checking for her approval. The entire episode lasted well over an hour. After we finished lunch and ventured into town, we found the same couple, same scenario, but different backdrop.

Teenagers know that their appearance matters. Photos and videos are carefully crafted with practiced poses and *Photoshop* edits to portray only the highlights of a seemingly perfect day and flawless appearance. "Roughly three-quarters (77%) of social media-using teens agree that people are less authentic and real on social media than they are offline."[166] The yearbook was once the only social platform where young people could gloss through each other's pictures. Now, even the most mundane activities are turned into compelling moments. Teens are required to look good on social media to show their friends who they hung out with, and more importantly, how good they looked doing so. The feedback you get on your posts is measurable. Hanging out is not about building relationships, but putting them on display.

Teens are born into a visual world of digital perfection, flawless appearances, and carefully curated profiles. If you look at any teenager's account, most of what you will find is a barrage of images featuring themselves. Developing adolescents hunger for positive affirmation. They yearn to be seen. Social media offers both. In the present selfie culture, teens become the product themselves.

This creates an incredible amount of pressure to look and act a certain way. Relational interactions have migrated online, making social media platforms the place to get noticed and affirmed. A teenager's greatest fear is anonymity. In an age where porn has gone mainstream and social influencers like Paris Hilton and Kim Kardashian West make their names by flashing their breasts in photoshoots and appearing in leaked sex tapes, young girls feel their only option for competing in the attention market is hypersexualization. Gail Dines, a radical feminist and leader of the internationally recognized anti-porn and pro women's rights organization, *Culture Reframed*, said it best: "In our society women have two choices: you are either f*ckable or invisible."[167] For most teenage girls, being invisible is simply not an option.

For most teenage girls, being invisible is simply not an option.

As Essena puts it:

> The culture of Instagram fame, sexism in media, the sexual objectification of women, the deception in paid posts, the idea that skinny starving girls get ahead, that if you're born into the body I have—you get a career out of it, you get an invite into all the parties, everyone wants to take you to lunch, everyone says they love you . . . I lived that life and felt so alone, shallow and lost . . . BECAUSE I WAS.[168]

Teenage girls are constantly bombarded with the unattainable standards of social media influencers; long, skinny legs, a larger-than-life butt, super thin waist, impossibly big boobs, finishing with plump lips, seductive eyes, and a pose that says, "Come and get it!" What do girls have to do to stand out on social media when this is the look of a successful woman worthy of our attention? Influencers like Kylie Jenner, Kim Kardashian West, or Paris Hilton are known as celebrities who are *Famous for being Famous.* They haven't earned their fame from the art they create, sports they play, or movies they're in. They're party girls who come from rich families whose lives of luxury are enviable. They stand out online because their bodies are inimitable, and yet somehow the desired standard. It would be impossible to emulate their looks without wiping food off the menu while spending a century on the stair master. Even then, no one can be both skinny and voluptuous at the same time without the help of plastic surgery or shapewear.

Image, Digital Intimacy, and Noodz

A British study by *the Royal Society for Public Health* found that "Instagram and Snapchat [rank] the worst for mental health and well-being. Both platforms are very image-focused, and it appears they may be driving feelings of inadequacy and anxiety in young people."[169] The game is rigged. There are few women that can measure up to these standards, leaving countless teenage girls frustrated and insecure. *Likes* and *followers* are rapidly becoming a costly endeavor. Typically, a hot, cellulite-free butt in a tiny bikini can get you more *likes* than a cute smile, which most certainly fuels existing insecurities and self-doubt.

Lisa

"When I walked into my classroom after recess, I overheard two seventh graders, Levi and Rose, yelling at each other, "No, it was not a nude! I was wearing my bikini. You just can't see it in the picture." Levi responded, "I will tell your boyfriend that you shared that stuff." The two of them went back and forth, having a vibrant discussion on how much skin should be exposed on Instagram without your partner getting jealous.

Nude pictures, also referred to as *nudes or noodz*, are typically intended to arouse a romantic partner, but not all respect their private nature. A massive sexting scandal unfolded at a high school in Louisa County, an area in rural central Virginia. The outcome left police, parents, and teachers stupefied. About a hundred pictures of naked teenage girls showed up on an Instagram account. All the pictures were of girls from Louisa County high school. Donald Lowe, the local police chief executive, had never witnessed a sexting scandal on this scale. Many of the interviewed teenagers who were in the pictures didn't understand the fuss about nudes, because they perceived sexting as a normal part of engaging with peers. The Louisa County Scandal revealed the gap between teenage culture and adult codes of conduct due to a lack of online sexual boundaries. Notably, a six-year-study that sampled almost 1,000 teenagers in Southeast Texas found that sexting is often the first sexual encounter among teens.[170] A study by Drexel University found that 54 percent of adolescents had received sexts before their eighteenth birthday. When I talked to one of my interviewees about social media, the seventeen-year-old reflected on sexting. In her opinion, it has become such a part of culture that it is not even reaching the news anymore. She shared:

> I know so many guys who have pictures [upon] pictures of naked girls on their phone, and they will show anyone. A girl will come up in conversation and they will be like, speaking of her, I have her nude. Do you want to see it?

She recalled a time when a nude photograph of a girl in seventh grade went viral in a neighboring school. The girl had sent it to her crush. In the end, nobody was held accountable, and the girl left the school with her reputation in ruins. She was the only one who suffered the consequences of spreading Child Sex Abuse Material. It's easy to judge her for choosing to take the photo, but the hyper-sexualization promoted by social media, combined with teenager's undeveloped brains, creates inevitable disaster. Most boys are gorging themselves with the latest trending filth on Pornhub. A simple nude request pales in comparison to what their porn-inspired fantasies demand. A girl's desire to be liked is becoming costlier in a *pornified* culture. Being alone in the safety and privacy of their bedroom, they feel they're in control, which creates a false sense of security. Teens are removed from the physical context of the situation they put themselves in. For the common teen, sexting is part of courting and flirting.[171] Nudes are collected like trophies. If you are the popular guy, you can get a lot of nudes. In one interview, a teen told me that she had lost track of how many times she had been asked for nudes. "If you don't go for it, you are considered a prude, if you do, you are a slut." Paul Roberts, author of *The Impulse Society: America in the Age of Instant Gratification,* explained the disturbing trend: "When I was in high school, if I had gone around saying, 'Here is a picture of me, like me,' I would have gotten punched. If a girl went around passing out naked pictures of herself, people would have thought she needed therapy. Now, that's just Selfie Sunday."[172]

RUMB Challenge

1. Study two opposite social media accounts, one that inspires you with positive values and one that reflects negative or shallow values.

Take a screen shot of both accounts and print them out. Label the accounts with the values they portray.

2. Make a list of five social media accounts that inspire you and five that you commit to unfollowing because they don't reflect what you would like to see in your own life.

Wildfires and Mink Slippers

Interactions between boys and girls have always been complicated by heightened sex drives during adolescence, but the digital age has removed almost all accountability. This is especially true in digital dating culture. One can scroll for hours through different dating profiles, sorting them by *hot, kind of hot, not hot, super-hot,* then decide who they want to message with no strings attached. *Ghosting* is a prime example of a lack of social accountability that has become mainstream. Teens avoid feelings of guilt associated with ditching their commitments. They don't want to be confronted by the emotional impact their actions have on another person; out of sight, out of mind. It doesn't allow for closure, and leaves the person guessing what he or she might have done wrong.

Our society is placing instant gratification on a pedestal. Social media and dating apps have granted us unlimited options to try someone new and pursue seemingly endless sexual opportunities. Consequently, they undermine the pursuit and value of faithfulness, trustworthiness, and endurance. Teenagers have mastered the quest of getting someone's attention online through *likes,* comments, photos, and the exchange of nudes, but they remain clueless when it comes to romance and healthy relationships.

How do our teens learn that relationships come with great responsibility? Successful relationships grow through giving and understanding, rather than taking. In the world of social influencing, what gets you ahead is primarily external: looks, possessions, and wealth. Being a person of character is secondary if relevant at all. Social media influencers are expected to use their platform for good, but people follow them for their appearance first before their integrity. When the 2020 wildfires were raging in Australia, Kylie Jenner shared her grief on social media regarding the tragic loss of over half a billion animals dying in the flames. However, her next post seemed to portray the opposite: Jenner then posted a shot of her mink Louis Vuitton slippers. [173]

Raw and Unfiltered

"Every single week we have a girl who comes to the ER after some social-media rumor or incident has upset her [and then she cut herself]"[174], stated Fadi Haddad, a psychiatrist at Bellevue hospital in New York City, in an article published by *Time Magazine.* Many teenagers turn to unhealthy habits to cope with their pain and feel alive[175] because their online profiles resemble a much shinier life than reality. With the rise of social media, teenagers often struggle to turn to the support of another human being. Tragically, seven in ten members of Generation Z state that they do not feel known or seen by those around them.[176]

Despite the possibility of enhancing real-life relationships, social media used without boundaries and intentionality evokes jealousy and loneliness. What makes the issues surrounding social media so complicated is that it simultaneously promotes both connection and distance, affirmation and insecurity. At the foundation of our behaviors lies questions of our own worthiness. Am I liked? Am I enough?

Social media offers quick, positive feedback to our feelings of insufficiency, superficially responding to our need for acceptance. In a fleeting moment, teenagers feel like they have a place in the world. They feel seen when people respond by liking their *selfie*, TikTok dance, or post, yet this type of social approval will always leave a gaping hole that only a healthy sense of self-love and deep relationships can fulfill.

It is time to question the values that govern our online choices. I talked to a thirteen-year-old about her screen habits. She shared that she had banned all celebrities from her Instagram feed after she realized that their unattainable lives and beauty standards had wrecked her confidence. If we don't equip this generation to question the values promoted by popular social media influencers, they will be shaped by what digital media throws their way.

If we don't challenge the values that drive a teenager's media habits, this generation will be swooped up by a world that defines success in terms of attention, wealth, and appearance. In a culture that demands quick feedback and physical validation, teens need to learn that relationships take time, investment, and work. Relationships that value the raw and unfiltered versions of ourselves are messy and unpredictable, but they are worth fighting for. Teens can only find meaning in real-life friendships if they are mindful of their life goals and aware of the values that require their fervent yes.

If we don't challenge the values that drive a teenager's media habits, this generation will be swooped up by a world that defines success in terms of attention, wealth, and appearance.

Discussion Questions:

1. How many hours a week do you spend on social media?
2. If your social media account could talk, what would it say?
3. What are some of the values promoted on your social media accounts?
4. How does social media affect the way you see yourself?
5. What does social media teach you about being a man or woman in our day and age?
6. Why is sending nudes to each other so normalized among your generation?
7. How do the videos and photos you consume make you feel?
8. Does spending time on social media bring out the best version of yourself? Why or why not?
9. If you could reinvent social media, how would it look? What would you leave out? What would you add?

Chapter 5: The Digital Playground

"Another 'F'! My stepdad, Dave, is gonna beat the sh*t out of me! I'm into French girls, not their stupid language," Jack muttered under his breath. With that thought, Jack's eyes jumped across the classroom to Clarissa, a senior honor roll student at Jacksonville High. He slouched down with his bleeding-red test carefully positioned over his phone and snapped a couple photos of his crush. He sent them to his best friend, Carle. "Do you think I have a chance?" Jack was annoyed by Carle's immediate response: "You have about as much of a chance with Clarissa as you do at passing French, lol." Jack sighed. "You're such a dork!" In a burst of ego-driven madness, he shot a text to Clarissa, "I hate French! Mr. Jones can move to Timbuktu! I hear they speak plenty of French there." To his amazement she texted back, "I know, right! This class is screwing my chances to go Ivy league, #supernerd. You coming to the bonfire tonight?" "What!?!" Jack was out of his mind, "You gotta be kidding me!" He screenshotted the text to Carle and sent, "Go home, hater!" Carle fired back, "Oh the irony. Your stepdad will never let you go . . . #so-close-yet-so-far." In that moment, Mr. Jones snatched his test out from under his elbow, exposing the smartphone. Busted!

Jack had a long walk home. He missed the bus because of detention, and Mr. Jones even confiscated his phone. "What an A-hole," he thought, "Mr. Jones is way too hardcore." The day was not a total loss. Clarissa would be waiting for him at the big bonfire that night. Then it dawned on him; he was super late, and Dave would be pretty wasted by this time. "He's such a psycho when he's drunk! If Dad was still around, he would kick his a** at the thought of how he treats Mom and me." Jack had not seen his dad since he was in middle school. He went MIA in Iraq four years ago. The government eventually pronounced him dead. Jack arrived home. He quietly cracked the door open and saw Dave passed out on the sofa. Jack's mom was at work. "What a pig," he thought. "A con like you just saw Mom as a chance to finance your booze!" Just then, he heard a knock at the door. "It's probably Carle, stopping by to get the juicy details about my unofficial date with Clarissa," he thought.

He swung the door open, and was startled to see Mr. Jones standing before him. He seemed very concerned, and pushed his way past Jack, closing and locking the door behind him. "It's just as I thought. They got to you first!" He slung Jack's now-dismantled phone onto the kitchen table. "What the hell are you doing! You destroyed my phone, A-hole. If you wake up my stepdad, we're both dead!" "Your pathetic stepdad is the least of my concerns!" Jones snapped back. "Look, I don't have time to explain, so you are just going to have to do exactly what I say!" "Are you threatening me? I'm gonna call the cops and you will be out of a job," Jack stuttered back. "Is that the best you got?" Mr. Jones mockingly replied. "Jack," Mr. Jones was now looking him square in the eyes, "he sent me for you." At this point, Jack was confused and a little worried. "I have been activated to retrieve you before it's too late." Just then, they heard car doors slamming shut. Mr. Jones peeked through the blinds to have a look. "Sh*t! They're here. Time for plan 'B'. Do you know Orion's Airfield? It's not far from here." He cracked open a black suitcase, "A little present from your dad." "My dad!?" Jack grew faint as his mind began to spin out of control. Mr. Jones grabbed him by the chin. "Stay focused!" He pulled out an assortment of passports, a stack of hundred-dollar bills, and, to Jack's terror, a black handgun. "What am I supposed to do with this?" Jack protested. "Nothing, I hope!" Mr. Jones replied. "Now get the hell out of here!" Jack hesitated. His heart was pounding. The front door's handle jiggled back and forth. "Jack, I will hold them off as long as I can, but you need to leave now!"

Are you hooked yet? Do you want to know how Jack escapes? What really happened to Jack's father? What will Jack say to his dad if he survives the journey to the airfield? Who is Mr. Jones really? Why are people after him? Jack is no longer a typical high school teen. He is now pulled into a world of international espionage, secret government plots, and mobilized crime syndicates. He will learn by doing. His journey will unfold in exotic locations to reveal the mystery surrounding his missing father. With enough wit, charm, and daring ambition, he just might survive long enough to take Clarissa out on a date. Welcome to the world of modern gaming, where reality and fantasy come together to create a version of life without limits.

Couch Heroes

Video games are more than just loud noises and flashing lights. They reflect fantasy worlds that have massively altered how Americans spend their free time. Most successful games are wildly creative, artistic, and complex in nature. They are designed to immerse players in a story that is far from reality. You are no longer just another "Joe Six-Pack" sitting on your couch. For countless teens, their online universe is the place where they encounter adventure, comradery, fun, and meaning. Through gaming, you could be an international spy or Commander of the Galactic Battalion. Maybe you are a modern-day Indiana Jones, making new archaeological discoveries while rescuing a beauty in distress. Today's video games play out like a blockbuster movie, but rather than being a spectator, players are an active part of how the plot unfolds. The plot thickens in a universe where other players from around the world can meet as sovereign characters in the same drama. These interactions with real people blur the lines between reality and digital fantasy. Your galactic fleet's mission to protect a civilian star cruiser from space marauders is only fantasy, but the multiplayer teamwork required to accomplish the mission is real. Your higher thinking brain knows deep down that this world is fictional, but the primitive side of your brain is experiencing every riveting moment of action, heroism, and teamwork as reality, pumping the brain with intense dopamine reward. What young person wouldn't want to be a hero among their peers? Just when your wingman thinks he's cornered by space marauders, you swoop down and cover his six to give him the chance to take out the enemy's lead ship. "Hot Damn, mission accomplished!"

As humans, we have an inherent longing to discover our purpose. Video games can hit our most sensitive nerve: our raw, human desire for significance. You can't be a hero unless you have someone to rescue; you aren't an explorer without uncharted territory to discover. You will never experience the thrill of making a difference in someone else's life until you become aware of the needs of others around you. The very elements that drive teens to play video games are the same core

Video games can hit our most sensitive nerve: our raw, human desire for significance.

components that give life its color. If our kids and teens don't experience purpose and adventure in the natural world, the universe of gaming is ready to step in at any time.

Gamer Nation

Lisa

"Alex was a fragile twelve-year-old boy who looked much younger than he was. He didn't want to participate in school lessons, he refused to take notes, he had no friends, and he would only engage with people on his terms. Occasionally, Alex would suddenly wake up from his zombied state and make an impressive contribution to the lesson. I could see a glimpse of the creative, intelligent, and thoughtful man hiding behind a blanket of mental haze. Alex was diagnosed with "school refusal syndrome", which allowed him to stay home if his parents were unable to motivate him to get out the door in the morning. Despite Alex's disengaged and avoidant behavior, he would brag exclusively about playing video games with eighteen-and-up advisory ratings. His parents worked after school, and Alex was left alone to his personal computer sometimes gaming up to ten hours a day.

One day, Alex's mother called the school in a fit of frustration to complain that her son had been treated unfairly. He was asked to tidy up the classroom after disrespecting a teacher. She voiced that he was already dealing with depression, and was now struggling with suicidal thoughts, which she also blamed on the faculty. Shortly after that incident, she pulled him out of school. It was apparent to me that Alex had chosen to live in another world. He had rejected the reality surrounding the rigors of education and the effort needed to build friendships, and replaced it with digital indulgence. In his virtual world, he could easily attain feedback, status, and respect. However, his engagement presented one glaring problem: it wasn't real! What would have happened if his parents empowered Alex to invest in activities that reflected healthy values and supported social skills, instead of relying on video games as a crutch for parenting? When the screen is removed, are teens left with blossoming friendships, new real-world skills, strengthened core values, and healthier bodies? For many teens, gaming is not just an exhilarating pastime, but a mind-altering addiction that trumps all other aspects of their life, including school, extra-curricular activities, and real-world friendship.

To date, nine out of ten teenagers between the ages of thirteen to seventeen play video games.[177] More than half of them have made "friends" online, and roughly a third of them have done so through gaming.[178] "[E] ight-in-ten [parents] say their school-age children play video games"[179] on a typical school day. Nearly eighty-five percent of teenagers say that they have a game console at home. The numbers continue to climb, with ninety-seven percent of boys and eighty-three percent of girls reporting that video games are a normal part of their free time activities.[180] Although young people often refer to their online community as friends, most of these "friendships" never blossom in the real world and they rarely meet their peers in person.[181] Remember James, who met his love through gaming? It was easy to fall in love with an online character, but he had never mastered the skills of maintaining a relationship and overcoming struggles of real-life companionship.

Currently, there are 2.5 billion active gamers worldwide. As of 2019, the gaming industry is among the wealthiest in the world, with a near 150 billion in estimated annual profits,[182] mobile gaming being one of the most profitable segments. With that money, you could buy 534,000 Ferrari 488 Spiders at a hefty price tag of nearly $281,000 each. The gaming economy is growing four times faster than the rest of the economy.[183] E-sports, led by games such as Overwatch, Dota 2, and League of Legends, has become a billion-dollar industry. It brought in over $900 million in 2018 alone. The prize money for winning Dota 2 gaming tournaments was more than $38 million in 2017. Despite the enormous amounts of money involved, E-sport gamers often burn out young.[184] As of 2020, Daniel Middleton (DanTDM) has a net worth of over $40 million dollars earned from reviewing computer games like *Minecraft* on YouTube.[185] Americans spend more money on video games than any other country in the world.

The purpose of presenting these statistics is not to demonize the act of enjoying gaming as a thrilling pastime, but rather to expose a driving force behind the development of these games: maximum profit. They are engineered to pull users into another reality, like a good movie that allows us to escape for a few hours. The feeling of being transported into an alternate universe with endless possibilities is gravitational. However, the major difference between gaming and films is that one has an ending and the other does not. In the universe of gaming, you are given a new identity, a purpose, and a mission. You are placed in a story that is all about making you feel good, accomplished, and special. The seemingly random sequence of events is actually a proven and tested formula to keep gamers playing. There is a legitimate fear that the life of the gaming alter ego can slowly take over.

The gaming industry has taken note of the primitive functions of the brain. Violent-sexist video games, full of objectification and sexual assault, are prevalent in a society that capitalizes on sexual images and abuse. The popular gaming store, Steam, features games with porn such as *HuniePop*, also referred to as *CandyCrush*, with more than 15,000 exceptionally positive reviews. *HuniePop* promotes a culture of lying to women in order to coerce them into sex. The user can earn sex with eleven women and a cat without them knowing about each other's affairs.[186]

The problem with games like *HuniePop* is compounded by the fact that the player is not just a passive consumer, but an active "player." Objectification in video games can severely impact both men and women. They alter users' perceptions of themselves and the world around them. It can influence their attitudes towards the opposite sex in real-life and further sexism, including "rape myths", solidifying the idea that women want to be raped.[187] Female users are used to a gaming culture where their objectification and harassment feels permissible, as gaming culture tends to promote such values. No matter the price, the industry knows how to design content to keep young users hooked. ”

The Irresistible Feedback Loop

Jason

“My roommate was a gifted college athlete, the classic jock. Getting girls was never a problem, but intellectual achievement was a different story. He was an avid gamer. I was a night owl, and would usually head to bed between one to three in the morning. He would be tucked away in a makeshift cave he built under the bunk, playing video games long after

I called it a night. His game of choice was *World of Warcraft (WoW)*. I would hear the mouse and keys clicking all night long. When I had finally had enough, I would demand that he put his laptop away. He would begrudgingly slap it shut and then set his alarm clock for 5:00 a.m. the same morning to get an early start on gaming the next day. I later found out that he was a highly rated player in the WoW universe. He used to brag that his profile was worth thousands on eBay. As of 2019, the website playerauctions.com is offering WoW accounts with price tags as high as $12,000. For my roommate, the world of WoW had become his reality of choice.

The economist Mark Aguiar and his team of researchers were surprised to find that men in their early twenties were deferring entrance to college and the workforce. Young men used to be the most reliable pool of workers that industries could draw upon, but this no longer seemed to be the case. Closer examination revealed that these young men were experiencing a failure to launch.[188] They were nestled at home, living with their parents. It became apparent that a significant number of these men filled their free time with gaming instead of filling out college applications or applying for a job.[189] Never in the last 130 years have young adults ages eighteen to thirty-four been more likely to live at home with their parents. More than thirty-two percent of those young adults fail to become self-sufficient.[190]

High school dropout Cam Adair is honest about how his passion for gaming became a life-altering obsession. Today, Cam Adair is a successful entrepreneur and speaker who leads a cutting-edge organization that offers freedom for countless teens caught up in similar circumstances. Adair argues that there are essentially four contributing factors that make games so compelling and can lead to addictive behavior. First, gaming allows you to escape your real-life problems. Instead

RUMB Challenge

Take a week-long vacation from all video games. Before you start, make a list of ten fun things you would like to do with the time you would normally spend gaming.

- How did it make you feel?
- What did you miss?
- What did you gain?
- What do you want to do more of?
- What parameters do you want to put around gaming in the future?

of dealing with a situation head-on, you get to take a break from it. Second, you can socialize and be whoever you want to be. Nobody cares who you are in daily life, if you get bullied, or if you are popular at school. Third, games allow you to feel a sense of purpose. You are on a mission, and what you do feels like it truly matters. Fourth, you get to experience a measurable reward for the effort you put in. You get instant, ongoing feedback for what you accomplish.[191]

Although the majority of teenagers don't think twice about using the digital playground of online gaming to unwind, this fantasy world has drastic effects on their social development. Time is our most precious commodity. It is a resource that we cannot earn back after it is spent. Gaming is full of content that is engineered to entertain. It can be a very enjoyable experience for those who seek to exchange their time for some good fun. However, problems occur when teens search for contentment, but only find more content. It is important that they recognize that gaming does not bring fulfillment as a reward for the hours they pour into their virtual endeavors.

In 2018, The World Health Organization added gaming disorder to their eleventh edition of the International Classification of Diseases (ICD-11) manual, labeling it a clinical condition and a diagnosable behavioral addiction. Behavioral addiction shares many parallels with substance addiction. The short-term benefits override the long-term negative effects. Positive feedback for our gaming efforts is constant and immediate. Instead of self-regulating, it is significantly easier for teens to find refuge in video games. Our reward system is hijacked. Gaming can be used to escape boredom and cope with stress, anxiety, or rejection. According to Psychologist Adam Alter, there is recipe that game developers use to maintain our committed engagement: "compelling goals that are just beyond reach; irresistible and unpredictable positive feedback; a sense of incremental progress and improvement; tasks that become slowly more difficult over time; unresolved tensions that demand resolution; and strong social connections."[192]

Even when teens are sent away from the luxuries of modern life, their phones go with them. I remember one youth retreat that took place in the Rocky Mountains. We had organized an inspiring guest speaker who had many years of experience engaging teenagers in deeper life discussions. The remote Colorado terrain provided the perfect haven for teens to unplug from their full-throttle city lifestyles. Despite his best efforts and the complete absence of internet connectivity, some teens still pulled their phones out to game, even while sitting in the front row just a few feet away from the speaker.

In the moment, gaming provides a deeply authentic experience that speaks to the identity of a player, but once the device is turned off, so is the reality that came with it. Thousands of hours of online gaming don't equate to rewards that carry over into real-life relationships. A Swedish study involving nearly eight thousand participants between the ages of thirteen to seventeen showed that young people who spend more than five hours playing video games a day were five times more likely to experience depression.[193] Unlike real-life adventures that deepen social bonds, strengthen emotional skills, and establish feelings of self-efficacy, the digital world provides no cushion for confronting the truth once you inevitably face reality: you are not the hero, fearless leader, or daring adventure extraordinaire you portrayed online. Youth need to be encouraged to explore the journey of self-discovery. If they learn to embrace who they are meant to be and face their personal struggles head-on with the help of caring adults, they stand a chance. Shame makes youth believe that they are unworthy of love, belonging and connection.[194] Often, it is a feeling of inadequacy and fear of rejection that causes a gamer to choose the virtual life over reality.

Game developers possess billions of hours of user data to help them create the most captivating games that keep users hooked. It's a formula that delivers profit, not value. They can see when users come online and, more importantly, what circumstances lead them to going offline. This data is immensely profitable, and often only requires minor alterations in the gameplay to coax users along. *Zynga,* the tech company that launched *FarmVille* in 2009, paid careful attention to users' gaming endurance. *FarmVille* offered a "pay-to-skip" option to accelerate players' progress, and freebies if the algorithm predicted that they would give up. Loot boxes can advance a player's earnings in the game by the millions and have made "free" downloads like *Candy Crush* immensely profitable. When a player opens a loot box, they will find random items that increase the game's value. Some countries such as Belgium and the Netherlands have banned most loot boxes as a form of illegal gambling. Dalton Combs, co-founder of *Boundless Mind*, an organization which combats the addictive nature of technology, observes, "If you're setting the consequences of someone's behaviors and you tie those consequences to learning machines so that the consequences shift according to individual markers, you really do have exquisite control over shaping that individual's behavior—over how he spends his time."[195] In recent years, games have become so much more addictive that even well-known public figures like Prince Harry, Duke of Sussex, have spoken out against them. Once a gamer himself, Prince Harry has since publicly announced his desire to see *Fortnite* (a game that has attracted over 250 million young players) banned because of its addictive nature. "It's created to addict, an addiction to keep you in front of a computer for as long as possible."[196]

Revenge of the Meter-Maid

Jason

My old college housemate Calvin was always dreaming of big ideas: joining the NYPD, becoming the next J.K. Rowling, or achieving video game superstardom in Silicon Valley, but nothing would ever come to fruition. He lived and breathed video games of all kinds. Our living room was essentially his gaming den. He was constantly glued to the sofa and could not hold down a job. He liked the idea of college, but failed all his courses because he never studied. We shared a two-bedroom apartment with four others guys to pay down the rent in Chicago. Although he was in his mid-20s at the time, Calvin was solely financially supported by his parents. He would talk about his job at a local gas station, which turned out to be completely fictional. Honesty was not his strong suit. One night, I witnessed the full extent of his addiction. Once a week, we had to move our cars to the opposite side of the road to make room for the street sweeper. It was a hefty fine if you did not move your car on those days. One of our housemates blew through the door to let Calvin know that his car was still parked on the wrong side of the street and the "meter-maid" was just around the corner. If he moved his car in that moment, he would be in the clear. Calvin's response stunned us. "Yeahhhh. Don't worry about it. It's fine," he casually replied. My roommates and I urged him to see the flaws in his logic. "How can it be fine? You are about to get a ticket! Move your butt!" I thought. The more we pushed him, the less interested he seemed in moving his car. He was glazed over. His eyes were attached to the screen as his hands frantically clicked away at the buttons of his controller. He ended up getting the ticket.

The Game is Rigged

Lisa

When gaming turns into an addiction, kids and teens are not the only ones who suffer. I vividly remember a mother's hopelessness as she revealed the extent of her son's deceit. Her shoulders hung low as silent tears ran down her cheeks. She told me in the presence of her son that he had been frequently skipping school for up to a week at a time. He would leave the house and sneak back in after his mom went to work so he could continue playing video games without anyone noticing. This had been going on for weeks until the school demanded answers for his absences. Her son complained that we simply didn't understand. He needed to play the game in real time, or he would lose points. He explained that he had a highly respected gaming rating, which would be destroyed if he didn't put in the time. His story was a common occurrence during my career as a teacher. Either kids would stay home pretending to be sick, or they would come to school dreadfully sleep-deprived. Downing cans of *Red Bull™ and Monster™* energy drinks was the common solution to surviving the day.

Game designer Ramin Shokrizade is honest about the industry's hard business directives. "The most aggressive companies will hire soft and hard scientists like myself, in addition to quantitative scientists, to optimize the

RUMB Challenge

Pick two afternoons this week to connect with friends:

1. Choose one afternoon to play video games and take note of how connected you felt with your friends during and after your virtual gaming session.
2. Choose another afternoon for a social activity with your friends (e.g. sports, board games, fishing) and discuss afterwards whether you felt more or less connected with your friends. Why? Why not?

exploitation of youth."[197] Dr. Douglas Gentile, an expert on adolescent media addiction, followed 3,000 kids for three years and discovered that children who struggle with mental health issues or attention disorders are more likely to display unhealthy gaming patterns. Gaming companies specifically target and abuse their desire to escape. Fascinatingly, children who game consistently from early childhood are more likely to develop attention disorders and social anxiety, making their social interactions in school far more difficult. This cycle intensifies mental health struggles and pushes them further into the world of online gaming.[198]

In a moment of vulnerability, Calvin opened up to me about his complicated relationship with gaming. He seemed to be somewhat aware that it wasn't producing positive results in his life. Calvin talked about being sick a lot as a young kid. He was frequently admitted to the hospital. His only way to pass the time was through video games. Calvin said that this was the origin of his obsession. He could sit in bed physically weak and broken down, but through video games he could experience a different reality. Like any addiction, if you want to break the cycle of constant gaming, you need to determine the psychological root of the attraction. What underlying human needs are driving the addiction?

China was the first nation that declared internet addiction a clinical disorder, calling it the greatest health threat to the present teenage generation. An internet addict is considered anyone who spends more than six hours a day online.[199] The Chinese have built more than 400 rehabilitation camps to treat Internet Addiction Disorder. One mom of a student in the rehabilitation camp discussed her son's concerning metamorphosis that alienated him from friends and family. "The games affected his mind. He had insomnia. He'd get dirty and smelly, but he wouldn't care. He wouldn't wash his face, body or feet . . . nothing. He changed into a different person."[200] A psychiatrist at one of the centers referred to gaming as electronic heroin, "[t]hey think that the real world is not as good as the virtual world. [. . .] Some kids are so hooked on these games they think going to the bathroom will affect their performance. So they wear a diaper."[201] The psychiatrists claim that the part of the brain that is responsible for social development stops developing and the inner age of the gamer remains immature. Addicted gamers often lack the ability to trust people, and have little desire to create and connect offline.

Chinese adolescents tend to have little company at home because of the one child per family policy that remained in effect until 2015. This fact, combined with parents who work long hours for little pay, breeds an environment that predisposes kids to escapist behaviors. However, Euro-America faces its own struggles with absent parents, lack of community, plunging birth rates, and overly-stressed teens. An absence of meaningful relationships drives countless teenagers to the online world to find self-worth, success, and validation. After viewing Cam Adair's *Ted Talk,* one teen had a riveting realization of the very real battle between people and pixels:

> I've been addicted to video games for about six years now. It takes a huge chunk out of my life. The reason I do all these is because at school I'm treated like I'm invisible, my teachers are jerks, and I'm depressed. Like you mentioned in the talk, online you are judged on how you play and how you interact with the community. I have made over 300 friends playing online who like me only for who I am.[. . .] But because of this I am failing my schoolwork and getting more depressed. I don't know why, but my addiction feels more like something glued me to my chair in front of my computer.[202]

There is nothing wrong with occasional gaming sessions with friends or retreating to one's room for a little "me time", but we should be wary that the virtual world doesn't slowly become the only place where our teens get their relational needs met. If we take the time to communicate that we see our struggling teen, that we are willing to ask questions and listen, even if we don't have all the answers, we effectively allow empathy to uncover the root issues of their escapist behavior. Youth need to be reminded who they truly are and who they were made to be.

Teens are desperate to feel significant. They long to be connected to a community that accepts them for who they are. Unlimited time in front of a screen will never produce socially mature behavior in the long run. It doesn't provide them with the tools to face the challenges of life head-on. Virtual fantasy worlds are built on principles of quick reward for minimal effort, which is contrary to the principles that lead to a flourishing life, such as perseverance, commitment, and resolve for reaching higher goals. Our teens need to understand that the offline world is messy and naturally requires more work, but the long-term rewards are worth fighting for. Teens can only find relational fulfillment, develop healthy coping strategies, and discover outlets to unwind if tech isn't a crutch to escape real life. Guiding our children and investing in their hidden passions is powerful during these developmental years. Remember, hardly any addiction develops after adolescence.

Discussion Guide:

1. What fascinates you about your favorite video game(s)?
2. What messages are the main characters conveying?
3. Have you ever seen gaming gone wrong? How?
4. What values do your favorite games promote? Which values are healthy, and which ones do you disagree with? Why?
5. Does success in the gaming world equate to success in the real world? Why or why not?
6. What do you value more than video games? How is that reflected in your life?

Chapter 6: Sex Gods and Zombies

Jason

In our interview, the former porn addict and reborn anti-porn activist, Gabe Deem, journeyed back to his first introduction to hardcore pornography.

"I was fourteen or fifteen at the time and believed porn was the answer to good sex. I thought it would turn me into a sex god, not a libido-less zombie! This is when my battle between pixels and real sex started."

Gabe described himself as an extroverted teenager who wasn't afraid to test boundaries and make his presence known. He was refreshingly honest about his experience growing up in a wired culture. When it came to his sexual development, he was all about finding the biggest thrill. Gabe and his friends used to brag about the porn they watched with girls they flirted with and even tried to get some to reenact their porn inspired fantasies in real life.

Porn welcomes consumers of all backgrounds, whether they are the captain of the football team, the mathlete, or the theatre kid. To date, nine out of ten teenagers are neutral, accepting, or encouraging when it comes to porn.[203]

If we want to empower this generation to take their values online, we need to understand what competing values the porn industry is throwing their way. When teens consume pornography, they are smitten by the outpouring of sexual euphoria blowing up their brain, leaving many unaware of the porn-inspired values they elect to align with. When I teach teens about the importance of choosing a value-driven life, I illustrate the message with dodgeballs. I ask a volunteer from the crowd to stand up. They represent my aspirations and goals. Similarly, teens also have dreams and ambitions to one day leave their own mark on the world. Many desire a family, a committed relationship, and practically everyone wants to experience great sex. However, if their value system isn't in alignment with their vision for success, they will become aimless dreamers, destined to wander but never fully arrive. I then throw the ball deep into the crowd, missing the lone volunteer by a mile. This goes on a few more rounds, until the teens are quite convinced that I have never touched a ball in my life. The moral of my silly shenanigans is then revealed. I pick up the final remaining dodgeball and explain, "Not every life value is equal or good. Some values we come to accept can lead us to very unpleasant places. We strive to succeed, but the values governing our lives cause us to miss the mark. However, carefully choosing values such as courage, community, or love to govern our actions can protect us from going down the wrong path when faced with difficult choices." I then launch the ball, backed with eighteen years of basketball experience, to nail my volunteer target.

The doctrine of porn promotes a selfish and destructive value system that is masked by pleasure, but in reality, derails the healthy development of countless teens. The harsh realities of producing and consuming porn are tragic and sobering, but it is critical that we as parents, teachers, or professionals working with youth understand the reality teens face on their own with their smartphones. Only from a place of understanding can we engage this next generation in deeper discussions about the values that govern their online choices.

The Fallacy of Neutrality

Internet pornography is defining an entire generation. It appeals to our most primitive and fundamental human desires. The kids who are growing up in today's world don't have the luxury of being neutral on this issue. They have two options: to become a consumer or a fighter. There is simply no middle ground. Almost every child is confronted with this fact each day they go to school, hang out with friends, or are alone in their room. The choice to say "yes" or "no" to pornography is a constant battle. The XXX store is waiting for them every time they check a message on their smartphone, and for many, pornography is simply a completely normal way of life. The boundaries to accessing internet pornography stretch as far as our kid's LTE 4G signal.

The message of porn teaches children and teens early on that there is a major disconnect between sexuality and love, affection, and tender care. Baywatch star Pamela Anderson, who was featured thirteen times as the cover girl for *Playboy* magazine, was fed up with the current sexualized culture. She joined up with Rabbi Shmuley Boteach to devote an entire book to the topic. Anderson explained, "Kids are growing up thinking sex is disconnected, painful, demeaning to women, involving many partners, and even violent."[204]

The New Sex Education

Jason

"One of my assignments as an educational integration expert placed me with an autistic eighth grader who struggled with severe anxiety. During one of his classes, the teacher played a sex education video that introduced the 101 basics. The video was nothing new for these thirteen- to fourteen-year-old teens. Porn was the established sex educator, so most of the class was astonished when the video highlighted that porn is fake.

What was once an awkward trip to an adult erotic store or uncomfortably sitting beside strangers in an adult movie theater, has now been replaced with the clandestine cloak of an internet browser. Today's children and teens have access to a virtually unlimited supply of pornographic material. Porn is so ubiquitous that it weaves its way into adolescent language and behavior; "it is not a matter of merely consuming porn but of becoming porn."[205] This rising generation of youth is so accustomed to being bombarded with erotic images that it has become increasingly normal to produce and share their own nude images. In other words, they are complicit in the production of Child Sex Abuse Material (CSAM) without even giving it a second thought.

Today, porn is mainstream entertainment. Some of the most popular celebrities, adored by teens all over the world, portray a glamorous life with a porn star side-hustle that launched them to fame. Kim Kardashian West initially entered the public eye after her sex tape went viral in 2002. She has since bolted up the list of top ten most popular celebrities, known for her incessant posting on Instagram. Many teens attempt to recreate her infamous "sink shot" booty pic (strategically sitting on the edge of a sink to accentuate her butt). Along with being *insta-famous,* she is among the most-searched adult actresses. Porn has become so prevalent in society that many don't even question the practices it promotes. *It's just for fun, and what's wrong with having a good time?*

Alice, the former porn consumer who we introduced in chapter three, started experimenting with porn at age eleven. She was twenty-three when she finally overcame her porn addiction:

> I lived a really sheltered upbringing that really didn't talk about sex, didn't talk about porn. As I was getting older, I asked what does this [sex] mean? I ended up finding it in porn. I used porn as my education. [. . .] While I was struggling with porn addiction from eighteen to twenty-three, I was at Bible college, I was working in the church and leading ministries. I had the 'good Christian girl' image. I won awards for my social justice and leadership work, I was quiet and well-behaved. No one would have guessed my secret addiction.

Her journey is one of many.

Nipplegate and Free Intimacy

To date, most porn sites follow YouTube's business model to profit through data harvesting, sidebar and banner ads, as well as click-bait. Between eighty and ninety percent of consumers watch free pornographic material, which includes bootleg copies and amateur videos.[206] In most cases, disclaimers and warnings regarding age are only mentioned *pro forma*.[207]

YouTube is the most popular social media platform to date, with seventy-three percent of Americans using its streaming services. Less known is YouTube's controversial origin. Its founders, Chad Hurley, Steve Chen, and Jawed Karim, divulged that the site was largely inspired by Janet Jackson's 2004 Super Bowl *Nipplegate* scandal.[208] They were surprised how difficult it was to find easily accessible online videos of her bare breast. The YouTube streaming model was born with huge success to follow. The site was purchased by Google for $1.65 billion USD in 2005, only a year after being launched. To date, 400 hours of video are uploaded on YouTube every minute. As soon as YouTube was launched, it was only a matter of time until a porn equivalent would follow. Sure enough, in the summer of 2006, adult entertainment sites such as PornoTube, RedTube, and YouPorn flooded the market with free content. Pornhub, launched in 2007, is now the most popular porn site with an average of 85 million people visiting their site daily.[209] To date, the porn industry is largely controlled by one multi-billion-dollar company, *MindGeek,* run by a handful of men in Luxemburg and operational offices in Montreal, Canada. Free porn is a lucrative business, contributing to porn's $97 billion global profits, with $10-12 billion a year in the United States alone.[210] In the U.S., porn revenue surpasses that of football, baseball, and basketball franchises combined.[211] In his presentation at Princeton University, Kirk Doran called pornography "a visual pheromone, a powerful 100 billion dollar per year brain drug that is changing human sexuality."[212] Online platforms like YouTube and Instagram are much more ambiguous about offering pornographic content, but one thing is clear: all are profiting from child and adolescent consumption. The white canvas of the teenage mind is easily intoxicated by curated sexual encounters. Who can forget the incredible rush of our first kiss or the heart-pounding dizziness of our sexual awakening? This healthy and natural predisposition to be sexually curious makes teenage consumption of porn a highly lucrative business. There are 830 million active teenagers online, and their raging hormones accompany them along the ride.[213]

With such numbers, there is little incentive to create effective boundaries to protect children from harmful media. Youth under eighteen are one of the largest porn-consuming demographics.[214] One study found that boys ages twelve and seventeen are the most frequent porn consumers.[215] According to Dr. Anthony Jack:

> [A]nyone with a high-speed internet connection can, if they choose, access more sexually arousing content in a few hours than the most obsessive and wealthy collector of a few decades ago could have amassed in a lifetime.[216]

In 2009, devices like smartphones became the go-to for countless internet users to access porn, driving online porn-related traffic to new heights. The industry blew up, with 420 million pornographic pages available online, 4.2 million adult websites, and 68 million daily internet search inquiries for online pornographic material.[217] In 2016, the most popular porn streaming site, Pornhub, recorded an astounding 4.6 billion hours (52.5 thousand decades) of porn consumed on their site in just one year.[218] In its 2017 end-of-the-year report, the company reported 95 billion viewings of its porn videos and 28.5 billion user visits.[219]

When Porn Gets Real

As porn goes mainstream, so does the message it preaches about sexuality. Girls are increasingly pressured by their boyfriends to perform like porn stars. Australian journalist Patrick Wood wrote in his investigative piece for *ABC News*, "There are wildly diverse views about online porn in this country, but one thing is clear: Australia has a problem."[220] In one of the most extreme cases, Wood reported about a young teen who was pressured into having group anal sex. Her bowels were so damaged in the abusive act that she lost her ability to pass stool and needed to have a colostomy bag surgically attached. An increasing number of girls have reported sustaining terrible injuries from their boyfriend's porn-inspired fantasies. "[Sex] tends to be using objects. It does tend to be quite violent or being tied up, and the girls often feel very powerless to say no,"[221] commented Susan McLean, a cyber safety expert.

Corrupted Intimacy

Pornography consumption is compelling. While it might be sexual curiosity and excitement that initially pulls a teenager in, over time it begins to fulfill a different role. Pornography provides instant gratification when facing stress, rejection, depression, or loneliness. The first time youth are exposed to online sex, the euphoria created by the dopamine reward is so strong that a powerful neurological pathway is formed between the reward and behavior. This phenomenon naturally occurs in the context of a loving relationship between two partners. It can motivate each partner to put their best effort into the relationship with a reward of sexual gratification. It pushes partners to maintain optimal relational health, where intimacy, vulnerability, and acceptance flourish. On the contrary, pornography introduces intense sexual rewards without being connected to any beneficial behavior. Pornography can seem like an authentic, meaningful interaction between consumers and actors. It feels vulnerable because a person in a video becomes sexually intimate when they allow consumers to cross all their boundaries and witness their most private moments. Alice drove the point home, stating:

> Porn is fake intimacy. It sort of pretends to be. The world we live in says sex equals intimacy and sex on a screen is free intimacy, with no risk of rejection and no risk of 'you suck at this' or 'I am not going to call you again.' You can just fantasize your life away and tell yourself, I am one of the sexy women that everyone wants.

How can vulnerability be experienced with videos that are made for the masses? How intimate is sex with an image on a digital device? Compulsive porn users often struggle with shame, low self-esteem, and mental health. It's no wonder the rising generation is developing concerning attitudes towards the opposite gender, sex, and intimacy.

Studies that analyze popular pornographic material reveal that eighty-eight percent of pornographic scenes portray physical aggression towards women.[222] These acts of aggression include spanking, gagging, open-handed slapping, hair pulling, choking, and bondage.[223] Other popular genres include acts of forcing a penis down a woman's throat to the point where she uncontrollably chokes or vomits.[224] We have to understand that pornography is flooding today's market with much more deviant images than simply portraying nudity. Pornhub boasts that among the most popular porn searches are "mom" and "teen" porn.[225] Studies of recent trends of pornography reveal that forty-one percent of mainstream adult movies show scenes where a man puts his penis in a woman's anus followed immediately by placing it in her mouth so that she can taste her own excrement.[226] These acts of sexual violence and humiliation are common and easy for children to discover online. Even hardcore, illegal porn is not out of a child's reach. Pornography has changed drastically over the past few decades. Perhaps the best way to illustrate how much more grotesque and brutal pornography has become is to follow the transformation of

RUMB Challenge

Make a list of values that are essential for true intimacy to exist between committed lovers. Make another list that reflects the values promoted through pornography.

Why does porn hijack true intimacy?

British journalist, Martin Dubney. As the former editor of the lad's magazine, *Loaded*, Dubney relied on softcore pornography in his magazine to ramp up sales. Years later, he was involved in the production of a documentary called "Porn on the Brain." When interviewing teenagers, Dubney's findings led him to believe that pornography is the "most pernicious threat facing children today."[227] He discovered that it was normal for teens to have been impacted by horrendous pornographic images, such as bestiality, even through seemingly innocuous channels like Facebook. He encountered teens who masturbated to porn as much as twenty-six times a day and girls who complained that they were asked to reenact what boys had seen in porn. Dubney has since become a radical anti-porn activist who educates people on the dangers of pornography.

If porn is so pervasive, without any borders to its consumption, it poses serious questions regarding its effects on the well-being and healthy physical, mental, and social development of children and youth. Perhaps the most alarming side effect of excessive pornography consumption is the erosion of sexual boundaries and an increasing acceptance of dating violence. Clinical psychologist Steiner-Adair, a leading expert in the field of media education, writes, "Abusive partners have always used belittling, derisive comments to control and punish their partner, and unfortunately, contemporary male culture has always included permission to openly rate and ridicule girls and women, especially in sexual terms. But the combination of media, sex and violence, online pornography, texting, and other social media has normalized this kind of behavior and the impulse to broadcast it."[228] Radical feminist, anti-porn scholar, and activist Gail Dines has spent three decades researching and uncovering the harmful effects of porn on society. She has observed a change in men's behavior. "I am not saying that a man reads porn and goes out to rape, but what I do know is that porn gives permission to its consumers to treat women as they are treated in porn."[229] According to Pew Research, almost one in seven teenagers "have pressured a partner into sexual activity they did not want to have."[230] There is no doubt that hardcore pornography consumption correlates with increased dating and sexual violence.[231] Cyber safety expert Susan McLean states, "I've had GPs [General Practitioners] tell me about the injuries they are seeing in young girls when they have been forced or coerced to do what is in porn videos. The girls in the video all appear to like it, so girls just think that's how sex is."[232] Alice shared that she had realized in retrospect that her boyfriend's sexual tastes were fueled by porn. "There was a distinct lack of eye contact. It wasn't intimate and gentle. He knew I didn't actually want to have sex. My pleasure was never even on the table. It was only 100% about him. I put up with all the crap that he did, and thought maybe he would love me one day."

Pleasure by Giving Pleasure

There is no greater form of communication that can more profoundly express intimacy, vulnerability, and acceptance than sharing a sexual relationship with someone you are committed to loving in their entirety, body, mind, and soul. Experiencing our sexuality with a significant other can be a way of summing up all our deepest thoughts, feelings, and desires in one beautiful act of vulnerability and acceptance. We are allowing someone else to cross over all personal boundaries to see us in our most private state of being. This requires a tremendous amount of trust between both partners. We must not only trust that the other partner won't exploit our vulnerability or trample on the shared intimacy, but also that the partner has a deep understanding of the value of a sexual relationship. The minute sex turns into something corrupted, deep emotional, physical, and psychological wounds follow. We believe that sexuality in its purest form is a physical representation of what has already been built into a relationship, like trust, love, care, desire, acceptance, and commitment. Sex that is built on a foundation of conquest (i.e., "You are just a one night stand to add to my list of achievements") or consumerism ("You are here to please me, and if you don't perform to my standards I am out") can only lead to pain and relationship ruin. It is a form of corrupted intimacy and vulnerability, absent of acceptance. Knowing you are capable of sexually satisfying your partner can be a very bonding and fulfilling experience. However, this requires a form of love that makes the other person's well-being the central focus. We learn to be pleasured by giving pleasure. This is sex 101, yet popular porn culture teaches teens the sheer opposite. Porn dehumanizes. Why else are there so many forms of sex that are designed for women to be subservient to men? Something is wrong when it is becoming increasingly normal for girls to be introduced to choking as their first sexual experience with a partner.[233] Where is the love?

Pornography teaches youth that the point of sex is neither to express love nor to have an amazing time with their partner, but to pleasure oneself in the context of being alone. Thus, it should no longer be surprising that sex, even in marriage, is on the decline. Some have called it a recession. Masturbation is on the rise, while sex is in a drought.[234] Teenagers growing up in a culture shaped by porn are learning to express their pornified sexual desires and expectations; however, without love for themselves and their partners, they will never know the joy and wholeness of sexual fulfillment within the context of a healthy and committed relationship, where the well-being of one another is the central focus.

What's Wrong with Pleasure and Limp Noodles?

Jason

In 2018, I participated in a fascinating group discussion at the *Global Summit to End Sexual Exploitation* in Washington D.C. The conversation shifted to porn as a possible influencer of increased sexual abuse among children in the United States. Everyone seemed to have their own take on how porn was fueling sexual abuse, when a young charismatic college student jumped in to ask a very important question: "What's wrong with pleasure, orgasm, and enjoying sex? Why should we be critical of something that gives people instant orgasm and intense sexual euphoria? Is it not strange to be against something that makes people feel good?" The answers to these questions are simple. Nothing is wrong with pleasure, orgasm, and sexual euphoria, but what if porn does not fuel one's sex life, passion, and desire? What if it sabotages the healthy sexual development of today's teens? The garbage that the porn industry is pumping into mainstream culture is poison, fundamentally shaping the hearts and minds of an entire generation. "I want to be real with kids about the effects porn can have on their sexual development," Gabe explained. "I never sugar-coat the truth. When I walk in a room with teens, I tell them just like it is, 'Hi I am Gabe Deem and I used to have a limp noodle'." What would drive someone to speak so honestly about a theme that most go to great lengths to keep hidden from others, especially the public eye? Like countless young teens, Gabe learned just how destructive and harmful pornography is for one's developing sexuality. He explained, "I want to help all those suffering from porn addiction and dependency and to refute the mainstream media's claim that porn is not a problem." Gabe does not claim a moral high ground on this issue. His motivation is simple: "People are going through hell!" He explained that his journey with porn started with girly magazines at eight years old. By the time Gabe entered college, the pixels had won the battle. When he reached his early twenties, he was incapable of having sex with his girlfriend.

This phenomenon among young males has left many confused and concerned about their sexual health, and terrified to pursue sexual intimacy with a real partner. These men are unable to achieve an erection when attempting to have sex with their partner.[235] Doctors are often unable to identify 'below the belt' physical malfunctions. Harvard urology professor, Abraham Morgentaler, observed, "[. . .] it's hard to know exactly how many young men are suffering from porn-induced ED [erectile dysfunction]. But it's clear that this is a new phenomenon, and it's not rare."[236] A Canadian study revealed among 258 adolescents, over fifty-three percent of males reported sexual difficulties, "[e]rectile dysfunction [ED] and low desire were the most common problems [. . .]."[237] This is especially apparent when adults and adolescents stop using pornography in an attempt to cure their psychogenic ED. Recent research suggests that sexually experienced adults (who have had years of physical sex with a real partner) recover from psychogenic pornography-induced ED faster than younger men or adolescents with little or no experience with a real partner.[238]

For Gabe, the journey of kicking porn to the curb was challenging. "When I couldn't get it up anymore, I freaked out!" He began to research the subject, and discovered hundreds of thousands of other guys in online forums were in the same panic as he was; "What was going on? We were all way too young." Gabe estimates that there are at least one million men registered with different online groups trying to resolve their porn-induced ED. "This only represents the men who are actually willing to come out and say they have a problem. I used to be a lurker (one who reads forums without being registered) before I officially joined the discussion." In his opinion, you can multiply this number by ten and that would generally represent the number of men struggling with porn-related ED issues. When it became crystal clear that porn had re-wired his brain, Gabe decided to drop it for good. After quitting porn, Gabe initially experienced symptoms like depression, lethargy, severe brain fog, stress, anxiety, and "the flatline", which he described as a period of time where you have no libido. "You feel like a ninety-five-year-old man with no testosterone and no drive to do anything, turning you into an asexual zombie."

Classroom Chats

Lisa

One could argue that culture has shifted, and sex as an expression of love and intimacy is outdated. One of my students argued that porn can be okay if managed properly. "Isn't it okay to indulge in porn as long as I am still able to have sex with my girlfriend?" he asked. This is a valid question, and deserves a legitimate answer. Porn accesses a powerful neurological system that hardwires sexual reward with behavior, creating strong adaptations in the adolescent brain. Thus, what teens view as a simple pleasurable experience has a profound impact on the development of their internal state of being. This does not only equate to physical sexual hindrances, like ED, but also very different attitudes towards romance, relationships, and intimacy, which are fundamental to pursuing a flourishing life.

Hot Sex and Cold Emotions

Hookup culture has flipped intimacy on its head. Many aspects of this lifestyle share attitudes with mainstream porn culture. Hookup culture is a modern phenomenon that is all about hot sex and cold emotions. Sex is uncommitted and casual. Even though many college students and teens alike have accepted hookup culture as normal, it is the very same young people who question it. Donna Freitas, author of *The End of Sex: How Hookup Culture is Leaving a Generation Unhappy, Sexually Unfulfilled, and Confused about Intimacy,* interviewed over 100 college students from seven different college campuses. She found that most students did not feel empowered by "hooking up" and showed little excitement, despite engaging in it. She further explained:

> [Hooking up] robbed them of healthy, fulfilling sex lives; positive dating experiences; and loving relationships. At its very worst, hooking up made students feel *miserable* and *abused*, and some students claimed that all it took was a hookup gone wrong and your college experience could be ruined—that one night could make or break your life at college for good.[239]

Freitas points out that kids use alcohol to desensitize their emotions in sexual encounters. Pamela Anderson discovered how an overabundance of porn has changed our values. She writes:

> We've abandoned sensuality, becoming uncomfortably numb. Men have to take drugs at a younger age just to get an erection because they're desensitized, bored, and overly indulged. Sexual partners have become products, and the range of sexual experiences offered by modern life is limited, flattened, and holds no fascination.[240]

To survive hook up culture, one must become emotionally devoid of feelings. "Catching feelings" in a hookup scenario is like catching the plague. Pornography teaches a generation to make a mockery of vulnerability and intimacy, which undermines the very foundation of relationship. Pornography is filmed prostitution. It twists sex into a consumable product where people are paid to be abused, humiliated, and degraded in front of a camera to feed the lust of a voracious sex market. Freitas states:

> Everybody is becoming a sex object, a sex toy; it's an exchange, an agreement. The mainstreaming of porn is tremendously affecting what's expected of them . . . What it means to have sex, a lot of the time, is to mimic what they see in pornography.[241]

This makes sense, considering how humans are wired. When a child or adolescent consumes hardcore pornography, the reward circuitry of the brain is flooded with dopamine for unnatural periods of time. Thus, the brain is rewarded for viewing the degradation of and violence towards another person, most often women.[242] The more often the behavior is repeated, the stronger the connections become.[243] The strongest natural achievable release of dopamine is through sexual stimulation.[244]

In Like a Needle, Out Like a Fishhook

Teenagers are curious about sex. They shouldn't be shamed for having the deeply human desire for sexual pleasure and fulfillment. We quite literally need this enticement to keep our species alive. Internet pornography provides a novel experience; there is always another video, another woman, another position, or "storyline" for customers to choose from. It exploits our human cravings for sexual discovery, so that the longing for intimacy and connection is never fulfilled. Thus, adolescents experience unending sexual excitement without ever finding sexual fulfillment. The porn industry is a highly saturated, highly competitive market which operates out of "business rationales and motivation."[245] Staying ahead of the competition depends on providing fresh sexual novelties to avoid user habituation and losing customers. This also explains why sexual content has gotten more deviant in recent years.[246] Scientists have dubbed the male appetite for sexual variety as the "Coolidge Effect." An experiment proved that male mammals who have mated with one female to the point of exhaustion and lack of interest in sex can recover immediately to sexual readiness when a new female is introduced to the environment.[247] This concept applies to porn consumption as well. Dutch researchers played videos of heterosexual intercourse to male test subjects who were initially sexually aroused, but with repeated viewings, their arousal yielded to habituation. However, with the introduction of a new erotic video, the males immediately returned to a state of high sexual arousal.[248] This suggests that pornography consumers can continually pump their reward circuitry with high levels of mine by introducing novel pornographic material. Dopamine is not only designed to create pleasure, but also to pursue pleasure.[249] Gary Wilson, author of "Your Brain on Porn," explains, "Bingeing on porn feels like a promise of pleasure but recall that the message of dopamine isn't 'satisfaction.' It's, 'keep going, satisfaction is just around the corner.'"[250] The brain is not meant to be exposed to such high levels of dopamine for extended periods of time and protects itself by shutting down dopamine receptors.[251]

This reduces the reward circuitry's sensitivity to dopamine, driving users to intensify their search for more sexual novelty. Wilson explains, "Porn goes in like a needle but comes out like a fishhook."[252]

Drugged

Porn addicts function similarly to drug addicts; they must increase the stimulus to achieve the same level of dopamine release, which can only be achieved by novel sexual stimulation. Pornography consumption can easily become an addictive pattern. Porn addiction is a chronic condition that doesn't go away just because someone stops using porn.[253] It takes about eighteen months to restore dopamine receptors to pre-porn condition.[254] Most porn consumers are unaware that they are hooked on porn until they try to quit. Many describe withdrawal symptoms that are similar to those of drug addicts. We talked to a professional counselor who works with porn addicts. He told us that it takes his clients a year with weekly counseling sessions to overcome their porn consumption. Will power alone is not enough. It requires tools, time, and a support system.

Constantly needing novel content to achieve the same results could also explain why popular pornography often contains shocking acts of violence and aggression. Such acts are consumed for the relentless search of a dopamine reward. As discussed in chapter three, the reward circuit is a primitive mechanism in the brain. It does not objectively process the content consumed, but rather the amount of dopamine released. This can have a devastating impact on the hearts and minds of today's teens, whose biomechanics can't help but attach the porn they watch (no matter how degrading or violent) to a euphoric sense of pleasure. This is very confusing for teenagers, as their identity and sexuality have not yet fully matured. The abuse and humiliation they are watching online looks wrong but feels good. The incoherence between biological sensation and higher moral understanding can lay the foundation for a corrupted and confused sense of self. A young boy might think that he is the type of person who enjoys sexual abuse when, in reality, his brain has been hacked by the porn industry. Consequently, porn can degrade a teen's identity, making them less likely to question when it crosses sexual boundaries. Sexual abusers are known to use a similar strategy against their victims. They violate someone's boundaries and then blame the victim for their biological response, claiming it makes them complicit. This effectively destroys the victim's self-worth, making them more vulnerable to future abuse and destructive behavior.

Why I Stopped

> ### RUMB Challenge
>
> Write down five characteristics that would describe your life in five years:
>
> a) With regular porn consumption.
> b) Replacing porn with thriving relationships.

How are young people expected to learn how to stand with a partner in a relationship, if they have spent years lusting after women and men of all shapes and sizes? Whether we believe it or not, porn will creep its way into a teenager's bedroom. For some, that might mean that they choose porn over the hassle of wooing a partner, facing possible rejection and entering a real-life relationship that requires work and emotional investment. While growing individualization and increased social isolation are considerable factors that have resulted in positive change, such as less unprotected sex and fewer teenage pregnancies, it is imperative to recognize the overdependence on technology, especially when teens choose pornography as a substitute over working towards a healthy romantic relationship.[255]

Attitudes in "porn-formances" have a deeply conditioning impact on the teenage brain. Porn is all about pleasure and gratifying personal desires without ever giving back. Therefore, porn consumption reduces empathy.[256] It interrupts the flow of communication and becomes a competitor between partners.[257] Specialist in sex education, Ran Gavrieli, whose TEDx talk "Why I stopped watching porn" has been viewed over nineteen million times, openly describes how his sexual fantasies and his views on women drastically changed through porn consumption. Gavrieli opened up his talk by stating:

> I stopped watching porn for two reasons, basically. The first one was that porn brought so much anger and violence into my private fantasies [. . .]. The second reason was I came to realize only by watching porn, I take part in creating a demand in filmed prostitution.[258]

Despite the common belief that porn-inspired fantasy can fuel sexual passion, lusting over other women or men while having sex is essentially masturbating inside another person's body. Numerous studies have shown that porn consumption correlates with less sexual satisfaction in a romantic relationship.[259] When romance is distilled to hot sex and cold emotions, sexual partners become disposable. Without emotional expression, there can be no true intimacy.

When Porn Wins

Although there are always multiple causes for marriages falling apart, Dr. Kevin Skinner found that twenty-five percent of all divorces in the United States are directly connected to porn consumption.[260] When we met Jenn, she was in deep despair. She was a stunning woman in her mid-twenties who had started a new family with her husband two years prior. When she confronted her husband about his porn consumption, wanting him to quit porn for the sake of their marriage, he made a choice. Porn had become his first love. He couldn't give it up, even if it meant his wife and son walking out of his life. Therapists Wendy and Larry Maltz, who have been working with porn addicts for more than three decades, conclude:

> Whenever we don't pay attention to how we relate to porn—what it means to us and where we are going with it—it's easy for porn to silently slip into the role of our 'Significant Other'. This is not surprising. We are likely to become emotionally and physically attached to anything we regularly turn to for emotional comfort and sexual satisfaction.[261]

Porn boils down to inflated body parts and staged intimacy. It undeniably changes the way consumers view the people they encounter in real life. According to a study published in the Journal of Applied Psychology, consumers are less sexually satisfied and perceive their partner as less attractive after consuming pornography over an extended time period.[262] Gabe recalled that the influence of porn actually decreased his interpersonal skills as his porn consumption increased. "It made me objectify women. I only saw bodies and never saw the souls inside. It made me more perverted." Women often feel unpursued or compared to actresses with doctored bodies, unable to measure up. Often, they feel like there is something wrong with them, instead of realizing that a disinterest in erotic activity and sensual pursuit is largely connected to their partner's porn consumption. Men also feel an increased pressure. Porn tells men that they are only able to be masculine and sexually pleasing to their partner if their genitals are far beyond the normal male proportion. Many men feel embarrassed or insecure in the bedroom, even though they are perfectly capable of pleasing their partner. A 2014 study that examined over 15,500 men around the world revealed that the average penis size was around 5.2 inches long, while no more than five percent of men had penises longer than 6.3 inches.[263] In contrast, the average penis displayed in mainstream porn is eight inches long.[264] A study conducted in the UK with 50,000 participants revealed that forty-five percent of men wish they could enlarge their penis.[265] Michael O'Leary, professor of urology at Harvard Medical School, found that the majority of men who seek penis enhancement surgery have a completely normal penis size. Tragically, most enhancement surgeries pose serious risks to reproductive health and often leave patients very unsatisfied with the results and side effects.[266] Dangerous, unnecessary surgeries are on the rise because young boys are under the assumption that the "normal" size penises they see in porn are actually irregular. According to the *International Society of Aesthetic Plastic Surgery*, there were 45,605 penis enhancement surgeries performed worldwide between 2013 and 2017.[267]

The Skeleton Key to the Heart

Porn is like a skeleton key to the heart and mind. It is a tool used to open locks without having one's conscious permission to enter. Once inside, porn begins to change a developing teen's worldview. Rather than seeing people, relationships, or the opposite sex through a healthy lens, the world is processed through a "pornified" filter of lustful deviance and lies about human sexuality.

Shame and guilt often surround the porn consumer like a weighted blanket that keeps them from rising up out of their bondage. Alice shared her journey, saying, "On the inside, I was dying with shame and secrets. I'd be using porn and masturbating and fantasizing every night. My personality was so divided, I had to keep up this 'perfect' image, which only increased my shame and secrecy over porn. I felt like two people. I felt fake and empty. I couldn't be truly real or honest with anyone, lest risk total rejection and horror." Shame is the chain that imprisons us from experiencing freedom through vulnerability and intimacy. It can perpetuate our negative behaviors, because it makes us feel like we don't deserve any form of connection, belonging, or even love.[268] Shame fuels addiction; we feel inadequate, cover up the pain of feeling unworthy, and the root cause of our pain never gets addressed. To combat the restrictive heaviness of shame, we need to remind teens of their self-worth and true identity. Empathy is the one and only weapon that has the power to drive shame away. Shame and empathy cannot coexist. If we engage in conversations that are honest, full of acceptance, and absent of judgement, shame will crumble. We should expose the porn industry for its corruption to remove the shameful lens through which teens view themselves.

RUMB Challenge

If your teen is struggling with porn, we recommend the organization **Fight the New Drug** (fightthenewdrug.org) for further educational resources.

If your teen is looking for a supportive network to kick porn to the curb, we recommend

Gabe Deem's organization, **Reboot Nation** (rebootnation.org).

If you are looking for a porn recovery program, we recommend **Fortify** (https://www.joinfortify.com). Fortify is specifically developed for teens. It empowers them to create their own battle strategies.

If you know of teenage girls that struggle with porn, we recommend Alice Taylor's organization, **The Grace Spot** (thegracespot.com) for further support.

For more conversation ideas for parents, we recommend the **Culture Reframed** Parents Program, (https://parents.culturereframed.org) a tool kit that helps you raise porn-resilient kids.

For a comprehensive school curriculum on the harmful effects of pornography, we recommend **Youth Wellbeing Project** (https://edu.youthwellbeingproject.info).

The Sexy Truth

Jason

"Gabe is a reminder that youth can adjust their online behavior to chase after what they truly value in life. He shared with me that even watching porn a few times can change your sexual tastes, and that alone is enough to keep him away. As he puts it:

> I avoid porn like I avoid cigarettes. The negative effects outweigh the short-term pleasure . . . If you want to find your true sexuality, you actually avoid the pornography like the plague because when you are on the internet you are only watching other people's fantasies. If you are truly trying to find yourself and explore your sexuality, that should be innately in you, and should not have to be influenced by something outside to discover what is inside of you.

His recovery from porn was a process that lasted two years before he experienced his peak sexual potential again. We chart the course of our lives and our brain will catch up. Gabe booted porn to pursue a genuine, loving relationship, and after some time his brain rewired itself to what he wanted: awesome sex inspired by love and commitment. In 2019, he ended up marrying the woman of his dreams and remains a passionate speaker and anti-porn activist to this day."

Porn Resilience Strategies

Empathy does not leave room for shame to exist. Over many years of working professionally with youth, we have observed that teens rarely talk to adults about their pornography consumption. Opening up with a trusted adult about struggling with porn is like turning the lights on in a dark room; it exposes it for what it really is—lustful exploitation. Porn addiction thrives in the shadows. This is the one place where it will never be broken. Martin Dubney, father of two, states:

> Like many parents, I fear that my boy's childhood could be taken away by pornography. So we have to fight back. We need to get tech-savvy, and as

toe-curling as it seems, we are the first generation that will have to talk to our children about porn. We have to tell our kids that pornographic sex is fake and real sex is about love, not lust. By talking to them, they stand a chance. If we stick our head in the sand, we are fooling only ourselves.[269]

When we address the topic with teens, there is often a sense of relief to be able to express their confusion and voice their questions about what they see. We will never reach that place of openness until we create a space of safety and understanding, and approach it with confidence. As Gabe Deem puts it, "We cannot sugar coat the discussion or teens will feel awkward or think you are hiding something." A study found that "[a] warm and communicative parent–child relationship is the most important factor"[270] in reducing porn use among children. Other factors that contribute to porn reduction are open parent–child conversation channels about sexual online experiences and sex education at home or school.[271]

RUMB Challenge

Start a conversation about porn:

1. Pornography portrays a type of sexuality that is harmful and fake. It hacks your brain.
2. Sex in the context of a loving and committed relationship is amazing. It builds a beautiful bond between you and your partner. What gets corrupted when you consume a type of sex that is created for the masses?
3. If you ever see anything on the web that feels wrong or shocking, know that you can always come to me. I won't judge you. I want to help you.
4. Fire drill: What is your plan when you are confronted with something pornographic?
5. I am talking to you about pornography, because I don't want you to miss out on real intimacy and amazing sexual satisfaction one day.
6. These days, people are trying to get your attention with pornographic content everywhere, how can we implement boundaries to avoid that? I trust you, but people will try everything to get you hooked. You are a true pioneer as you learn to be intentional with what you watch (praise positive efforts).
7. Tell your own story, "I saw something and did not know what to do..." (be relatable and empathetic).

Intimacy and the Naked Screen

Teens need to be reminded that they are not passive victims of this corruption, but are destined to be the change that dismantles what they themselves are not responsible for creating. It takes a warrior's heart to rise out of this mess and claim back the life they were meant to live. Rather than feeling shameful, they should be angry. Porn promises sexual freedom, while it robs them of everything that truly matters. Pornography is hungry. It preys on our fundamental human needs: our desires for something more; our longing to be in control. The reality is that pornography consumption is never stagnant. Consuming porn is like being taken down a fast-moving river. Once you fall in, the current pulls you downstream. The void for intimacy, passion, love, and acceptance will always ache to be filled, but it is up to us to inspire youth to channel their sexual energy towards real goals, beautiful life-giving relationships, and a fulfilling love life to keep them from remaining lonely consumers in front of a naked screen.

Discussion Questions:

1. Why do advertisers promote their products with hypersexualized women or chiseled men? What kind of reaction are they trying to get from you?
2. Why does pornography consumption make people feel good and bad at the same time?
3. Why does Gary Wilson, the author of "Your Brain on Porn", say that "porn goes in like a needle and out like a fishhook?"
4. What does porn promise? What does it actually give you? (examples: bondage, ED, poor sexual performance)
5. What are some of the messages porn sends about being male, female, how to love?
6. What effects can porn have on somebody's self-image?
7. Why is porn toxic to present and future romantic relationships? Why does porn hijack intimacy and fulfilling sex?

Part Three:

Relationships: The relationships between parents and teens are sacred. Current laws and internet legislations are allowing major tech companies to supersede a parent's ability to guide and set boundaries in the digital age, all while making a profit from the exploitation of youth online.

Understand: We want to empower parents and professionals working with youth to make a stand against online exploitation. By understanding how exploitation can be normalized within societal practices and laws, we can learn to expose injustice and demand for accountability and change to protect and empower our teens online.

Mentorship: When injustice is brought into the light, we are no longer passive victims. We have an opportunity to lead the way by actively standing against exploitation. When we know what we stand for, what is broken, and what needs to change, we will have the confidence to confront the problem head on.

Boundaries: While we have the power to set healthy boundaries in our own homes or classrooms, we will always be at a disadvantage when competing with a trillion-dollar tech industry that knows little to no boundaries. We must unite together as parents and professionals working with youth to demand the necessary boundaries around industry practices that make pornification a choice, not an inevitability.

Chapter 7: The Normalization of Injustice

Jason

"My former college housemate, Calvin, was never hard to find. He was almost always parked on the living room couch with a sprawling array of video game controllers, glowing screens, and wires woven throughout the room. His ability to multitask was second to none. He would engage in mass online gaming while messing with his handheld device, simultaneously hanging out on social media on his laptop. He had entertainment down to a science! I learned a lot about the lifestyle habits of an avid gamer from Calvin. One aspect that especially stuck with me was the kind of expression gamers engaged in during their online battles. No one held back their emotions, thoughts, opinions, or frustration. Insulting, cursing, taunting, provoking, or "chewing out" other players made up most of the online chatter, usually without cause or reason. I remember Calvin, who was kind and gentle in nature, trying to reason with the other players. He would question their outbursts and politely ask them to be respectful when playing, but it was as if he was talking to people who had their headphones turned off. It fell on deaf ears. I was a college basketball player at the time, and thought about how insulting another player in such a way would probably end with a trip to the emergency room; in the world of online gaming, however, no one can touch you. There are simply no real consequences for degrading others."

The Sanctity of Speech

The internet grants unprecedented freedom to those savvy enough to wield a mouse and keyboard. Upgrade to a touchscreen, and surfing the web becomes a lot more like finger gymnastics. The internet is a powerful tool to share a wealth of knowledge, culture, and ideas, which creates the basis for the freedom and development of Euro-American society.[272] Our access to information and our ability to share our thoughts and opinions through the web allows us to exercise our fundamental human right to the freedom of speech at a level that has never before been possible in human history. The Universal Declaration of Human Rights refers to the freedom of expression as, "[everyone's . . .] right [. . .]to hold opinions without interference and to seek, receive and impart information and ideas through any media and regardless of frontiers."[273] The declaration is recognized by the global community as a "[. . .] common standard of achievements for all people and all nations."[274] It is a milestone document that unites the global community by a universal understanding of fundamental human rights. According to the Human Rights Committee, the freedom of expression, together with the freedom of opinion, is instrumental in providing the necessary conditions for the development of a human being, which establishes the cornerstone of liberty in all democratic societies.[275]

Benjamin Franklin said, "[w]hoever would overthrow the liberty of a nation must begin by subduing the freeness of speech."[276] The freedom of expression is of critical value for creating active participation in civil life; where self-actualization in a diverse and tolerant society is possible through uninhibited access to scores of ideas, thoughts, and philosophies.[277]

No longer does the common citizen have to take up their position on their humble soapbox in the town square to make their thoughts known. The open plains of the web offer almost everyone their own digital stage. Standing face to face with our toughest critics and deliberating our personal thoughts and political opinions on the streets of Washington D.C. would require heaps of courage in comparison to posting a simple tweet or updating our social media status.

Boundless Consumption

According to *Statista*, in April 2020, fifty-nine percent of the world's population—4.5 billion people—were online active users.[278] The natural social and cultural barriers that once limited a youth's ability to access unfiltered information and express themselves in the broader community are virtually nonexistent.[279] Two factors that contribute to the power of the online world are anonymity and equality. No one will ever know who username *surfer-dude88* is, but everyone can hear or read what he has to say. People can hide behind the screen and engage with one another as equals. No one would know if *surfer-dude88* just got out of prison or made a fortune in the stock exchange, or if maybe he's a fourteen-year-old deliberating his political ideals like a young Stephen Colbert. In the end, everyone can be anyone, making the internet unique to those who wish to be measured by their words, not their social status, cultural background, or age. This is especially relevant for youth whose status as a child often disqualifies or undermines their participation in public debate.[280]

Humanity online represents a new era where the enjoyment of the freedom of expression by both children and adults has become a central component of societal living.[281] We don't have to look far to see how Trump's Twitter account, Obama's Facebook campaign, or the Kardashians' *insta-drama* has influenced culture and politics. Kim made porn pop; Obama "liked", "followed", and "friended" his way into office; Trump, for better or for worse, tweeted; and Hillary learned that not all email is created equal. A vital role of the freedom of expression is to critique government and to question policy with the intention of being heard. It allows citizens to seek the support of the people to pursue common interests, alternative policies, and thoughts that are often contrary to the government in power.[282] Everyone, including youth, has the ability to play the role of the 'public watchdog' without the bias of corporate interests; a role which used to be limited to mass media firms.[283]

Stolen Innocence

Even though the expansion of the freedom of expression into online territory has greatly benefited our society, it has also given people an incredible degree of unchecked autonomy to use these networks for their own devices. Pornography consumption has flooded the internet under the protection of free speech (freedom of expression). Our infatuation with unbridled freedom has dissolved both legal boundaries and societal values that once separated child, adolescent, and adult expression. This has created an exploding exploitation market, where dehumanization is monetized. Children and teens don't have to seek out harmful digital media; rather, billions of hours of the most grotesque content is dumped on the digital streets for all to discover. Disturbing adult sexual fetishes and degrading acts of sexploitation wander their way, like trash caught in the wind, onto the digital playgrounds of our children's online world.

The Economics of Aggression

Jason

"I recently encountered a pop-up ad on my smartphone while reading the news. It advertised an app where users could use the swipes of their finger to beat and batter a sexy 3D-looking woman. As the video ad previewed the game, it showed a user's finger aggressively swiping over the female character, who would respond as if being struck or punched. The woman's response to being beaten was downright cynical. She would giggle and get back up as if she wanted more.

As a teen, I can remember the constant temptation to check out porn on YouTube. I would browse for videos about typical young guy interests, such as cars, surfing, paintball, sports, etc. After clicking on a specific video related to my search, YouTube would display what were supposed to be related videos on the side of the screen. Somewhere in the lineup, there were suggested clips showing naked women holding rifles, sitting in cars, or even playing sports. It was just waiting for me to click and enjoy the show. I guess that is where it all could have started, and usually does for countless young men and women. Sexual expression is designed to be found and viewed. The porn industry takes advantage of the right to freedom of expression. More clicks, more money; it's as simple as that. With 830 million teens online, there is money to be made. We talk about porn as the dark corner of the web, but it is much more like the "city of lights," Las Vegas. Companies will do whatever they can to get you through the door and make money.

The online sex industry and its overwhelming influence on the development of children and adolescents alike represents a culture that has been slowly worn down. Porn has gone mainstream and has become an inevitable part of our daily lives. In October 2014, Pornhub stepped into the public eye in the middle of Times Square in New York City with the advertising slogan "All you need is hand"[284] and their website address posted underneath. In 2015, people lined up around the block to see *Fifty Shades of Grey*, which was followed by *Fifty Shades Darker* in 2017 and *Fifty Shades Freed* in 2018. As porn continues to find acceptance in mainstream society, tech companies, who are profiting by the billions, aren't expected to develop safeguards to protect youth from the seductive draw of online sex.

When I worked in the school system, I remember hearing a fourteen-year-old girl gushing about how she and her friends were going to see *Fifty Shades of Grey.* What kind of effect does a movie that celebrates and sexualizes male dominance and violence against women for the sexual pleasure of men have on a young girl? It's very possible that she left the theater thinking, "So this is what men think is beautiful and sexy." According to CDC and United Nations (UN) reports, nearly one in five women have experienced rape or attempted rape[285] and thirty-five percent of women have been attacked physically and/or sexually by an intimate partner or non-partner in their lifetime.[286] The harsh reality is that kids in Euro-America have effortless access to online content that makes *Fifty Shades* look like a *Disney* movie in comparison. Most major tech companies wash their hands of responsibility but make huge financial gains from their involvement. It's always the same excuses: "It's too expensive"; "We're just a platform, and what people upload is not our responsibility"; "It's impossible to protect children without damaging the freedom of expression." At the end of the day, no one is willing to sacrifice a slice of the fortune to end online sexploitation, protect children, and assist parents in developing feasible alternatives to secure their children's online experiences.

What would happen if other industries, like the car industry, were allowed to behave this way? What if they placed all responsibility on parents to protect their kids? They could simply say that they just manufacture the cars. It is the parents who drive them. It is their job to keep their kids safe. Think about how much money the car industry would save without having to engineer their automobiles for safety or to be environmentally friendly. The auto industry invests an incredible $100 billion a year in R&D,[287] where a value for safety and environment are critical focal points. If the tech industry was expected to behave in a similar way, where consumers, not maximum profit, are the central focus, childhood innocence and adolescent development would have a fighting chance. The problem isn't necessarily politicians, industry leaders, or even the porn industry, although they all have their part to play. The biggest problem is us. We have swallowed the pill of passivity. We don't fight for our parental rights to protect the best interests of our children and teens. Our society has overwhelmingly bought into the ideology that the internet is too vast and too open to protect our children from harmful media content. We have accepted the fact that whatever happens to them online is largely beyond our control. It's as if the porn industry and Big Tech have been given a free pass in comparison to the incredible standards that other industries are legally required to meet. Let's be real for a moment and sober up to the kind of industry online porn has become, and whether we should question, at a societal level, if we are okay with how it takes advantage of the right to freedom of expression. ”

Sexploitation

Pornography consumption goes hand in hand with an increased demand for commercial sexual exploitation. Sex educator Ran Gavrieli explains:

> Porn is marketing for sex trafficking both directly and indirectly: directly because online and offline hubs for trafficking use pornographic images to draw the buyers, indirectly because of porn's influence on the culture. A key ingredient to the success of commercial sex is the belief that people (women especially) are sexual commodities, and Internet pornography is the ideal vehicle to teach and train this belief.[288]

Porn sites like Pornhub are known for profiting from trafficked women, rape, and child abuse.[289] On February 10th, 2020 the *BBC News* released the heart-wrenching account of Rose Kalemba, a fourteen-year-old teenager who was kidnapped at knifepoint by two men. She was forced into their vehicle and driven to another location, where she was repeatedly raped over the course of twelve hours. A third man recorded her assault, adding another layer of dehumanization to her horrific torture. The videos they made of her assault and rape were uploaded to Pornhub with the title, 'teen crying and getting slapped around', 'teen getting destroyed', 'passed out teen.'"[290] Two months after Rose's horrifying ordeal, she stumbled upon the Pornhub links to her rape on social media, which led to a wave of vicious bullying at her school. She spent six months pleading over email for Pornhub to remove the videos, but it wasn't until she changed her email address and posed as a lawyer with a fictitious lawsuit that the site responded and took the videos down within forty-eight hours. To date, a campaign by *ExodusCry* to shut down Pornhub has been signed by almost two million people from more than 192 countries and endorsed by over 300 anti-trafficking and children and women's rights organizations.

The Other Side of the Camera

In front of the camera is the seemingly always willing and "give me more" persona of the porn star; however, on the other side of the camera lens is a criminal world built on dehumanization and exploitation of vulnerable human beings. Supporters of the porn industry lean heavily on the hollow argument that online sex reflects a free market where women can choose to profit from their involvement in the production. Dr. Donna M. Hughes, co-founder of *Citizens Against Trafficking*, fights to expose the plight of women who are used to produce mainstream porn. In her article, *Sex Trafficking of Women for the Production of Pornography*, she shares the traumatic stories of former porn actresses which reveal how porn and sexual exploitation are intertwined with demand and consumption. Like most sex traffickers, porn producers and agents alike make a business out of exploiting society's most vulnerable. Porn is essentially filmed prostitution. It is the act of paying someone for sexual favors. Prostitution is illegal in most states because it is a breeding ground for sexploitation and organized crime. It robs the vulnerable and marginalized of their humanity, reducing them to an object to be bought and sold. However, "purchasing" someone to have sex in front of a camera with the intention of reselling the abuse online is somehow considered a legal, protected work of art. The correlation between sexual abuse and prostitution is high. A sample study based in New York found that 95-98 percent of women involved in human trafficking had a history of childhood abuse and neglect.[291] Sexual abuse is a horrific act that breaks down self-worth and damages the natural boundaries that protect our sexuality from the ill intent of others. A child or adolescent survivor of sexual abuse may feel that their value as a human being is reduced to their physical body, creating a major vulnerability for future abuse to occur. One in four girls and one in six boys become victims of sexual abuse before they turn eighteen years old.[292] One in five women will get raped in their lifetime.[293]

Dr. Hughes explains, "[porn performers'] first experience making commercial pornography is often brutal and traumatic."[294] Threats, drugs, and alcohol are commonly used to coerce and numb their victims from the unspeakable trauma. Alexa's introduction to porn was far from what she had expected. "My first movie, I was treated very rough by three guys. They pounded on me, gagged me with their penises, and tossed me around like I was a ball! I was sore, hurting, and could barely walk. My insides burned and hurt so badly. I could barely pee and to try to have a bowel movement was out of the question."[295] Other women Dr. Hughes writes about described a world where no matter how loud they pleaded for the beatings and humiliating subhuman treatment to stop, the cameras kept rolling. One actress refused to perform and wanted to go home after getting tricked by her agent to show up to a shoot, where seventy-five men who answered a newspaper ad were lined up to ejaculate in her face. Her hesitation was met with a threat of a fictitious lawsuit if she didn't agree to be the victim of this hugely degrading production. Fear and intimidation are constant undercurrents surrounding the industry side of porn.[296] Shelly Lubben, a former pornography performer, testified, "Women are lured in, coerced, and forced to do sex acts they never agreed to do . . . [and given] drugs and alcohol to help [them] get through hardcore scenes . . . The porn industry is modern-day slavery."[297] Imagine how these depictions of exploitation corrupt the core values of developing adolescents. It's impossible for youth to pleasure themselves to online prostitution and learn to respect human dignity at the same time.

The Normalization of Injustice

Every time society sees injustice but accepts it as a part of life, terrible atrocities follow. We must only turn the pages of history to see injustice repeat itself over and over again. We need to be wary of corrupted culture and common societal beliefs, because the very nature of a corrupt society is to normalize injustice so it is hidden behind popular opinions, one-sided arguments, and legalization.

> Every time society sees injustice but accepts it as a part of life, terrible atrocities follow.

Harriet Ann Jacobs was born into

slavery on February 11, 1813. In her autobiography, *Incidents in the Life of a Slave Girl*, she recollects the raw, real, and horrifying realities facing one who is born into a corrupt culture; a society that legalized the act of owning another human being as personal property. Jacobs' story is unique in the way she exposes the normalization of injustice, wherein every possible rationalization, no matter how absurd, was employed to vindicate this cruel trade of owning and selling people.[298] The history of slavery in America exposes how culture can be blinded to the point where the average citizen sees their "lawful" involvement as just and right.

RUMB Challenge

Give three examples of normalized injustice today (*e.g. products produced through child labor*)

1.
2.
3.

If people know that an injustice is wrong, why is it still legal?

If porn is a breeding ground for exploitation and degradation of human dignity, why is it so widely available to kids and teens without any legal recourse?

When reading the chilling accounts of Ms. Jacobs' plight of being born and raised a slave, it's difficult not to wonder how people residing in the "land of the free and home of the brave" justified slavery as an ethical, moral, and inevitable way of life. Jacobs' childhood and adolescence were tragically stolen from her by the bonds of slavery. Sexual abuse and morbid beatings plagued what should have been the best years of her life. The cruel, inhuman treatment of African Americans was beyond the pale of even the darkest imagination. Jacobs described one particular punishment where a slave was bound to a wooden beam, feet hanging from the ground, and beaten to near death. "[N]ever before, in my life, had I heard hundreds of blows fall; in succession, on a human being. [. . .]."[299] Jacobs eventually escaped the horrors of slavery and became an abolitionist, reformer, famous author, and speaker.

This is only a glimpse of her life, and doesn't do her story and accomplishments justice; however, her firsthand account highlights how the normalization of injustice brings unfathomable pain and suffering to those who don't have a voice, or who have been stripped of their rights for the benefit and financial gain of others. The history of slavery in the

United States reveals the destructive nature of a culture where there is a collective opinion that is so established and normalized within societal living that the legal framework itself supports such injustice. Slavery was so ingrained into everyday life that one of the main arguments supporting its existence was that society itself would crumble into economic ruin if it was abolished.[300]

Perhaps some of the most empowering and equally beautiful words ever written come from the United States Declaration of Independence: "[w]e hold these truths to be self-evident, that all men are created equal, that they are endowed by their Creator with certain unalienable Rights, that among these are Life, Liberty and the pursuit of Happiness."[301] This declaration was written in 1776. Slavery wasn't abolished until 1865 in the 13th amendment of the US constitution, nearly ninety years later. How many African Americans suffered unimaginable atrocities against their humanity in someone else's pursuit of liberty and happiness?

Despite the abolition of slavery almost 160 years ago, between 100,000 and 300,000 youths are trafficked and sexually exploited within the United States every year.[302] Like an aggressive weed, exploitation and systemic injustice may be cut down, but if the roots aren't addressed they will grow back under the guise of popular culture. Pornhub serves as a prime example.

Pornhub actively approves and profits from racist sexual exploitation on its site. One current video on their site, titled "Black slave gets f***** by white master", received 240k views. In light of videos like this, Pornhub's attempts to appear anti-racist and philanthropic could not be more cynical. Their donation of $100,000 following George Floyd's death, claiming that they stand in solidarity with injustice and racism,[303] cannot cover the true nature of their online content. International speaker, author, domestic violence expert, and cultural sensitivity trainer Dr. Carolyn West explains, "The images found in porn predate the founding of the United States."[304] Today's porn industry monetizes erotic images that normalize oppression, exploitation, and violence against women (and men) of color. It draws on the images of unimaginable suffering from hundreds of years of slavery, oppression and social injustice.[305] Porn turns the cruelty and exploitation that has been around for hundreds of years into profit. Dr. West explains that it is dehumanizing, degrading, loaded with racism, sexism, and aggression towards women of color.[306]

As we've previously argued, sexual stimulation has a deep impact on the development of the adolescent brain. It creates powerful neural pathways that hardwire the consumption of racist porn with self-pleasuring and consumerism. As Dr. West concluded in her interview with Gail Dines from Culture Reframed, "I see no evidence that you can consume hours and hours of some of this racialized content and be a better human being for it."[307]

A Societal Parasite

Porn piggybacks on the momentum of current events. As Dr. West states, "We are living through a global pandemic and now we have pandemic porn" making a mockery out of a crisis where hundreds of thousands have lost their lives. She went on to say that the moment Bill Cosby was convicted, the porn industry made a parody about his crimes against women as if to make a joke out of the Me Too movement. This trend has now continued into the social justice movement. Dr. West recounted finding porn that co-opted the language of the "Black Lives Matter" movement by producing a genre of porn called "Black Wives Matter." Dr. West explains, "It's a way of minimizing, trivializing and marginalizing [social justice movements]. It becomes a space where you can say the most horrifically racist things that you can't say in mainstream media."[308] If we want to confront injustice in our nation and combat sex trafficking, exploitation, and the corruption of core human values, we must question the practices of freely accessible mainstream porn. We have to question how many young people we will

RUMB Challenge

Freedom is like water. We need it to survive and thrive. However, too much water can lead to drowning.

Sit down as a group or family and discuss five issues regarding the internet where people are "drowning" in someone else's unchecked freedom (*examples: fake news, cyberbullying, data harvesting*)

Are there any effective efforts underway to change laws regarding these issues you chose? Why or why not?

What boundaries do we have in the offline society that are disrespected or non-existent online? Why?

allow to be swallowed up in the name of freedom before history reveals our society's shameless passivity and acceptance of this trade.

Breaking Free

When society and culture no longer reflect ethical truth, we cannot wait for politicians or industry to make a corrective course. Instead, a grassroots movement is needed to rise up and speak on the behalf of those who are unable.

The age of the internet has created a new and untamed frontier, where freedom and human rights are enjoyed at a higher degree than any other time. However, we must not forget the cruel and grim lessons of history. With more freedom comes more responsibility. Freedom exercised without restraint is not true freedom, because unchecked freedom can greatly harm the rights of others. Freedom is a beautiful gift, but without regard for others, it can be someone else's prison. If we want this rising generation to tackle some of the greatest societal challenges of our time with dignity and respect, we must take a stand against the exploitation, degradation, and racism depicted online.

Freedom is a beautiful gift, but without regard for others, it can be someone else's prison.

However, before we can take an effective stand against a billion-dollar industry, we need the right equipment. We cannot go to battle without a weapon or a shield. Understanding our fundamental rights, the rights of our children, and the rights of parents to guide and protect their families is a critical step towards finding our collective voice together. Changing systems and reforming exploited internet legislation takes courage and a deeper understanding that speaks to the principles and foundations that our right to speech was built upon. When we expose the link between online sexploitation, pornification of youth, and the way tech companies take advantage of legislation and the freedom of expression to justify their corruption, we begin to see how we can fight against injustice and reform a broken web.

Discussion Questions:

1. Why is it important to learn from our historic failures to protect human dignity? How can these hard lessons expose normalized injustice today?
2. Why is it impossible to consume pornography and respect human dignity at the same time?
3. Why does mainstream pornography rely on images that portray violence, aggression, and racism?
4. What are some of the dangers of complete anonymity online?
5. Have you ever seen exploitive images on the web? What was the context?
6. What can we do to stop an exploitation online?

Chapter 8: How to Pick a Fight with Goliath

In May 2020, President Trump filed an executive order to limit how tech companies can interfere and censor political opinion just days after one of his tweets was flagged for fact-checking.[309] In his fury over the discrediting of his words, he blasted tech giants like Facebook, YouTube, Google, and Twitter for selective censorship of free speech. As frustration on both sides of the political aisle mounts over Big Tech's handling of online expression, a fundamental flaw in internet legislation is revealed. Tech companies have unprecedented control over online speech. They profit from virtually every form of online expression, even illegal content, justifying their actions by referring to the legal immunity provided under Section 230 of the 1996 Communications Decency Act (CDA). Trump's executive order states:

> Section 230 was not intended to allow a handful of companies to grow into titans controlling vital avenues for our national discourse under the guise of promoting open forums for debate, and then to provide those behemoths blanket immunity when they use their power to censor content and silence viewpoints that they dislike.[310]

When imagining the origins of the web, no one would have envisioned a piece of internet legislation as the foundation that the online world was built upon. Rather, many of us conjure pictures of a 1960s laboratory loaded with giant machines, flowing wires, and twinkling interfaces as the backdrop to the digital universe we experience today. However, this is like giving the inventor of the wheel credit for the creation of a Formula One race car. There are clearly other minds at work that lead to such modern marvels. As obscure and equally boring as this legal reference may sound, it created the path that led to the establishment of tech superpowers who successfully brought the web from a humble information-sharing network to an immersive digital world.

The Twenty-Six Words that Created the Internet

Jeff Kosseff, author and cybersecurity law professor at the U.S. Naval Academy, concludes that the web as we know it today was birthed out of Section 230, or as he boldly states in the title of his book, *The Twenty-Six Words that Created the Internet.* He is referring to the actual legal text of Section 230 of the CDA: "No provider or user of an interactive computer service shall be treated as the publisher or speaker of any information provided by another information content provider."[311]

To date, companies like Google, Facebook, Amazon, Microsoft, and Apple are sovereign demi-gods birthed out of the unprecedented legal immunity provided by Section 230. Google was recently called into question when asking conservative news site, *The Federalist,* to remove its comments section or risk being demonetized. Google holds the power over what media content gets published as it regulates almost all online advertising. Virtually every establishment depends on this tech giant for funneling customers and generating revenue. In response, Senator Josh Hawley introduced new legislation to give citizens the means to sue Big Tech enterprises if they use selective censorship of political speech.[312] Hawley explained, "Section 230 has been stretched and rewritten by courts to give these companies outlandish power over speech without accountability."[313]

Section 230 and Children

The future success of this rising generation is intertwined with the digital frontier. It is in their best interest to learn the ins and outs of cutting-edge technology. Scouring the web for useful research, using it as a tool to share information, or simply keeping up with current events plays a vital role in teens' development. However, the current state of the internet and the industries that rely on Section 230 to squeeze maximum profit from the exploitation and degradation of the vulnerable has placed the well-being of youth and the rights of parents in harm's way. The realization of a youth's unparalleled exposure to deeply disturbing forms of online expression leaves parents and professionals baffled about how we arrived here today.

The Runway to Unprecedented Immunity

In the 1990s and early 2000s, the internet was rapidly developing into the dominant platform for public engagement of all kinds. As revolutionary as this new form of media was, it demanded that a very important question be answered: who is responsible for illegal expression? Section 230 was the government's answer to this question. You can't write libelous, slanderous, or obscene expression in newspapers or broadcast such communication on public television or radio networks, but the internet has taken over the function of these aging mediums and absorbed their audiences.

One would think that the rules that existed for decades over these fading mediums would be adopted into the online frontier, but it isn't that simple. Internet service providers weren't ready or able to keep track of millions upon millions of different private and public forms of communication that pass hourly through their networks without incorporating clumsy filters. Websites that allow third parties, such as private citizens, to post freely on their site regarding a multitude of topics claimed that they would be faced with a similar problem if they were held liable for someone else's content. To make matters more confusing, websites that did incorporate community standards were taken to court for failing to meet these standards in every circumstance, which took away any incentive for them to self-regulate out of fear of getting sued. This created a formidable barrier for all online businesses that allowed third parties to post freely on their platforms to achieve a scalable business model without getting sued into oblivion before they reached critical mass. Section 230 relieved this tension by granting legal immunity to websites that published and promoted third-party content. The new legislation allowed social media sites like Facebook, Myspace, and YouTube to get off the ground without fear of being shut down in a legal black hole if a social media user posted something online that was against their community standards or even illegal. Without fear of lawsuit, the freedom of expression online exploded among common citizens, forming the internet into what it is today.[314]

Innocence Offline

"Ring... Ring... Ring..." chimed the doorbell. Mrs. O'Connell wasn't expecting any visitors. For a split second, she thought about pulling down the door blinds and going upstairs to avoid rejecting another overly enthusiastic sales pitch. Her curiosity got the best of her as she slowly cracked the door open. Shocked by what stood before her, she froze in silence. A fully nude couple was standing at the door. The man's chiseled physique and the women's impossible curves made the moment feel even more ridiculous. "What on earth is going on?" she thought. Still in shock, she couldn't find her words. The couple spoke first. "Hi, I am Nero and this is my girl, Electra. We are here to see Billy. We always hang out together around this time." Electra jumped in, "Yes, we have some new moves to show off." Just then, eleven-year-old Billy came bumping down the stairs to see what was going on. Upon seeing Nero and Electra standing before his mother, he grew cold and pale, and his laptop dropped out from under his arm as his smartphone slipped from his fingers. They both tumbled down the stairs. No one seemed to notice, given the awkwardness of the situation. Mrs. O'Connell gasped, "You know these people?" Electra smiled as she explained, "Of course he knows us. Billy has been checking in with us regularly for a year now. Nero waved, "Hey Billy." "We have been educating him," Electra proudly stated. If this story feels terribly inappropriate, then you are having a healthy reaction. Maybe you are outraged. You should be, because there is nothing okay about what you just read. The story was based on an internet safety video launched by New Zealand's Department of Internal Affairs.[315] Its purpose is to wake people up to the reality facing children and teens online, because this

RUMB Challenge

Use New Zealand's government campaign as a conversation starter about the ease of access to porn. You can find the internet safety campaign here:

https://www.keepitrealonline.govt.nz/parents/pornography/

What makes the video seem so absurd?

is exactly what is happening to the vast majority of youth born into the wild plains of the digital frontier.

"Never before in the history of telecommunications media in the United States has so much indecent (and obscene) material been so easily accessible by so many children in so many American homes with so few restrictions."[316] This statement was provided by the Department of Justice in the case *ACLU v. Reno.*[317] In this exemplary case, the United States government argued in favor of the CDA[318] in fulfilling the legitimate aim of the government to protect children from harmful internet content. It was one of the first major cases brought before the United States Supreme Court that called into question the far-reaching right of adults to freedom of expression online.

The CDA served a two-fold purpose: first, to create safeguards to shield minors from indecent, harmful, and obscene expression online; and second, to protect distributors of third-party online speech from lawsuits. However, the U.S. government's attempt to regulate children's access to internet pornography through the CDA was deemed unconstitutional by the Supreme Court on grounds of violating adults' First Amendment[319] right to freedom of expression. The legislation exposed internet platforms and citizens to criminal prosecution for inadvertently subjecting youth to patently offensive or indecent speech as measured by contemporary community standards. The law was unclear to the common citizen of the exact definition of what was considered illegal and left them at risk of criminal charges, effectively chilling free speech. This failure to create a constitutionally sound legal remedy canceled out the first legitimate aim of the government to shield children from an exploding online sex industry, leaving only the second aim of the State intact, known as Section 230. This became a runway to grant unprecedented immunity to internet service providers (ISPs) and online web-based media platforms from any legal ramifications of the content that was promoted, posted, and edited on their site, regardless of the harm caused to minors.

The Good, the Bad, and the Ugly

The controversy surrounding Section 230 is complex in nature. It should be applauded for the many positive functions it provides, but ignoring or using these benefits to justify the atrocities taking place online, with no resolve to confront the problem head-on, is a travesty to future generations. Fire was an epic discovery to humankind, but it wasn't long before humans used it to burn down their neighbors' houses. We need to protect a free internet, but demand that the same innovation that reels in profit be channeled to also protect the integrity of the online world. The algorithms that are used to predict our every move online should be capable of stopping child porn, sexploitation, and the death of childhood innocence.

Sex-for-sale sites profit by the billions under the protection that Section 230 provides. As long as they aren't the ones producing the media from scratch, sites like Pornhub are free to post, promote, and push the most deviant and deeply harmful content in front of our children's eyes with absolutely no fear of legal consequences of any kind. The porn industry doesn't care about how the product was made; whether the actors were coerced, abused, trafficked, groomed, or exploited to produce degrading sex videos. They also don't care about the age of the consumer or how it harms their well-being. Through Section 230, these companies have been granted legally protected tunnel vision. It's not personal, it's just business.

In May 2020, both President Trump and his presumptive Democratic Party opponent, Joe Biden, called for the repeal of Section 230. As this book is being written, the outcome of Donald Trump's executive order regarding this repeal is unknown. The fact that lawmakers and global leaders are beginning to push back on blanket immunity legislation will awaken a sleeping industry juggernaut that will not relinquish its grip on monetized obscenity and sexploitation.

A Step Towards Truth

There is probably nothing more sacred to the American way of living than the freedom of expression. In the infamous words of George Washington, "If the freedom of speech is taken away, then dumb and silent we may be led, like sheep to the slaughter."[320] James Madison was in agreement when encapsulating the freedom of speech in the very First Amendment in the Bill of Rights.[321] In accordance with the jurisprudence of the United States Supreme Court, the government has no constitutional authority to limit the freedom of expression on grounds that such speech promotes ideas, opinions, or values that go against the majority population's beliefs.[322] The Supreme Court has largely ruled that the freedom of expression is only to be limited in "extraordinary circumstances", and even expression that may promote "undesirable or illegal conduct" is not necessarily grounds for government interference.[323] However, there are certain boundaries in place to protect citizens from those who would use their First Amendment right at the cost of greatly harming others. The Supreme Court refers to such expression as having "low First Amendment value."[324] This expression was defined by the Court in the case *Chaplinsky v. New Hampshire.*[325] The Court provided examples, such as lewd, obscene, profane, libelous, insulting, or fighting words (speech that is spoken for the sole purpose of causing physical violence). The Court ruled that such expressions have "no essential part of any exposition of ideas, and are of such slight social value as a step to truth that any benefit that may be derived from them is clearly outweighed by the social interest in order and morality."[326]

The challenge surrounding the protection of minors from pornographic exposure is compounded by the fact that pornography has no legal meaning, making it difficult to classify which sexual content found online would fall under the category of obscenity. In the case *Miller vs. California*, the Supreme Court came up with a three-prong test to identify obscene speech. Rather than creating a list of categories that obscene expression could fall under, they relied on societal values. It requires that the average person would be able to apply contemporary community standards to identify

RUMB Challenge

Support the EARN IT Act. The EARN IT Act was formed by NCOSE to "develop recommended best practices for providers of interactive computer services regarding the prevention of online child exploitation misconduct." Patrick A. Trueman, president and CEO of the National Center on Sexual Exploitation, states, "While Big Tech argues against more accountability, we know that by creating a commission of experts, the right balance between privacy protection and child protection can be found." For more information visit: *https://endsexualexploitation.org/articles/statement-earn-it-act-will-give-big-tech-needed-accountability/*

that the expression in its entirety is only designed to respond to the lustful interests of its consumers. Second, that these same community standards would find the expression "patently offensive." Lastly, "that a reasonable person would find that the work, taken as a whole, lacks serious literary, artistic, political, and scientific value."[327] Something has gone terribly awry in the values that are driving internet legislation forward. The current interpretation of laws and policies in place are clearly designed to protect profit over people.

Much of pornography is designed to attract and arouse the most habituated and committed audience, which creates an enormous market for shocking, sexually abusive online content that spills into a large minority of whom are not yet adults and are still developmentally vulnerable. There is no possible argument that would consider the act of seventy-five men ejaculating in a woman's face "a step towards truth." It's fair to question the current state of the internet and a child or adolescent's overwhelming ease of access to such content. We, as a community of parents and professionals whose job is to provide an environment that kids and teens can thrive in, rather than have to heal from, should boldly challenge how the porn industry distributes its filth. Our cries for corporate digital responsibility should be justified, "by the social interest in order and morality." Pornhub's outrageously slow six-month-long response to Rose Kalemba's multiple pleas to remove her attackers' recording of her rape and torture serves as a prime example of how these industries profit from their own apathy. Only when profits were threatened did Pornhub see any reason to take down this revenue-generating crime.

In a time when sixteen U.S. states have declared porn a public health crisis, young people should have the right to explore and experience the many indispensable benefits the internet offers without their sexual curiosity being exploited. Furthermore, parents, guardians, and caregivers have the right to be supported in their responsibility of raising future generations in a manner that secures their developmental well-being.

Here lies the strongest tension between the legitimate aim of government to protect the well-being of children, and to secure the rights of adults to live in a society where the extension of rights reflects the age and maturity of the subject or holder of those rights. As was decided by the Supreme Court in the case *Butler v. Michigan*, the government is not to enact or interpret laws that "[. . .] reduce the adult population [. . .] to reading only what is fit for children."[328]

There is a conflict between two equally important aims of governmental oversight: to protect both children and adults in the digital age. If the issue was simply a matter of protection, we would kick kids and teens off the web, but this would be detrimental to their holistic development and preparation for adulthood in the digital age. Thus, a minor's access to digital expression and participation in the online world should be protected; meaning, the integrity of the web should not be reduced to a trash pile of filthy adult sexual expression, ready to make a quick buck on our kids and teens. The current interpretation and jurisprudence surrounding Section 230 has created a lack of incentive for the tech industry, such as internet service providers, open mass media platforms like YouTube, or the millions of mainstream porn sites, to invest in the necessary tools to protect minors.

A Global Pandemic

The digital exploitation of youth is a pandemic. It is a global crisis that stretches far beyond the borders of the United States. Countries around the world are struggling to protect children online. The United Kingdom has taken extensive steps to regulate children's access to pornography by announcing a plan to block adult webpages that do not require age verification technology.[329] In 2015, the Indian government denied its citizens access to 857 adult websites.[330] In 2016, Pornhub was banned in Russia for allegedly violating child protection laws.[331]

The porn industry has wandered into nearly every family home, and it wants us to believe that this is not only normal, but inevitable.

The porn industry has wandered into nearly every family home, and it wants us to believe that this is not only normal, but inevitable. We, as a global community, have welcomed with open arms the countless benefits the internet offers, but not without a price. If we want to see sustainable change regarding the protection of children online, it is crucial to start a global conversation. We must understand our role as parents to protect our children's best interests online, just as we would in the physical world.

What I learned from Driving Lessons

Jason

When I was sixteen, my parents enrolled me in Driver's Ed. My driving instructor was exceptional. She went beyond the call to teach me how to be a safe and competent driver on the road. She even took me to a local military base to learn how to make special maneuvers in emergency situations. It was an awesome experience, except for one factor: Nancy. My fellow Driver's Ed student had some serious problems, mostly with understanding the fundamental basics of driving, like making turns or using brakes. Fortunately, our driving instructor had her own set of controls that could override ours. Quite frankly, this setup saved our lives. Nancy would screech into turns at top speed and shamelessly admit that she forgot that there were brakes in the car. I learned to close my eyes and trust that our driving instructor would jump in at the right moment, which thankfully, she always did.

This analogy can help us, as global community, understand how we can use international law to strengthen our argument for higher industry standards to ensure the safety of minors online. Think of children's rights as a driving instructor's car. If the vehicle represents the rights of a child, then the parent represents the driving instructor who has his or her own set of controls designed to override the child's actions, with the goal of safely reaching the destination of adulthood. For example, a child might want to use social media to exercise their right to freedom of expression, but parents are there to make sure this is done safely and responsibly. The goal is for a child to eventually drive their own vehicle, exercising their rights on their own, but they need supervision to protect their best interests in accordance to their developmental capacity. Sometimes, parents and children can only team up so far as the road allows them to drive. When successful parenting online is impossible, due to current industry practices, it is up to the state to assist parents by creating a reasonable path for parents to protect their child's well-being. In this instance, the state can be thought of as the construction crew that builds the roads for the vehicle to drive down, while parents are responsible for overseeing youth's safe and competent operation of the vehicle that propels them forward to their goals.

Legal Armaments: "Family First" Rights

The car analogy illustrates how the framework of human rights can empower parents across the globe to place the necessary pressure on the state to support them in guiding youth in the digital age. While the U.S. is a signatory to the United Nations Convention on the Rights of the Child (UNCRC) and has played a pivotal role in drafting the UNCRC, they have not yet ratified the convention. This statement is not to be misunderstood as a lobby for the United States to ratify the UNCRC. The controversy surrounding this debate is nuanced and deeply rooted in the volatile state of U.S. politics. Arguments in favor and against U.S. ratification deserve their own dedicated book to amply explore this debate before suggesting any conclusive thoughts. However, there are empowering principles enshrined in the treaty that places a child's well-being and the plight of parenting in the digital age at the center of policy making and judiciary interpretation of laws. For example, the drafting, passing and legal interpretation of Section 230 would have looked very different if the situation of the child and the role of parents in guiding children in the exercise of their rights was given due weight. Furthermore, the legal principles enshrined in the document can serve as a foundation for parents around the globe to confidently stand upon when facing a culture that has bent over to the will of the adult industry.

Children's rights only function when parents or guardians are given legal authority and protection to guide their children in the exercise of their rights with the child's best interests as the central focus. Essentially, children's rights provide a legal platform for parents to stand on when confronted with threats against their children's well-being. Well-known human rights expert John Tobin states, "[r]ather than pitting the rights of parents against those of children, the [UNCRC] actually advocates a model that enables parents to make claims upon the State, and by implication the broader community, to provide them with the assistance necessary to meet the demands of parenting."[332] Therefore, when addressing the unlimited access children and teens have to pornography in all its forms, parents are given a framework to construct a legal argument that demands a change in the porn industry's distribution of adult content online. Youth should enjoy freedom of expression online, as it is critical for their holistic development, insofar that parents guide them to exercise these rights in accordance with their best interests. In the words of Tobin:

> A young child may only see the ball on the road whereas an older person will (hopefully) see the oncoming car; a young child may see the gratification that comes from eating candy whereas an older person will (hopefully) see the health consequences; an adolescent may see the peer acceptance that comes with taking drugs or drinking alcohol but an older person will (hopefully) see the health and lifestyle consequences.[333]

Adults can exercise their rights to the point of their own demise, if they so choose, while minors are accountable to their parents or caregivers, who protect them from misusing these rights. Children are by nature in a process of maturation, and are dependent on others. They are developing and their independence grows over time.

International Human Rights Law not only seeks to protect children, but also views them as holders of human rights, meaning children have a right to practice and develop their ability to exercise their rights online (subjects of the law). This is an important distinction, because it is a fundamental principle of human rights that one person's freedom cannot be exercised at the expense of someone else's protected rights. Thus, the role of parents to protect the well-being of their children and to guide their children in the safe exercise of their rights should be considered when discussing the scope of application of an adult's limitless right to distribute and access hardcore pornography.

The freedom of expression is not an absolute right. Article 19(3) of the International Convention on Civil and Political Rights, places special "duties and responsibilities" on holders of this right. Therefore, in accordance with law and what is considered necessary, the right to free speech may be restricted on grounds of respect for the rights of others; or for the protection of public health and morals.[334] In this case, the term "others" refers to children and the role of parents in guiding their children in the exercise of their rights online to protect their well-being and development.

Profit over People: Examining Societal Values

The formation of human rights and the legislation that incorporates them into daily life is driven by a societal value system that prevails over the injustices of our past. This is a continuous process where progression, not arrival, is the aim. We must constantly wrestle with popular culture to identify whether current trends and progressive ideas are in alignment with the value system that evolved into the human rights we enjoy today.

According to U.S. state reports submitted to the Human Rights Committee, the U.S. considers it reasonable to limit harmful but legal expression to protect the environment or the value of private property. For example, pamphlets can be limited by law to avoid littering.[335] City zoning policies can forbid adult movie theaters or porn shops, if the secondary effects of these actions cause harm to other businesses or reduce the value of surrounding homes.[336]

From the perspective of parents or those working with kids, it seems absurd that property value, the damage caused to surrounding businesses, or the potential that offensive sexual content could litter our streets are grounds to limit harmful media distribution, but the well-being of children does not carry the necessary weight to challenge how businesses distribute such expression online.

A Value-Driven Change

Neither the industry nor governments are going to make major changes until we stand up in unity to say enough is enough. In the words of civil rights activist, Dr. Martin Luther King Jr., "Change does not roll in on the wheels of inevitability but comes through continuous struggle. And so, we must straighten our backs and work for our freedom. A man can't ride you unless your back is bent."[337]

We don't have to demand the regulation and restriction of adult expression. Rather, we can ask for reasonable actions to be taken to protect the development of children. A trillion-dollar industry should make responsible investments towards children and teens' online safety, and not be allowed to hide behind Section 230 as the cure-all to their troubling business practices. The government has no problem requiring the auto industry to adhere to environmental and safety standards, incentivizing manufacturers to design efficient vehicles that are safer for the consumer and better for the planet. Everyone benefits from these goal-based regulations. There is no reason why the tech industry, Google, internet service providers, mainstream porn businesses, or social media platforms should be exempt from implementing protective measures to make the job of guiding our children's internet use feasible. When countries are clear about their boundaries and the values they stand for surrounding the well-being of youth, it is amazing how tech companies are suddenly able to change their business practices to protect minors when profits are on the line.

Former U.K. prime minister David Cameron is a pioneer in demanding industry responsibility to empower parents and protect childhood innocence. In his daring speech, he shared his motivation:

> [Parents are] told the internet is too big to mess with; it's too big to change. But to me, the questions around the internet and the impact it has are too big to ignore. The internet is not just where we buy, sell and socialise; it's where crimes happen; it's where people can get hurt; it's where children and young people learn about the world, each other, and themselves.[338]

The U.K. has taken a global leadership role by taking extensive steps to combat children's online access to pornography, as well as abolishing child abuse images. Cameron explained his motivation, saying, "Now, I'm not making this speech because I want to moralise or scaremonger but because I feel profoundly, as a politician and as a dad, that the time for action has come. This is, quite simply, about how we protect our children and their innocence."

The U.K. has taken extensive steps towards developing age verification technology to prevent child exposure to pornography. They have also implemented digital hashtags to block and erase child abuse images. The U.K. also requires ISPs to block pornographic content by default, so new costumers over eighteen are required to contact their ISP to have access to porn enabled.

If we want to restrict youth's access to pornographic content, we need to recognize that pornography is fundamentally different than any other form of expression. It is a brain virus that hacks the primitive functions of a teen's reward circuitry. As previously stated, sexual euphoria is the highest attainable reward the brain can produce, similar to drugs. No speech should ever be limited based on people's beliefs or opinions; this would silence anyone opposing mainstream views or ideas. I highlight this differentiation between harmful or offensive speech and online sex to bring clarity to a long-standing misconception. It is a fallacy to argue that guidelines placed on the production and distribution of porn, which would serve to protect both actors and consumers, would ultimately lead to the chilling of free speech in all other forms. There is no other kind of speech that elicits orgasm on demand.

RUMB Challenge

For more information about organizations advocating to protect youth online, we recommend:

- National Center Against Sexual Exploitation– https://endsexualexploitation.org/
- Enough Is Enough– http://www.enough.org/

Please visit wiredhuman.org for a more extensive list.

Boots on the Ground

Ending exploitation and protecting the well-being of children is a team effort. Each player needs to get involved and do their part. Governments, parents, internet providers, web-based platforms, educators, and nonprofit organizations need to demand higher industry standards.

We must make our voices known and stand against exploitation. We encourage you to join the grassroots movement that is emerging all around the world to combat digital exploitation and the devastating impact it has on childhood development. As we are concluding this book, The National Center on Sexual Exploitation (NCOSE) is hosting its first virtual global summit with over 22,000 attendees from around the world. NCOSE is the leading organization exposing the links between all forms of sexual abuse and exploitation. They raise awareness, lobby on Capitol Hill, and demand responsible action from leaders in the tech field.

If we want to see fundamental change, we have to ensure that internet-based platforms like Pornhub and many others cannot hide under blanket immunity by utilizing Section 230 to avoid legal prosecution.

NCOSE's fight to bring Backpage.com to justice for offering a flagrant online platform to purchase human beings for sex serves as a prime example of how exposing corruption and demanding justice can have real-world impact towards ending sexploitation. Corruption thrives in societal apathy and crumbles when exposed by those with a steadfast resolve to say enough is enough. Backpage.com was an advertising platform that made millions off of prostitution and sex trafficking through their model of online classified listings, and even provided word suggestions to advertise trafficked children. Backpage used the content for profit, while hiding behind the immunity provided under Section 230 to justify their actions. In 2017, the mother of sixteen-year-old Desiree testified to a Senate committee about the devastating loss of her daughter. Desiree was trafficked on the site, which resulted in her murder. This horrific tragedy exposed the vile nature of backpage.com. NCOSE joined forces with other organizations to pass federal legislation known as FOSTA-SESTA, a bill aimed at fighting online sex trafficking. It marked a monumental shift that resulted in backpage.com being taken down. It removed blanket immunity from internet platforms that knowingly profit from the facilitation of sex trafficking and prostitution. It provided a way for survivors to testify against websites that function as "virtual pimps."[339] The removal of backpage.com serves as

RUMB Challenge

- Sign petitions to shut down porn sites that promote trafficking (e.g. https://www.traffickinghubpetition.com/)
- Write a letter to your congress(wo)man about declaring porn a public health crisis.
- Support leading organizations such as The National Center on Sexual Exploitation (NCOSE).
- Report misconduct to social media safety centers.
- Get educated about the „Dirty Dozen List" that highlights twelve companies that contribute to sexual exploitation in America.
- Research three grassroots movements that are taking a stand against exploitation and the pornification of the internet and post their campaigns on social media.

For more detailed information and updates on latest current events, please visit our website: wiredhuman.org a powerful example that digital exploitation cannot prevail over united action against injustice.

The Egg Crate Method

Jason

As Liza Smoker approached the podium at the 2019 Coalition to End Sexual Exploitation Global Summit in D.C., I was unsure what to expect. Above all the speakers, high-level lawyers, tech industry pioneers, academics, and top-tier NGO leaders, her workshop on grassroots advocacy through engaging the legislative process was by far the most empowering part of the global summit I experienced. Many might believe that walking the halls of Congress to educate our leaders and advocate for change is a job for a high-powered, well-funded lobbyist with a sharp suit and the trademark briefcase. As ordinary citizens, it can feel unrealistic to think we can storm the halls of Congress to demand justice and inspire change to build a path forward for our youth.

Smoker will tell you otherwise. She is no stranger to advocating for justice in the halls of Congress. However, she began her journey of grassroots lobbying at the state level, describing how nervous she was when she stood outside the office of a Florida legislator. Armed with a powerful message of truth, social justice, and an egg crate box on wheels to carry her various materials, she approached the door. In that moment, it blew open. A member of the legislative staff was noticeably agitated as they escorted another slick, high-paid industry lobbyist out of their office. He looked the part, with a thousand-dollar suit and a five-hundred-dollar leather briefcase that seemed to give him the coveted license to lobby. At this point, she described feeling completely out of place. It was obvious from her choice of clothing attire and her silly box apparatus towed behind that she did not at all fit the mold of a high-rolling lobbyist.

As she shared her story, a deep sense of solidarity overwhelmed me. I could identify with her situation of feeling the weight of injustice surrounding digital exploitation and the feeling of being inadequate to join the fight myself. However, the conclusion of her story immediately erased these false feelings. In the words of St. Augustine, "The truth is like a lion. You don't have to defend it. Let it loose and it will defend itself." Ms. Smoker boldly entered the room and made her case before the legislative staff. To her amazement, everyone was very receptive to what she had to say. They gave helpful tips, and even offered to call other offices to let them know she was coming.

She wondered about the lobbyist they dismissed moments prior. If he wasn't welcome, how did she manage to earn their favor? As she was leaving, she admitted to the staff that she was not a professional lobbyist, but there as a private citizen. A staffer confidently responded, "Oh, we know!" Smoker was curious, "What gave me away?" Without hesitation, the man whirled around, pointed conspicuously to her plastic cart and said, "That!" Feeling exposed by her gaffe on wheels, she promised to rid herself of the contraption, to which he responded, "No! Keep it. That helps you." He explained that she represented the common citizen who was coming with a legitimate concern. She was not paid to stand in the office, but put herself on the line out of a deep commitment to making a positive change in her community. From their perspective, she represented what the halls of the Florida Legislature and the doors of their offices were made for—to be a space where the ordinary citizen can make their voice known on behalf of those who do not have one.

We want to encourage you to assess your space of influence. If we unite, educate, equip, and empower, Big Tech will have to yield to consumer demands and create more accountability. Starting somewhere can look as simple as signing a petition to shut down sites that promote trafficking, educating your kids on the harmful effects of pornography, or supporting local organizations that promote internet safety. We decide what values to teach and model for the kids we live and work with—not the tech industry, and certainly not mainstream porn. ”

Discussion Guide:

1. Why does Section 230 serve as a breeding ground for exploitation online?
2. Why can we find disturbing content online that would never be allowed on public broadcasting or in public spaces?
3. What are examples of Big Tech choosing profit over people?

4. What companies/products/media have you stumbled upon that contribute to sexual exploitation?
5. When a nation's legal policies and laws enable injustice, what does it reveal about their societal values?
6. How can Big Tech companies become part of the solution?
7. What can we learn from the actions other countries are taking to improve online child safety policies?

Part Four:

Relationships: The greatest tool we have at our disposal for guiding teens towards healthy media choices is the relationship we have with them. That is why stewarding a healthy connection with a teenager by being present in their lives and modeling what a value-driven life looks like is critical for an adolescent's development.

Understand: The internet is loaded with a multitude of values that are thrown at our teens every time they pick up their smartphone. Many of these values represent the interests of industries seeking to profit from their interactions online.

Mentorship: When we become aware of the power of being present in someone else's life, we can inspire our teens to build boundaries that protect their offline world from digital distraction. We want to empower teens to identify values that promote healthy lifestyles and to reject those choices that seek to exploit their time and attention.

Boundaries: When teens learn to see their values as an intricate piece of who they are, their choices online and the boundaries that protect their vision for life come from a place of identity, rather than what people are telling them to do.

Chapter 9: The Power of Presence

Lisa

“Google Maps must have had a glitch. The main road we had been following was rapidly deteriorating in both safety and structural integrity. “As if driving up the side of a skyscraper was possible? This mountain requires an elevator,” I thought. The Swiss Alps were a stunning backdrop to our vacation location, overlooking the majestic Lake Como in Italy. In that moment, a monster SUV came around the bend of the dirt road. Without hesitation, it pulled alongside of our VW Golf and signaled us to roll the window down. “You don’t have a chance in that thing,” the driver told us. I thanked him for his concern. “You’ve been warned.” He pulled away with a little smirk on his face. I wasn’t about to give up so easily after driving five hours from our home in Freiburg, Germany. I reluctantly pulled forward. It didn’t help that some tourist had ripped off his oil pan on a jagged boulder protruding from the center of the road. Their bleeding river of car fluids guided our way. Suddenly, the car made a loud screech as it bottomed out in the dirt, leaving us teetering between ground and wheels. We got out and unpacked our bags. The lighter load allowed the wheels to dig into the dirt and we were on our way.

This vacation was one of the most memorable times I shared with my family. Every time I think back on our adventure together, the feelings return immediately. I can smell the crisp mountain air. I can hear shepherds herding their flocks and the bells of mountain goats ringing. I can feel my baby boy warmly snuggled up against my chest and my husband’s hand in mine. We were completely unplugged. No cell phone signal, no social media, no email, no distractions. All our senses were completely engaged in the present moment, creating vividly joyful memories. We felt fully alive.

As we were slowly making our way back down the mountain, I reflected on my own media consumption habits. Was digital media working for me, or was I working for digital media? I had squandered many hours away binge-watching Netflix, getting lost in the endless selection of news apps, and scrolling through my Instagram newsfeed until my eyes hurt. Yet, it had brought me no closer to the people around me. Slowly, my brain had chosen images over the effort it takes to engage in the present moment. I was missing out on what I have come to call "the real deal." If I was susceptible to the seductive draw of digital entertainment, teens who are still learning the fundamentals of self-control have their work cut out for them. If we want this rising generation to learn to engage with the world around them with all their senses, we need to get off the couch and invite them into a world of unplugged adventures, never to be forgotten. ”

Change Starts with Us

It only takes a short drive down the roads of America's capital to remind me that life moves quickly. You would be lucky to travel three miles without getting cut off or blasted by someone's horn. Working hours are long, rent is high, and somebody needs to make sure food gets on the table before bedtime. Juggling family, friendships, and a career is a daunting challenge. Most families require a double income to make ends meet. Being available 24/7 to respond to work calls, check notifications, and answer emails has become a cultural norm. Today's teens don't have it much easier. Their lives are dominated by a performance-driven value system, where grades and extracurricular activities are mandatory for a competitive college application. Even though teenagers spend more time at home, they spend less time conversing with their parents. Instead, they zone out to enter their digital world of choice. If we want youth to live a life that prioritizes people over pixels, and own tech habits that reflect their values, we need to question our priorities. There is simply no way to address healthy media interaction if we do not model what we wish to see in our teens' approach to digital media. Children and teenagers absorb everything; they learn intuitively from us, even when we don't think they're paying attention. Observational learning is a key component of

> We need to create sacred spaces in which the here and now is what we treasure above anything else.

human behavior. We need to create sacred spaces in which the *here* and *now* is what we treasure above anything else.

Lisa

"When I would come home as a teenager, my mom eagerly awaited me in the kitchen. She would lean in closely, displaying deep and genuine interest in what I had to say. Her body posture, eye contact, and intentional questions about the most mundane moments of my day revealed that she was fully present. To this day, my mom is an excellent listener. She responds to what I have to say, and she remembers the little details I share months later.

Those brief conversations meant the world to me. They signified that my life was important to my mother, and that what I experienced mattered to her. My mom's active listening communicated, "What is important to you is important to me." She didn't judge. She didn't vent or make it about what she had to say. She simply created the space to let me be. These times were special moments of bonding where I felt seen and known. Today, we have to protect these uninterrupted moments more than ever, as distraction is just a click away."

Counterintuitive Truth

Teenagers are hesitant to express their need for true connection, especially when it comes to sharing with adults or any authority figures like teachers or parents. Many teens might not be aware of their deep need for intimacy and express that they are uninterested in quality time.

The University of Toronto and Bowling Green State University tracked the hours of 1,600 children to better understand the impact of adolescent-parent relationships. Even though teens express their desire for independence and display a less interested attitude of engagement towards their parents, the study revealed that six hours of "family time" a week with parents "actively engaged" had a fundamental impact on adolescent wellbeing. The study suggests that teens who spend more intentional, unstructured quality time with their parents are emotionally better off and less likely to get into trouble than their peers. Regular family dinners, marked by an open and present atmosphere, are proven to lower risky teenage behavior such as drinking, smoking marijuana, eating disorders, and sex.[340] A study involving 5,000 adolescents in Montana found that frequently sitting around the dinner table resulted in lower rates of depression and suicidal thoughts.[341] Children that had become victims of cyberbullying recovered faster if they often shared a meal with their parents. Children that routinely sit around the dinner table with their parents are also proven to have better family relationships and experience less stress in life.[342] The reward of winning the battle over screens at the dinner table is worth the effort.

The Denmark Model

Denmark has been ranked the happiest nation in the world three years in a row. The Danish have a happiness trick up their sleeves known as *hygge*. Meik Wiking, CEO of The Happiness Research Institute, explains, "To *hygge* is to build sanctuary . . . We shelter each other when we invite people into our homes, when we give time, listen well, or provide a bed for the night; when we offer privacy, a winged armchair, anonymity, a tent in the garden."[343] All it needs is atmosphere, turning off digital gadgets, space for pleasure, thankfulness, togetherness, an attitude that values "we" over "me", a safe space, and the willingness to celebrate your "tribe." In other words, we must learn how to treasure the people in front of us over digital entertainment, productivity, and profit.[344] The Danes have come to understand that screen-free activities such as playing a board game, having a picnic, reading a book, or simply enjoying human company will ultimately lead to a more flourishing life.

All of us have the ability to be truly present with someone else, to listen intently, show interest

RUMB Challenge

Develop a family media plan to protect what matters most to you. Use the following link:

https://www.healthychildren.org/English/media/Pages/default.aspx#wizard

and compassion, and to ask meaningful questions. In a time of information overload, and as things change rapidly, with the possibility to be elsewhere at any time through our devices, it is more important than ever to learn how to fully live and engage in the moment. We set the tone and decide what, when, and how to consume.

What is Driving your Online Habits?

Most of us have the tendency to gravitate to one of two poles when addressing digital media: either we feel defeated, or respond in panic because we are overwhelmed by the vast and unstoppable progression of digital innovation. Being passive or indifferent, denying access, sleuthing through text messages, and exploding when our kids don't follow our instructions undermines our efforts to empower youth to steward sustainable media choices that promote their core values. It is not nearly as important how our kids interact with digital media when we are present as it is in our absence. College is the ultimate testing ground for graduating high school teens who are venturing out on their own for the first time. Suddenly, they are responsible for creating the life they want to lead. We need to raise a generation that has learned how to steward life-giving media habits that strengthen their self-esteem, support their life goals, protect their relationships, and know how to implement healthy boundaries.

The RUMB Method

In order to speak into a teenager's life, we need to take the time to understand and value their digital world. Instead of just telling our children or teens to get off the screen, it is essential to develop an interest in their unique online experience. Perhaps it means taking the time to learn the world of a certain game or playing it with them. The same applies to social media. Look into who your kids are following and why. Check out the apps they enjoy and see what appeals to them. Our understanding deepens the relationship, which leads to mentorship and healthy boundaries, otherwise known as RUMB.

Jason

"There is no one who taught me more about the transformative power of RUMB than Daniel. Daniel was a highly intelligent and creative thirteen-year-old boy on the autism spectrum. He struggled to make it a full day without completely losing control and the school calling his parents to pick him up. On his worst days, he would simply run away.

I have spent years advocating for kids and teens on the autism spectrum in the German public school system. The problematic behaviors and struggles are easy to identify, but speaking into these issues is another story. Kids and teens on the spectrum have a unique and fascinating perception of the world around them. While most of their classmates followed the unwritten social norms, the high schoolers I worked with wrote their own.

I was completely baffled on how to change Daniel's hardwired tendencies to melt down or run away at the slightest infraction of a classmate or teacher. I quickly realized that none of my insights, thoughtful wisdom, or suggestions made any difference in his behavior. He didn't care what I had to say. After months together, I began to crack the code. I had overcomplicated my approach. It wasn't until I took a legitimate interest in the things that were most important to him that I began to have a breakthrough.

The teens I worked with who were on the autism spectrum were often captivated by a specific topic. It could be superheroes, farm animals, or world history that dominated their thoughts. Some colleagues found these obsessions to be annoying, but I learned to make them my door of entry to build our relationship.

Daniel was fixated on airplanes. He had practically memorized every kind invented. I learned to listen and take authentic interest in all things aviation. I would ask lots of questions, and occasionally contributed some interesting points when I could. We talked about the character and discipline needed to be a top-level pilot, and how these traits could be displayed in other areas like school and friendships. When Daniel felt that the things important to him were also important to me, his attitude began to change. There was an openness to hearing my perspectives, and out of respect for our relationship, he began to value my insights. This resulted in a complete transformation of behavior at school. He no longer wanted to run away and stopped looking for reasons to melt down. He was a pleasure to be around, and began to succeed all across the board, both relationally and academically.

We don't have to approve every online behavior, but a teenager needs to feel seen before they will choose to listen. Two of our biggest mistakes as parents or professionals working with youth is to stay completely removed from their online encounters or to monitor without asking the deeper questions."

Lisa

"When my student stood in front of me, the weight of his shame and guilt was palpable. It wasn't his choice to receive a circulating nude photo of his classmate Kerry, but the fact that he had seen it on his phone was haunting him with disgrace. I had a choice to make. I could respond in panic and get upset by the severity of the situation, or I could recognize the courage it took to be the only one in his entire school to confront the situation head-on. He trusted me as his teacher to find help for Kerry, alert the proper authorities, and address the student body to discourage future instances.

Empathy starts with listening with a heart that wants to understand. Risky online behavior often arises because of issues at home, psychological struggles, substance abuse, or problems in school.[345] If teenagers struggle in real life, chances are high they struggle online. Our kids' media choices are an expression of a deeper—often unfulfilled—longing.

When we plant a garden and the vegetables fail to grow, we do not blame the vegetables; we look at the reasons they aren't flourishing. We investigate the soil and examine the amount of sunlight. We water the plants and apply fertilizer. With equal care, we need to explore the "why" behind our teens' misuse of digital media. Instead of blaming them for their online behavior, we need to look closely and examine what is driving a teenager's digital habits. By looking at the ingredients that stunt their growth from a place of understanding, we can create an environment that allows them to blossom. If we allow empathy to guide our conversation surrounding tech, shame will cease to exist.[346] Addressing our children's fundamental human needs to be seen, known, and accepted will set this generation up for success, rather than digital dependency.

We encourage you to choose one night a week to talk about

tech-related challenges with a heart of empathy and continually process the values that drive your family's online choices. Challenging this generation to explore the "why" behind their digital habits will uncover how they can make healthier tech choices.

Jason

In one of my workshop sessions with teenagers, the topic of committed relationships and sexual exploration came up. The teens were curious about the "why" behind setting boundaries on sexual pleasure. I affirmed the validity of this question. Sex is fun, and humans aren't confined to being attracted to just one partner. Why would anyone choose to put boundaries on their sex drive, rather than living out as many sexual experiences possible through porn or multiple partners? Everyone agreed that they one day wanted a committed relationship with a loyal and loving partner. With this goal in mind, I explained how sexual encounters have the most profound effect on our brain's reward circuitry. If we train our brain to crave variety over commitment, we aren't setting ourselves up for long term relationship success. Armed with a deeper understanding of the "why" behind their choices, and their goals at the forefront of their actions, they were able to make the connection that porn and one-night stands will not bring them closer to what they truly desire.

From Screen Addicts to Sustainable Consumers

Digital devices are here to stay. Demonizing technology doesn't help anyone; it is merely a question of *how* we use it. Phones have become so prevalent that forty-three percent of eighteen- to thirty-four-year-olds check their phone during foreplay.[347] Every tenth person checks their phone during sex, with eighteen- to thirty-four-year-olds being twice as likely to do so. Even when people are doing their "business," smartphones are there to fill the time, with fifty-nine percent of people checking their phones on the toilet. *iPass*, a mobile connectivity company, found that sixty-one percent agreed that it is impossible to give up Wi-Fi, which was ranked higher than sex and junk food.[348]

Establishing Healthy Boundaries

Boundaries protect what we value most in life. The younger our kids are, the more important it is that we enforce boundaries. We suggest holding off on giving your kids a smartphone until at least eighth grade. The older and more mature our teens become, the more we can help them reflect on *why* those boundaries are necessary. If teenagers understand that boundaries are there to protect their life goals, values, and health, it becomes easier to implement them.

As families take time to explore what boundaries they need to set around technology use, they will likely uncover the extent of their unhealthy habits that may even border or cross the line of addiction.

Will power alone is not enough to overcome addictive cycles. There are many factors that feed into addiction, ranging from childhood trauma to struggles with intimacy. It is essential to create a safe place for whoever is struggling without blaming or labeling them. True healing always happens in the context of community, restored intimacy, and a life with purpose and direction. However, it is wise to involve professionals to uncover the underlying roots of addiction and develop a plan forward.

Jean Twenge and her team of researchers found that teenagers are happiest when they spend less than an hour a day online.[349] If we want our teens to find long-lasting satisfaction, we need to work towards that goal. How we can achieve that goal will differ from family to family, classroom to classroom, and setting to setting.

A teacher wanted to make sure that smartphones wouldn't turn into a distraction in her classroom. She built little smartphone beds with her students. The phones would sleep during class, to be retrieved after the lesson was over. Chris Beard, a basketball coach at Texas Tech, decided to start a radical experiment. He previously decided to ban smartphones during team mealtimes and during their two-day bonding retreat. After they lost three times in a row, he took his idea a step further. He would collect the phones every night before his players would head to bed. Without the accessibility of smartphones at night, the whole momentum shifted. The team went on a winning streak and finished second in the NCAA championship.[350] A high school teacher decided to take her class sailing for a couple of days. She shared with me, "When I explained that I didn't want students to bring their smartphones, you can imagine that most of them were not happy to hear that. I explained my heart behind the decision: 'Disconnection from family and friends allows us to focus on the present and the people we spend time with. It prevents homesickness and the misuse of photos and videos students easily post on social media platforms.' After we returned from our week of adventure together without their devices, my students shared that none of them missed the access to their smartphones, but all of them were excited to get home and get their devices back. Leaving our devices at home allowed us to fully engage with each other, strengthened our sense of belonging, and helped us to feel like a stronger team."

We must determine how our values and priorities reflect our engagement with our devices. Ultimately, we should be training our kids to tune into each other instead of devices. France has passed a law that forbids digital devices on school grounds for anyone under fifteen. While France found their way to limit tech, we need to work on finding what boundaries work best for our individual families and social settings.

As mentors in our teenagers' lives, it is part of our job to encourage them to strengthen the muscle of self-control. However, for adolescents to fully understand that concept and come to appreciate boundaries is its own challenge. The world-famous "Marshmallow Experiment" is proof that the ability to access self-control is the foundation for a successful life. Researchers Angela Duckworth and Martin Seligman discovered that self-control is two times more important than IQ when it comes to predicting high-school performance, school attendance, and final grades.[351] We need to teach our kids to deflect their attention from technology onto life-giving, in-person relationships. Information itself does not change behavior. Instead, reason and willpower function like muscles that need to be exercised repeatedly.[352] Small, habitual actions make all the difference. The same principle applies any time we want to change our behavior, from trying to lose weight to learning a new skill. We must constantly interrogate how and why we use technology.

RUMB Challenge

Make a list of ten screen-free activities and prioritize them in order.

Make sure that the activities are active or social. Instead of pulling out your phone when you feel bored, stressed or lonely, choose an activity from the list.

e.g. building a project in the backyard, playing volleyball with friends

RUMB Challenge

Commit to boundaries that reflect your values.

Examples:

- Hold off on the smartphone and get your child a "Relay" (a cellular walkie talkie) or a "Gabb" phone (unlimited talk and text, without apps and internet browser) to reflect their age and maturity.
- Use a filter to block pornographic sites (we recommend "bark", "netnanny" or "covenant eyes").
- Create tech-free spaces. For example, no screens at the dinner table, in bathrooms, or in bedrooms.
- Have all devices in an allocated area at night.
- Encourage no screens during homework.
- Create a screen drawer.
- Create screenless family traditions (e.g., no screens during a holiday celebration).
- Create a "tech budget". Allow teens to decide what to spend their tech time on and treat it like a weekly allowance. If they want to game with their friends on a Saturday night, they can save up their tech time to spend on a special occasion.
- Decide together what influencers to unfollow that negatively affect your teenager's self-image and values.

Guiding Mentorship

Teenagers are developing adults who want to make sense of the world. We need to give them a chance to reflect on which tech consumption habits bring them life, and which ones stand in the way of living life to its fullest. They will feel empowered if they have all the information to choose for themselves. Society has previously applied this concept when it comes to bad eating habits, smoking, or alcohol consumption. We discuss and set healthy boundaries and teens make their choices. Unfortunately, we haven't learned how to successfully integrate digital media into those discussions. Eating a healthy diet doesn't mean that we can never have our favorite ice cream or fast food. It's all about moderation and intentionality. Digital media follows similar rules. There are plenty of healthy ways to use the web, and just as many ways to be abused by it if teenagers aren't intentional. Perhaps this equates to capping the selection of apps we use, the number of times we play video games or scroll through our newsfeeds. These boundaries may sound intimidating, even for adults, but we can learn together. Our teens will respect when we are authentic and admit to failure. In the social media age, it is a powerful hallmark when people can feel safe enough in a relationship to admit to their mistakes. If we have proper boundaries, technology will no longer have the power to hijack our goals, and wreak-havoc on our relationships.

RUMB Challenge:

Ask your teen to imagine life ten years down the road:

What dream career do you want to pursue? What kind of relationships and people do you want to be surrounded by? Do you want a committed romantic relationship built on trust and intimacy? Do you want to have your own flourishing family?

Once you have a picture of the ideal life you want to arrive at in ten years, would this outcome look different if your tech habits never changed?

What online habits have the potential to become stumbling blocks to pursue the best version of your life?

The Tech Revolution

We need a revolution to challenge our behaviors and priorities. The truth is, it starts with us. Christoph, a high school teacher and father, shared his experience:

> I realized how important the smartphone had become to me. When I didn't have my smartphone on me, my two-year-old daughter would bring it to me, as if I had forgotten something really important. One night, my friends and I talked about how great it would be to abstain from the smartphone for a while. I immediately had to think of all the things I would miss. That reminded me of the time I quit smoking. I had all these positive associations with a bad habit. I was afraid smartphone fasting would make me uninformed and socially excluded. That night, my friend put his smartphone on the table and asked if I was 'in.' It was one thing to talk about it in theory, but another to do it. I decided to hand my smartphone to my friend. Seven weeks went by. I

> needed to find new ways to entertain myself when waiting for the doctor or fighting boredom. I realized that I craved my smartphone a lot more when I am stressed and asked myself *why*. I definitely missed out on a couple things, because it was harder to get in touch, but after fasting my smartphone, it felt like a fresh start that allowed me to give the smartphone its rightful place in my life.

Christoph provides an extreme example that wouldn't be feasible for most of us, but even short smartphone breaks are beneficial to our health. Digital detox is worth fighting for. A 2014 study conducted by University of California, Los Angeles (UCLA) revealed that sixth graders who spent five days at an outdoor camp without any access to screens were significantly better at reading human emotions than they were before attending the camp.[353]

In a day and age where nine out of ten teens recognize spending too much time online as a problem among their peers (including sixty percent who say it's a major problem, and more than fifty percent who admit spending too much time in front of screens themselves)[354] we must challenge the status quo and help our kids navigate this new territory. We need to be bold enough to fight for and protect tech-free space, whether it be an hour a day, a day a week, or a week a year. Our kids might not thank us now, but they will likely thank us later.

Fully Unplugged

Lisa

As I interviewed former students who are now grown adults, I was surprised to hear how utterly positive they reflected on the boundaries their parents had set around technology. They expressed a deep gratitude that someone had taught them how to exercise self-control, not to game their lives away, and to carefully select how to use social media. Mia, a seventeen-year-old who worked as a camp counselor during summer break, talked about her favorite aspect of the camp. The camp directors didn't allow for any digital media devices for the entire month she was there. She loved the fact that people were simply focused on people. Looking back, she treasured the time without any digital distractions.

She raved about the fact that everyone simply enjoyed being with each other.

Let's be real; intentionally choosing the tech we choose to spend our time on according to our values and implementing digital breaks will probably be difficult for most of us, but if we look at what we will gain in return—deeper friendships, closer, connected families, and healthier lives—it is more than worth the effort.

Discussion Questions:

1. Imagine a family vacation without phones? What would it look like? What would make it better? What would make it worse?
2. What are three social settings that you would like to experience without having a phone *(e.g. dinner, game night)* What did you lose? What did you gain?
3. How does it make you feel when you are talking to someone who is on a device?
4. Why is personal success linked to incorporating digital breaks *(e.g. Texas Tech, NCAA basketball championship)*? Think of five benefits of taking digital breaks.
5. How can parents and mentors support you in making wise tech choices?

Chapter 10: Who We Are is Where We Go

Jason and Lisa

Instagram influencer and adventure photographer Lennart Pagel had just wrapped up another off-the-grid photo expedition, which started in Mongolia and ended in South Tyrol, Italy. In our interview, he shared how he had just learned to ski, dogsled with huskies, galloped on tribal horses, and watched trained hunting eagles catch prey. He found refuge with nomads and their families, tasted wild cuisines, and learned to play games with local kids. Lennart is one of the most influential German landscape photographers, with an Instagram fan base that is about to crack the 500k marker.

He grew up in a small town on the North Sea. As a teenager, he wrestled with boredom and found himself in frequent small-town trouble. He and his friends eventually passed the long afternoons sitting around and smoking weed. Things got real when high school graduation came and went. He described having a deep yearning for something more. "I felt stuck and knew I wanted more in life; more passion, more direction, and more adventure."

His quest for purpose led him to the high deserts of Redding, California. It became his laboratory, where he learned to capture the unique and rugged wilderness terrain. "I cultivated a value for being in the now. This is a key ingredient in my art. Nature is happening right now, and if I am distracted by the noise of yesterday or tomorrow, I will miss the beauty right in front of me," he stated. He wanted to share his art with others and found Instagram to be a powerful platform to catalog his unique perspectives on the world around him. His following began to grow. Upon his return to his motherland, he was discovered by a collective of German Influencers who made creating over consuming their mission.

Through continuous hard work, investment, and the joined adventures with other photographers who shared his passion, his fanbase blew up. To date, the collective of young men, known as the German Roamers, has accumulated millions of followers all over the world, been featured in Walden and Spiegel magazine, released their first book, and have partnered with name brands like Olympus, Adidas, and Mercedes Benz. The outdoor collective provides a window for people to catch a glimpse of the planet's most remote and wild terrain.

We asked Lennart about the values that guide him as an influencer. Lennart explained:

> For one, my mission is to make a living off something I'm passionate about—photography, adventure, the outdoors. Besides that, I want to inspire my followers to realize the miracle of the planet we live on. I also love it when someone messages me and tells me that my pictures made them leave the couch to go outside, explore nature, often times with a camera on their side. This adds a lot of meaning to my work.

Lennart was real about what life looks like on the other side of the camera. He shared stories about sleeping in the rain and pushing through days without proper food or a comfortable bed, in order to reach the remote locations featured on his Instagram page. Living out of a backpack, unexpected inconveniences, and spending endless nights behind a laptop editing and sorting through photos are all part of the job description. To him, the price is worth it.

"What about the fame and wealth that comes with being an influencer? Do these factors ever cause you to comprise your values?" we asked.

Lennart clarified his position:

> If I decide to work with a brand in promoting them or their products, it's because it's a good fit with who I am and what I do. I don't want to push products on my followers and use them for my benefit. Unfortunately, I don't see this sincerity in most influencers. Something else that distinguishes me from others in my field of work is the abbreviation "HE›i" on my Instagram account. It means that God is greater than me. I try not to see myself as the center and origin of everything, but rather to see my work and income as a gift I get to steward.

We dug deeper. "But how do you handle the consumerist side of social media?"

His answer was honest:

> I think anyone who's part of society is a consumer. Every creator is a consumer, too. The difference is, I don't leave it at that. I consume, but then I try to take it as an inspiration and create something from it. For example, when I see a picture that really speaks to me, I try to understand, "What makes this picture so great? How can I implement this into my own photography?" I try not to stay in consumption mode.

We continued, "How do you stay present with those around you, especially because being on your phone is part of your job description?" Lennart reflected:

> I always have my phone on silent and vibrations turned off. When I'm with people, I try to not look at my phone at all unless it's really necessary. When I'm in bed I turn my phone on airplane mode until the next morning. Those are a few things that help me. I favor offline connections over online feedback. At times, this means that online connections have to wait, but that's okay.

What separates Lennart from other influencers is how he stewards and protects his core values. He is willing to pay the price to make them guiding forces in his life. Some values he directly reflected on in our interview and others are inherent in the life he chooses to live each day. Choosing courage over comfort has become an integral part of the way he lives. His life clearly reflects his values for community, faith, adventure, and risk-taking, to name a few. Holding on to your values does not have to be a struggle if your values become an integral part of who you are. As Brené Brown puts it:

> Our values should be so crystallized in our minds [. . .] that they don't feel like a choice—they are simply a definition of who we are [. . .]. Because [this] is integrity—choosing courage over comfort; it's choosing what's right over what's fun, fast, or easy; and it's practicing your values, not just professing them.[355]

The link between values and identity is critical when reflecting on a teenager's interaction with digital media. Their values aren't just ideals to strive for; they represent who they are. In practical terms, respecting human dignity and rejecting pornography becomes a position of, "this is who I am", rather than, "this is what I should do." When our teens learn to see their values as a reflection of themselves, their ability to make healthy choices online is less about what adults are telling them to do and more about who they want to be. Therefore, rejecting sexploitation, choosing creation over consumption, and stewarding healthy offline relationships reflect their core identity. If we want teenagers to self-regulate, we need to teach them to plug technology into their values. "

RUMB Challenge

Make a list of your top three films. Choose one film to watch together as a group or family.

Examine what core values the main characters are portraying.

Which values (e.g. courage, family, selflessness) lead the key protagonists closer to accomplishing their goals?

Which values (e.g. selfishness, lying, power hunger) cause hardship?

Analyze your life as a film. You are the lead protagonist. What values do you want to see portrayed in your life? What values sabotage your success?

Values Online

Within minutes of opening their laptops or picking up their smartphones, teens are introduced to a myriad of competing values promoted online. Hypersexualization, posing, objectification, bullying, and violence are omnipresent in the media this rising generation consumes. To some degree, the exposure is inevitable and won't harm youth, if they know their values and are willing to fight for their own stance in life. However, if they haven't yet been given the opportunity to decide which values they are committed to and why, they can't be expected to make sense of what they are confronted with in the digital world.

A Shift of Focus

As parents, teachers, or professionals, we have a privileged window of opportunity in which to help our youth recognize the incredible impact an externally focused life has on their health and wellbeing. Valuing others over self-indulgence is in opposition of the design of digital media, because technology is engineered to bring the consumer satisfaction, making them the center of their online experience.

When teens are hyper-focused on themselves, even if it isn't out of a selfish heart, life tends to get very heavy. Personal weaknesses, deficiencies, and emotions become magnified. When teens are given the opportunity to make a positive impact in someone else's life, they focus their attention on their talents, natural gifts, and sphere of influence. The only thing that can truly help struggling teens is to learn how to focus on and invest in others. When they choose to live a life that's about investing in others, health and happiness will follow.

Learning to cast their attention onto others adds meaning and purpose to their relationships. It isn't a coincidence that the final step of Alcoholics Anonymous' twelve-step program is giving back to others by supporting recovering alcoholics on their journey to recovery. The act of serving others gives their relationships purpose within the community they build, helping to overcome their desire to drink. This rising generation needs to learn that they hold the power to spread

RUMB Challenge

Research possibilities to volunteer, support, or positively influence those in your circle.

Commit to doing one activity a week that is focused on others.

RUMB Challenge:

Develop a value-driven screen contract that you commit to as a group or family.

Example:

- Today, we commit to using digital media for creation over consumption.
- Today, we commit to spreading kindness instead of pain.
- Today we commit to honoring human dignity instead of treating each other as a means to an end.
- Today, we commit to using media to strengthen our core friendships rather than collecting a following.

kindness over pain, encouragement over gossip, and authenticity over objectification. The truth is, life-giving values can be learned.

Denmark is the first country that turned the value of "empathy" into a school subject. Similar to studying math or a foreign language, the Danes identified empathy as a life skill that must be learned and mastered. This rising generation needs to realize that they hold the power to practice empathy when encountering exploitive or hurtful situations online. Their empathy allows them to interfere when a classmate is bullied, hurt, or exploited, even when it happens behind a glass screen. If empathy governs their life choices, they won't remain numb, but will instead master the courage to seek help and demand justice.

Casting Vision

When examining life values, a great place to start is by casting vision. When a young child is asked about their dream career, the classic answer seems to fall in the category of firefighter, doctor, or police officer. Who wouldn't want to be the hero helping those in need and saving lives? Protecting, serving, and rescuing are amazing core values to live by. Fast forward to the smartphone generation; the most common answer to the "what-do-you-want-to-be" question is alarming. In 2018, *The Washington Post* published an article based on a survey conducted by the U.K. travel agency, First Choice. When 1,000 kids ages six to seventeen were asked about their dream career, seventy-five percent aspired to be a YouTuber or a "vlogger."[356] Teens who learn to make choices on the basis of their core values develop their own internal compass that will guide them towards meaningful lives filled with purpose.

Jason

"Over twenty years ago, my father gave up business to pursue his passion for mentoring and coaching leaders from around the world to help them reflect on life outside of their career. He turned down wealth and notoriety to make his life about family and loving others well. He made time in his busy schedule to coach our basketball teams. He came to all our important events and never missed a birthday or graduation. If you judged my dad's success by the kind of car he drove, you might come to the wrong conclusion, but my father knew better than to think of success in such narrow terms. His life is flourishing with abundant love and gratitude from those who know him. He exemplifies a life led by his commitment to the values that are most important to him: family and meaningful relationships.

A few years ago, my father was diagnosed with an aggressive form of cancer. When word got out that he needed help to beat this horrible disease, a flood of support came from every corner of his life. His wife and five kids surrounded him, the leaders he worked with organized the best doctors in the country to look after him, and hundreds of friends sent letters supporting him in prayer and many gave financial gifts. People offered their homes when they heard he needed to travel to California for treatment. The teens my parents once mentored in a local youth group, who are now fully-grown adults, rallied together to help support my dad in any way they could. Kids he used to coach in basketball grew up but never forgot the impact he had on their lives and wrote him letters of support and encouragement. Even members of Congress, who had cherished his friendship for many years, held a time of prayer for him at the Congressional Members Bible Study on Capitol Hill. In his moment of need, his social capital was revealed. A lifetime of loving, serving, and investing in others created more fulfillment than money or notoriety could have ever delivered. Such love can only be found in the trenches of relationship and the values that have our unwavering yes. Today, my dad is cancer free.

There is a common misconception among teenagers that building a fulfilling life is something they don't need to be concerned about until they are older. Building a lasting community and committed romantic relationships are goals for people in a different stage of life. One day they will follow suit, but the present is all about fulfilling their immediate desires. The dating culture among Gen Zers and Millennials is a prime example. Sexual expression is often absent of committed love, because this value is a hindrance to one's fundamental primitive desire for recreational procreation. Self-indulgence through porn and sex outside of a value system is justified in the name of being young. However, a flourishing life is built on a foundation of virtuous values, not inwardly focused escapades. Adulthood draws upon what our teens have wired their brains to as a road map to pursue their vision and purpose for life.

When the Rubber Meets the Road

Jason

"It was the middle of the night, and the only thing that I could do to keep myself from going over the sanity rails was to drive. I felt like I was suffocating in hopelessness. As a sophomore in college, I couldn't think of one person to call on for help. Although I knew coaches, professors, and many fellow students at the university, my internal turmoil made me feel incredibly vulnerable. I couldn't imagine sharing my raw and unfiltered life with someone who wasn't family. The crippling effects of loneliness had me on the ropes. Looking back, I probably would have had a long list of reasons why my suffering was the result of the unfair world around me. In reality, "adulting" had my number. I was far from home, and learning to self-regulate was proving to be a substantial chore.

It has been ten years since I struggled with such intense loneliness. I keep this memory close as a reminder to be understanding of those who share my battle. The worst part about loneliness is the feeling that I am unique in my despair. This is what gives loneliness its power: the belief that everyone else is living "the dream", while you are alone in your suffering. This could not be further from the truth. A national survey of 1,502 college students showed that sixty percent felt emotionally unprepared for college life and relationships.[357] All of us struggle with feelings of disconnectedness at one point or another. Living by our values strengthens the most important relationships in our lives. On the other hand, compromising our core values leads to passivity, pain, and relationship ruin."

Lisa

"I bumped into a counselor that worked next to my office. She had just finished a session with a mom whose daughter dropped out of college. As we engaged in a deeper conversation about this rising generation, we realized that we had encountered numerous families with similar struggles; their kids were wrestling with the idea of giving up on college. Friendships seemed impossible to come by, as students preferred to stay in their rooms and connect through social media. Their kids weren't prepared for the lack of social engagement and the awkwardness of face-to-face encounters. This often led to feelings of intense loneliness that caused their children to question whether college was the right choice. If parents aren't raising pioneers who are willing to plow a new path forward in the digital age, then their teens are in for a rude awakening.

What is the Life You Want to Live?

Jason

When I was a junior in high school, I participated in a thought-provoking exercise where we had to write down a list of qualities that we wanted to see in our future partner. I painstakingly put together a detailed description of the magnificent person I intended to put a ring on one day. When everyone was finished, we gathered back together and read them aloud, only to have the instructor reveal the trap we'd fallen into. She challenged us with a bold question: "Do you exemplify this list of qualities in your own life?" It was a simple but powerful truth: we attract what we are. The same can be said for community and friendship. If I feel hyper-connected yet alone, chances are I am searching for community, rather than building the community I want to see. I have personally never experienced a meaningful friendship I found; rather, I built meaning into friendships I said yes to. The truth is, friendship and community are forged through intentionality, selflessness, and sacrifice. You cannot withdraw what you haven't deposited, and you won't attract what you don't exemplify in your own life. Too often we hear teenagers say, "I just don't have good friends," as if they should miraculously land in their lap. Meanwhile, they are squandering hours away watching their friends' lives unfold behind a screen.

Teens are growing up in an era where everything seems instantly available, so why not friendships?

RUMB Challenge:

Robin Dunbar found that people are biologically limited to managing five intimate friendships.

Write down the five people in your life that are closest to you. Write down five things you can do to help prioritize and protect those relationships.

The average teenager's online social network is far beyond what is humanly possible to manage. Even though these online interactions fuel connection, most of the time they don't equate to friendships that teens can rely on when the going gets tough. Famous anthropologist and evolutionary psychologist Robin Dunbar found that people are biologically limited to managing five intimate friendships, which he describes as the supportive relationships that belong to one's most inner circle of companions. Beyond this circle is only space for a maximum of ten sympathetic friends, thirty familiar acquaintances, and 100 miscellaneous introductions. The average Facebook user has accumulated 500 friends, with the majority likely falling into the miscellaneous category.[358] Managing and appeasing the random friend category can be a distraction from the friends who deserve our attention the most—our supportive friends. Teenagers need to learn that searching for the right friends starts with becoming the friend they want to meet. ”

Walk the Talk

As parents, teachers, or professionals, we have to recognize our sphere of influence and challenge ourselves to evaluate the values that guide our own choices. We need to model a lifestyle that promotes people over pixels, reflected in how we balance work and family and how we build community.

Make healthy values a team priority in your family or classroom. Ask your kids and teens what areas of your life are points of frustration for them and commit to working on them. When we show our commitment to healthy values in a way that is meaningful to our youth, it opens a door to discussing the values that are influencing their online habits. If we are dissatisfied with our teen's consumption habits, we need to offer them alternate ways to build a life centered around community, healthy relationships, and purpose.

As it is with any unhealthy pattern of behavior or addiction, when something gets taken away, we need to replace it with something meaningful that reflects our values. Willpower is never enough to break a bad habit, let alone an addiction. For Alice, the radical anti-porn activist, a key turning point in overcoming her porn addiction was to become physically active. She enrolled in roller derby and Olympic weightlifting.

Instead of feeling sluggish, she gave herself permission to take up space and be strong. She now lives her life for others. Her mission is to create safe spaces for women to talk about their struggles with porn and find freedom in vulnerability and purpose.

What I Learned from Language School

Jason

"When I moved to Germany, the government required that I pass a language and culture proficiency test to be eligible for the German equivalent of a Green Card. This involved seven months of full-time language courses to prepare for the exam. During this time, the German Chancellor, Angela Merkel, had made a controversial political decision to allow millions of immigrants to enter the country in response to the Syrian refugee crisis. This decision resulted in a massive influx of asylum seekers from around the world longing for protection and security behind German borders.

My language cohort consisted of roughly twenty-five individuals, and nearly everyone was from a different country and cultural background. We spent five days a week cramped in a small room learning German together. I could have never imagined that some of these individuals would one day belong to my inner circle of friends. The cultural divide between us was so wide that misunderstandings and offense were common in our interactions. There were virtually unlimited anthropological landmines hidden from sight, ready to set the classroom ablaze. Consistency was key. Over time, we got to know each other's stories. Behind the great divide was a unique and powerful life journey.

Yesoph was in his early thirties when I met him. After observing him for a few weeks, I had made many false assumptions about his values, background, and motives. After months of language classes, I started to realize that I had him all wrong. I invited Yesoph over to our apartment for dinner with my family and a few friends. I was shocked by his story. He shared that he belonged to the Christian minority in Syria, and had to flee after ISIS murdered five of his closest friends. In Syria, he was highly educated, respected, and loved. In Germany, he was no one. His degree was unrecognized, making it difficult to find work. To most people, he was just another immigrant looking for a better life, but Yesoph and I called each other brothers.

As we journeyed through language class, consistent interactions broke down the walls around us, follow-through kept us bonded outside of the classroom, and outward focus made space for each other's stories without judging or taking offense, which led to authentic and meaningful community. Over the course of my five-year stint in Germany, many of the people in my language class became my family.

When loneliness strikes, I look to the areas of my life that need my attention. I have found that consistency, follow-through, and outward focus are key contributors to strengthening friendships and promoting mental health. If I don't constantly monitor these values or ignore the signs, life runs like a car with its dashboard lit up, costly breakdown imminent. ”

Values in Action

Teens have little unstructured free time and a million ways to spend it. Unwinding time is precious, so they seek opportunities that will give them the quickest gratification in return. This creates a tension between possibilities and consistency. My work with youth and young adults is a constant reminder of how challenging it can be to follow through with our commitments when the world is always dishing out reasons to back out. I have noticed a shift in scheduling culture, especially in young adults and teens. Those belonging to Generation X and older welcome the opportunity to schedule meetings out in advance, while Generation Z and Millennials find it very stressful. The consensus is always the same. What if a more attractive opportunity comes up? The preferred method is to make plans while leaving wiggle room; "I think I can make that work" or "I should be able to come," only to cancel the day of. In the moment, they are rewarded by a more enticing opportunity, but they lose the long-term reward that accompanies consistency and follow-through. If we aren't careful to protect our yes to consistency and community, the result can be a fragmented social life, which leads to half-backed relationships.

A lack of meaningful friendships harms a teen's well-being and drives them to screens. Loneliness reduces cognitive control, which makes teens far more susceptible to the design and purpose of digital media: to capture their attention by offering immediate gratification, undermining healthy emotional regulation. The most appealing ways to spend our time aren't always the best choices. Therefore, consistency always requires a high value for follow-through.

The key to developing follow-through is closely related to emotional stability. Our emotions are like the unruly kids in the back seat of our life-mobile; the minute we allow them to take over the driver seat, things get messy. Emotions aren't truth, they are feelings. Although our feelings are valid, they shouldn't have absolute authority over our choices and behavior. When the time comes to follow through, what is driving a teenager forward—their values for what they have said *yes* to, or a fleeting moment driven by how they feel? Just as digital media is engineered to respond to our feelings and not our cognition, our brain desires to make choices based on instant reward rather than long-term goals.

Whether you are a teacher managing tech in your classroom or a parent fighting to put devices in their rightful place, building a strong value for long term goals helps teens to understand the *why* in what they are fighting for. If boundaries are only understood as rules to follow, teens won't learn to self-regulate outside of being told what to do. However, if we help youth to understand the intent behind these boundaries and cast a vision of a destination worthy of their efforts, we create ownership over what they have said *yes* to in their lives.

Vision is the life and blood of persistence and tenacity, but vision without a purpose is a hollow shell waiting to disappoint. Teens struggle to find contentment with the world's version of success: achieve the best grades, go to the most prestigious university, and find

RUMB Challenge

It takes a minimum of twenty-one days to rewire your brain and start a new habit.

Choose one "bad" tech habit you want to kick to the curb. This habit needs to be tangible as well as measurable (e.g. scrolling through social media, watching porn, taking your phone to bed, using tech while eating).

Decide on a "good" habit to replace the "bad" habit with (e.g. reading a chapter in a book, calling one friend a day, going on a daily jog).

Log your daily progress. No need to fear failure. The joy is in the journey!

a high-paying job. These goals are worthy pursuits, but without centering them on others, they will leave us feeling empty. If we want youth to live and use their devices with intention, we need to help them determine where they want to go in life. The desire to get married one day is just one example of a vision that eighty-eight percent of Americans have in common.[359] Teens can choose their lifestyle, but they need the tools to make their goals possible. The foe of deeply felt purpose is inwardly focused lives.

Purposelessness kills. It drives people to fill the void and pushes them towards a counterfeit, which often surfaces in the form of addiction. Deep down inside, teenagers yearn for their efforts to be worthwhile and for their actions to mean something. If media consumption turns into compulsive behavior, it uncovers a void that is longing to be filled. If you talk to any porn consumer that decided to quit for good, they will tell you that they needed something to live for, something to fill their time with and people to join them on their life journey; they needed a sense of purpose and direction. A teen's vision for life and the values driving them forward govern their media choices. Their interaction with digital media can take on an entirely new form as they put devices to work for them, rather than being consumed by them.

Mia, thirteen, decided to turn her life around:

> Last month, I decided to delete Snapchat and Instagram off my phone. When you delete social media, you realize that there are people who actually want to talk to you and not just respond to your stupid stories. For the first time in a long time, I feel like I have friends who care about me. I have way less drama in my life now that Snapchat and Instagram are gone. I feel better about myself, but I also feel it has made me a nicer person. I struggle with anxiety a lot, but Snapchat and Instagram made everything worse. I used to waste hours a day on social media. I would scroll until I felt completely numb. I was so consumed with my smartphone that I didn't even pay attention to the people I really cared about. I was too hooked on unbroken Snapchat streaks and likes from people who do not really know me or care about me. Without the fog of social media, I suddenly realized that there are people out there who actually love me.

I also do more things that I love, like running or painting. I feel so much better about myself. It's like my mental health is so much better. I used to hurt myself, but now I am learning to accept myself just the way

I am. Now, it's all about discovering who I truly am and what I want to do with my life.[360]

Let's empower this generation to harness the benefits of technology and build a life that is so rich, even tech cannot hijack their goals. Let's inspire this generation to make tech work for them, to cut out the messages that undermine their self-esteem, push them toward hypersexualization, and lead to loneliness, depression, and anxiety. Let's challenge this generation to form new habits that support their goals and well-being. It's up to us to sow seeds and cast vision of a life that is more unplugged, present, full of adventure, meaning, and community.

Conclusion

Lisa and Jason

"We don't have to accept what we are given when it comes to our children. We envision a world where parents are back in the driver seat, where innocence is enjoyed and protected, where the excitement of the first kiss, the rush of a first date, and symphony of friendships aren't stolen or corrupted by the danger lurking in the wild plains of the digital frontier.

Let's take our stand, both parents and all advocates for youth, to demand new digital legal boundaries that make pornification a choice, not an inevitability. We want our children's internet habits to reflect that friendship matters, and that love is worth the effort. We want them to use tech to achieve their goals, empower their lives, reflect their values, and strengthen their relationships.

We want them to be fully alive and well when they enter their adult years. We want them to launch with their wings fully spread and nothing weighing them down so that they can live a fuller life with more opportunities than we had. Let's inspire our kids to use digital media, not be used or abused by it. It is time for a life without the tight grip of tech; a life where we are the masters of our choices; a revolution that values *people* over *pixels*."

Discussion Guide:

1. Do you agree with this statement? "Becoming a pioneer in the digital age is the only path forward to reaching my vision and purpose in life." Why? Why not?
2. What are examples online where poor life choices are glorified and portrayed as a successful life?
3. How can you use "values" to blaze new trails in the wild plains of the digital frontier?
4. What difference does it make in your life if you saw your values as a part of who you are, rather than something you simply profess?
5. How do you respond when you are placed in a situation online that compromises your values?
6. How can you continually grow in your RUMB journey together?

Contact

We would love to hear from you! Please reach out for questions, resources, and subscribe to our newsletter for the latest tips on healthy media choices. We are also available to speak at your conference, event, school, or church on a range of topics regarding empowering youth to practice value-driven media use.

Website: wiredhuman.org
Email: info@wiredhuman.org
Facebook: wearewiredhuman
Twitter: wearewiredhuman
Instagram: wearewiredhuman

Find out more about Jason and Lisa Frost and Wired Human at:
wiredhuman.org

Acknowledgements

This book was by far the most challenging project we have ever taken on. That we stand here at the finish line is nothing short of a miracle. We are so grateful for the people who believed in us, the people we met along the way, took an interest, lent us their stories, the students we interviewed, and friends that gave financial gifts.

Thank you to Daniel Broderick for dreaming with us when this was just an idea. Many thanks to Stef and Christoph, who were the first to sow into our project. Your belief in us launched us forward. Thank you to Dan Frost, Anke Pagel, Gabe Deem, Alice Taylor, Christoph Brandt, Lennart Pagel, and Dorothee Wörner for sharing a piece of your story. Thank you for taking the road less traveled and for leading lives that inspire.

Thank you to our families, Daniel and Lori Frost, Ryan and Rebekah Frost, Megan and Brad Haynes, Nathan Frost, Aaron Frost, Anke and Manfred Pagel, Jonas and Krissi Pagel, Lennart and Patricia, Jannis Pagel, and Anna Pagel for listening to our thoughts, reflections, and ideas, for creative ideas, and for processing the never-ending book topic, for sending us articles, checking in, and looking after our little ones.

Thank you to Lori Frost for modeling a value-driven life, where family and relationships were always placed at the forefront of her life choices. We are grateful for her constant encouragement, prayers, and the many moments she looked after our kids. Lori was the first to read our manuscript and believe in us before anyone else could see what we were doing.

Thank you to Manfred Pagel for his wisdom and counsel. You listened to many of the early ideas and gave us invaluable feedback throughout the book journey. You have captured the importance of this topic before anyone else did. We are grateful to have you as a role model in the way you live your life.

We are so grateful for journeying through life with friends that live by their values and supported us along the way, Laura K., Simon, Doro, Debbie N., Tini, Nathan T., Laura and Daniel, Hannah and Alex, Janna and David, Annegret, JJ and Letitia, Dori and Jonas, Annika and

Christian, Elisabeth and Jürgen, Joana, and so many more we could mention.

We like to thank Chevas Wong for sharing his thoughts and wisdom when we really needed it.

A huge thank you to our phenomenal editor, Olivia Buckley. Your ability to craft words and your sharp mind and eye for detail has turned this book into what it is today.

Thank you to our children, Noah and Amelia, who were so patient with us. Raising kids with close to zero screen time and writing this book as parents of little ones in every waking hour came with many challenges for us and the kids. This book was written in the middle of the night and early mornings long before the sun would rise, on car rides, during the kid's naps and while playing together. We promise that we will make up for some of the lost family time. We will take you on new camping adventures and river walks and will give it our very best to practice what we preach. You are and will always be our utmost priority in life.

References

1 Hedges & Company, Vehicle Registration Statistics, accessed August 20, 2020, https://hedgescompany.com/automotive-market-research-statistics/auto-mailing-lists-and-marketing/.

2 "1900-1930: The Years of Driving Dangerously," The Detroit News, April 26, 2015, https://www.detroitnews.com/story/news/local/michigan-history/2015/04/26/auto-traffic-history-detroit/26312107/.

3 Ibid.

4 "Car Crash Deaths and Rates," National Safety Council, accessed July 11, 2020, https://injuryfacts.nsc.org/motor-vehicle/historical-fatality-trends/deaths-and-rates/.

5 All Interviews were conducted in March 2019 in the greater Washington Metropolitan Area. Interviewees were between thirteen and eighteen years old at the time of recording. Names and identifying details have been changed to protect the privacy of individuals.

6 Maria Elizabeth Loades, Eleanor Chatburn, Nina Higson-Sweeney, Shirley Reynolds, Roz Shafran, Amberly Brigden, Catherine Linney, Megan Niamh McManus, Catherine Borwick, Esther Crawley, "Rapid Systematic Review: The Impact of Social Isolation and Loneliness on the Mental Health of Children and Adolescents in the Context of COVID-19," Journal of the American Academy of Child and Adolescent Psychiatry, June 02, 2020 DOI: 10.1016/j.jaac.2020.05.009.

7 "Experts Around the World Warn Parents to be Vigilant as Cyberbullying Increases During Lockdown," accessed July 21, 2020, https://www.cybersmile.org/news/experts-around-the-world-warn-parents-to-be-vigilant-as-cyberbullying-increases-during-lockdown.

8 Nellie Bowles, Michael H. Keller, "Video Games and Online Chats are 'Hunting Grounds' for Sexual Predators," New York Times, December 7, 2019, https://www.nytimes.com/interactive/2019/12/07/us/video-games-child-sex-abuse.html.

9 Olivia Solon, "Child Sexual Abuse Images and Online Exploitation Surge During Pandemic." NBC News, April 23, 2020, https://www.nbcnews.com/tech/tech-news/child-sexual-abuse-images-online-exploitation-surge-during-pandemic-n1190506.

10 James Atkinson, William Mountaine, Epitome Of The Art Of Navigation. Or, A Short, Easy and Methodical Way to Become a Compleat Navigator (W. & J. Mount, 1753).

11 In 2019, 3.2 billion smartphones were used worldwide, but the trend is rapidly growing, especially in emerging economies. https://www.statista.com/statistics/330695/number-of-smartphone-users-worldwide/.

12 Melinda Gates, "I spent my career in technology. I wasn't prepared for its effect on my kids," Washington Post, August 24, 2017, https://www.washingtonpost.com/news/parenting/wp/2017/08/24/melinda-gates-i-spent-my-career-in-technology-i-wasnt-prepared-for-its-effect-on-my-kids/?utm_term=.1a6f86a90671.

13 Depending on the study, scholars estimate that teenagers spend between 6,5-10 hours in front of screens. In the case of this study conducted by Common Sense Media, nine hours consists of the time in front of all screens combined, even when used simultaneously. Common Sense Media, November 2, 2015: "Tweens, Teens, and Screens: What Our New Research Uncovers." https://www.commonsensemedia.org/blog/tweens-teens-and-screens-what-our-new-research-uncovers.

14 Jean M. Twenge, "Have Smartphones Destroyed a Generation?," The Atlantic, September 2017, https://www.theatlantic.com/magazine/archive/2017/09/has-the-smartphone-destroyed-a-generation/534198.

15 Ibid.

16 Ibid.

17 Amanda Lenhart, Pew Research Center, Teen, Smartphones and Texting, p. 2.

18 Misra, Cheng, Genevie, Yuan, Miao, "The iPhone Effect: The Quality of In-Person Social Interactions in the Presence of Mobile Devices," in Environment and Behavior, 48, no 2 (July 2014), https://www.researchgate.net/publication/270730343_The_iPhone_Effect_The_Quality_of_In-Person_Social_Interactions_in_the_Presence_of_Mobile_Devices a 2017 University of Texas study

19 Almost every other teenager admitted in a study, conducted by Pew Research in 2018, because of smartphones they are online "almost constantly," compared to one in four in 2015. Pew Research Center, May 2018, "Teens, Social Media & Technology 2018"

20 "U.S. Loneliness Index," Cigna, https://www.multivu.com/players/English/8294451-cigna-us-loneliness-survey/docs/IndexReport_1524069371598-173525450.pdf p. 6ff.

21 Stefanie Marsh, Teenagers on Loneliness: 'We want to talk to our parents. We need their Guidance', The Guardian, April 8, 2017, https://www.theguardian.com/society/2017/apr/08/teenagers-loneliness-social-media-isolation-parents-attention.

Jena Mc Gregor, "This Former Surgeon General Says There's a 'Loneliness Epidemic' and Work is Partly to Blame, The Washington Post, October 4, 2017, https://www.washingtonpost.com/news/on-leadership/wp/2017/10/04/this-former-surgeon-general-says-theres-a-loneliness-epidemic-and-work-is-partly-to-blame/?utm_term=.488de9ca1610.

Rebecca Harris, The Loneliness Epidemic. We are more connected than ever, but are we feeling more alone?, The Independent, http://www.independent.co.uk/life-style/health-and-families/features/the-loneliness-epidemic-more-connected-than-ever-but-feeling-more-alone-10143206.html.

22 Loneliness is measured by the UCLA loneliness scale, which consists of 20 questions that measure the subjective feelings of perceived isolation.

23 Cigna U.S. Loneliness Index using the UCLA loneliness scale https://www.multivu.com/players/English/8294451-cigna-us-loneliness-survey/docs/IndexReport_1524069371598-173525450.pdf, p. 6f.

24 Vivek Murphy, "Work and the Loneliness Epidemic," Harvard Business Review https://hbr.org/cover-story/2017/09/work-and-the-loneliness-epidemic.

25 John T Cacioppo and William Patrick. Loneliness: Human Nature and the Need for Social Connection. (New York: W.W. Norton & Co), 2008.

26 Cacioppo; Patrick, Loneliness, p. 14.

27 Ibid., p. 34-45.

28 Brian A. Primack, et al., Social Media Use and Perceived Social Isolation Among Young Adults in the U.S. in the American Journal of Preventive Medicine, 53, no. 1, (July 2017) p. 1–8. http://www.ajpmonline.org/article/S0749-3797(17)30016-8/fulltext.

29 Pew Research Center, Teens, Kindness and Cruelty on Social, Network Sites, p.2. http://pewinternet.org/Reports/2011/Teens-and-social-media.aspx.

30 Pew Research Center, May 2018, "Teens, Social Media & Technology 2018 http://assets.pewresearch.org/wp-content/uploads/sites/14/2018/05/31102617/PI_2018.05.31_TeensTech_FINAL.pdf.

31 Jean M. Twenge, iGen: Why Today's Super-Connected Kids Are Growing Up Less Rebellious, More Tolerant, Less Happy-- and Completely Unprepared for Adulthood and What This Means for the Rest of Us. (New York, First Atria Books, 2017), p.75.

32 "Dealing with Devices," Common Sense Media. (2016). Dealing with devices: The parent-teen dynamic. San Francisco, CA.

33 Adam Alter, Irresistible. The Rise of Addictive Technology and the Business of Keeping Us Hooked, (New York: Penguin Press, 2017) p. 4.

34 Susanna Schrobsdorff, "Teen Depression and Anxiety: Why the Kids Are Not Alright," Time Magazine, October 27, 2016, http://time.com/magazine/us/4547305/november-7th-2016-vol-188-no-19-u-s/.

35 Jackie Salo, "'Oh, He Just Died': Teens Mock Drowning Man in Disturbing Video," New York Post, July 20, 2017, https://nypost.com/2017/07/20/oh-he-just-died-disturbing-video-shows-teens-mocking-drowning-man/.

36 Sara H. Konrath, Edward H. O'Brien, Courtney Hsing, "Changes in Dispositional Empathy in American College Students Over Time: A Meta-Analysis." Personality and Social Psychology Review, 15, no.2 (2011), 180–198.

37 Ibid.

38 Das Erste, Hakenkreuze und Gewaltvideos, accessed July 13 ,2020, https://www.daserste.de/information/reportage-dokumentation/dokus/videos/exclusiv-im-ersten-hakenkreuze-und-gewaltvideos-video-100.html.

39 Lisa M Jones, Kimberly J Mitchell, and David Finkelhor, "Trends in Youth Internet Victimization: Findings from Three Youth Safety Surveys 2000-2010," Journal of Adolescent Health 50, (2012), p. 179-86. Although numbers vary, depending on the country and research conducted, similarly high numbers can be found in various international studies. A Swedish Study among high school students for example revealed that 98 percent of male and 76 percent of female test persons stated that they had viewed pornography. See: Häggström-Nordin et al., 2005.

40 Covenant Eyes, Stats on How People Perceive Porn, accessed July 21, 2020, https://www.covenanteyes.com/pornstats/.

41 Ibid.

42 Wendy Waltz; Larry Waltz, The Porn Trap: The Essential Guide to Overcoming Problems Caused by Pornography, (Harper Collins, New York, 2008), p. 25.

43 Shawn McDowell, Michael Leahy, and Clay Olson, "Forum: Talking to Students," The Set Free Global Summit, April 6, 2016, https://vimeo.com/173068565/64df8d9e63 (accessed June 7, 2018).

44 Helen Fisher, Justin R. Garcia, "Singles in America: Match Releases Largest Study on U.S. Single Population for Eighth Year," https://www.prnewswire.com/news-releases/singles-in-america-match-releases-largest-study-on-us-single-population-for-eighth-year-300591561.html.

45 Sophie Davies, "Revenge Porn Soars in Europe's Coronavirus Lockdown as Student Fights Back," Thomson Reuters Foundation News, May 5 2020, https://news.trust.org/item/20200505165904-e8umi/?utm_campaign=trending&utm_medium=trendingWebWidget&utm_source=detailPage&utm_content=link4.

46 Helen Fisher, Justin R. Garcia, Singles in America, PR Newswire, February 1, 2018, https://www.prnewswire.com/news-releases/singles-in-america-match-releases-largest-study-on-us-single-population-for-eighth-year-300591561.html.

47 Justin R. Garcia, quoted in Nancy Jo Sales, American Girls: Social Media and the Secret Lives of Teenagers, 24 January 2017 (Vintage, New York 2017), p. 185.

48 "Is Yubo 'Tinder for Teens' and Should Parents Be Concerned,?" WebWatcher, accessed July 21 2020, https://www.webwatcher.com/blog/is-yubo-tinder-for-teens-and-should-parents-be-concerned/.

49 Smriti Bhagat, Moira Burke, Carlos Diuk, Ismail Onur Filiz, Sergey Edunov, Facebook Research, February 4, 2016, https://research.fb.com/three-and-a-half-degrees-of-separation/. The numbers are based on 1.59 billion people active on Facebook at the time of the study in 2016.

50 Twenge, iGen, p. 92.

51 Cacioppo; Patrick, Loneliness, pp. 92-112.

52 Twenge, iGen, p. 93ff.

53 Substance Abuse and Mental Health Services Administration. (2017). "Key substance use and mental health indicators in the United States: Results from the 2016 National Survey on Drug Use and Health" (HHS Publication No. SMA 17-5044, NSDUH Series H-52). Rockville, MD: Center for Behavioral Health Statistics and Quality, Substance Abuse and Mental Health Services Administration. Retrieved from https://www.samhsa.gov/data/ Caroline Simon, More and more students need mental health services. But colleges struggle to keep it up, USA Today, http://college.usatoday.com/2017/05/04/more-and-more-students-need-mental-health-services-but-colleges-struggle-to-keep-up/

54 Joe Sugarman, "The Rise of Teen Depression," John Hopkins Health Review, https://www.johnshopkinshealthreview.com/issues/fall-winter-2017/articles/the-rise-of-teen-depression

55 Bessiere K, 2010, Effects of Internet Use on Health and Depression. A Longitudinal Study. Journal of Med Internet Research 12:e6; Campell et al. 2006,Internet Use by the socially fearful. Addiction or Therapy? CyberPsychology & Behavior 9, 68-81, Morrison and Gore, 2010, The relationship between excessive internet use and depression. A questionnaire-based study of 1319 young people and adults. Psychopathology 43, 121-126 Kotikalapudi et al. 2012, Associating depressive symptoms among college students with internet usage using real internet data, http://web.mst.edu/~chellaps/papers/TSM.pdf.

56 Manfred Spitzer, Einsamkeit - die unerkannte Krankheit: schmerzhaft, ansteckend, tödlich, (München: Droemer, 2018), p.305-306.

57 Maggie Fox, "Major Depression On the Rise Among Everyone. Biggest Increase in Diagnoses Seen in Teens," NBC News, May 10, 2018, https://www.nbcnews.com/health/health-news/major-depression-rise-among-everyone-new-data-shows-n873146.

58 Benoit Denizet-Lewis, "Why Are More American Teenagers Than Ever Suffering From Severe Anxiety?" New York Times, October 11, 2017,

https://www.nytimes.com/2017/10/11/magazine/why-are-more-american-teenagers-than-ever-suffering-from-severe-anxiety.html

59 Stephanie Pappas, "Cyberbullying on Social Media Linked to Teen Depression," Live Science, June 22, 2015, https://www.livescience.com/51294-cyberbullying-social-media-teen-depression.html.

60 Shirley Cramer, "Instagram Ranked Worst for Young People's Mental Health," Royal Society for Public Health, May 19, 2017, https://www.rsph.org.uk/about-us/news/instagram-ranked-worst-for-young-people-s-mental-health.html

61 Sally C. Curtin; Melonie Heron, "Death Rates Due to Suicide and Homicide Among Persons Aged 10–24: United States, 2000–2017", National Center for Health Statistics, October 2019, https://www.cdc.gov/nchs/data/databriefs/db352-h.pdf.

62 Sabrina Tavernise, "U.S. Suicide Rate Surges to a 30-Year High," New York Times, https://www.nytimes.com/2016/04/22/health/us-suicide-rate-surges-to-a-30-year-high.html.

63 American Academy of Pediatrics, "Children's Hospitals Admissions for Suicidal Thoughts, Actions Double During Past Decade," May 4, 2017, http://www.aappublications.org/news/2017/05/04/PASSuicide050417.

64 Jean M. Twenge, Thomas E. Joiner, Megan L. Rogers, Gabrielle N. Martin (2017). "Increases in depressive symptoms, suicide-related outcomes, and suicide rates among U.S. adolescents after 2010 and links to increased new media screen time." November 14, 2017 Clinical Psychological Science, https://journals.sagepub.com/doi/abs/10.1177/2167702617723376.

65 Donald, J. N., Ciarrochi, J., & Sahdra, B. K. (2020). "The consequences of compulsion: A 4-year longitudinal study of compulsive internet use and emotion regulation difficulties." Emotion, Advance online publication, 2020, https://doi.org/10.1037/emo0000769 .

66 Melinda Gates, "I Spent my Career in Technology. I wasn't prepared for its Effect on my Kids". The Washington Post, August 24, 2017, https://www.washingtonpost.com/news/parenting/wp/2017/08/24/melinda-gates-i-spent-my-career-in-technology-i-wasnt-prepared-for-its-effect-on-my-kids/?utm_term=.e9beab429bcb.

67 William Ralston, "Who really killed Avicii?," GQ magazine, 25 September, 2018, https://www.gq-magazine.co.uk/article/who-really-killed-avicii.

68 Brené Brown, Dare to Lead: Brave Work. Tough Conversations. Whole Hearts (New York: Random House, 2018), p. 186.

69 Social capital has been formally defined as, "[…] connections among individuals- social networks and the norms of reciprocity and trustworthiness that arises from them." Robert D. Putman, Bowling Alone. The Collapse and Revival of American Community (New York: Simon & Schuster, 2000), p.19.

70 John Grahmlich, “5 Facts About Crime in the U.S.,” Pew Research Center, accessed July 22, 2020, https://www.pewresearch.org/fact-tank/2019/10/17/facts-about-crime-in-the-u-s/.

71 Ben Sasse, The Vanishing American Adult. The Coming-of-Age Crisis-and How to Rebuild a Culture of Self- Reliance (New York, St. Martin's Press, 2017), pp.28-45

72 Ben Sasse, The Vanishing American Adult. The Coming-of-Age Crisis-and How to Rebuild a Culture of Self -Reliance (New York, St. Martin's Press, 2017), p.5.

73 David Brooks, The Social Animal. The Hidden Sources of Love, Character, and Achievement, (New York: Random House, 2012)189, Kindle.

74 James S. House, Karl R. Landis, Debra Umberson, “Social Relationships and Health,” Science, July 29, 1988, New Series 241, no. 4865, p. 541.

75 Roy F. Baumeister, Mark R. Leary, “The Need to Belong: Desire for Interpersonal Attachments as a Fundamental Human Motivation,” Psychological Bulletin 117, no. 3, (1995) 497-529, p.506.

76 Debra Umberson and Jennifer Karas Montez, “Social Relationships and Health: A Flashpoint for Health Policy.” Health Social Behavior, 2010; 51(Suppl): S54–S66. doi:10.1177/0022146510383501. p.2.

77 Juliana Holt-Lunstad, Timothy Smith, Bradley Layton (2010) “Social Relationships and Mortality Risk: A Meta-Analytic Review.” PLoS Medicine 7, no. 7: pp. 8-9. e1000316. doi:10.1371/ journal. pmed.1000316,

78 Nicole Lyn Pesce, “U.S. Life Expectancy Rises for the First Time in Four Years — Here's How Much Longer Americans are Living,” Market Watch, January 31, 2020,”https://www.marketwatch.com/story/americans-are-living-a-month-longer-as-us-life-expectancy-rises-for-the-first-time-in-four-years-2020-01-30

79 Meilan Solly, “U.S. Life Expectancy Drops for Third Year in a Row, Reflecting Rising Drug Overdoses, Suicides,” Smithonian Magazine, December 3, 2018, https://www.smithsonianmag.com/smart-news/us-life-expectancy-drops-third-year-row-reflecting-rising-drug-overdose-suicide-rates-180970942/#033JaTLLWzd4mAUg.99.

80 George E. Vaillant, Triumphs of Experience. The Men of the Harvard Grant Study, (Cambridge: Harvard University Press, 2015), p. 1, position 70, Kindle.

81 Liz Mineo, “Good Genes Are Nice, but Joy is Better,” The Harvard Gazette, April 11, 2017, https://news.harvard.edu/gazette/story/2017/04/over-nearly-80-years-harvard-study-has-been-showing-how-to-live-a-healthy-and-happy-life/.

82 Ibid.

83 Ibid.

84 Manfred Spitzer, Einsamkeit - die unerkannte Krankheit: schmerzhaft, ansteckend, tödlich. (Munich, Droemer, 2018), p. 314.

85 George E. Vaillant, Triumphs of Experience. The Men of the Harvard Grant Study, (Cambridge: Harvard University Press, 2015), p. 1, p. 27, position 453., Kindle.

86 Naftali Beder, "What Technology Can't Change About Happiness," Nautilus, September 17, 2015, http://nautil.us/issue/28/2050/what-technology-cant-change-about-happiness.

87 Scott Stossel, "What Makes Us Happy, Revisited," The Atlantic, May 2013, https://www.theatlantic.com/magazine/archive/2013/05/thanks-mom/309287/.

88 Jean Twenge, "Teens Have Less Face Time with Their Friends – and are Lonelier Than Ever," The Conversation, March 20, 2019, https://theconversation.com/teens-have-less-face-time-with-their-friends-and-are-lonelier-than-ever-113240.

89 Diane Sawyer, ScreenTime, ABC News, May 3, 2019.

90 Based on nine hours a day, recorded by Common Sense Media: Landmark Report: U.S. Teens Use an Average of Nine Hours of Media Per Day, Common Sense Media, November 3, 2015, https://www.commonsensemedia.org/about-us/news/press-releases/landmark-report-us-teens-use-an-average-of-nine-hours-of-media-per-day.

91 Mike Mills, "Facebook our Friends Manifesto," 2015, https://vimeo.com/122149315.

92 Stuart Wolpert, "UCLA Neuroscientist's Book Explains Why Social Connection is as Important as Food and Shelter, "Newsroom, October 10, 2013, http://newsroom.ucla.edu/releases/we-are-hard-wired-to-be-social-248746.

93 Amanda Lenhart, Aaron Smith, Monica Anderson, Maeve Duggan and Andrew Perrin, "Teens, Technology and Friendships." Pew Research Center, August, 2015. http://www.pewinternet.org/2015/08/06/teens-technology-and-friendships/, p. 21.

94 Diane Sawyer, ScreenTime, ABC News, May 3, 2019.

95 Research by Professor Albert Mehrabian's of the University of California in Los Angeles that was conducted in the 1970s and highly influenced the discussions surrounding non-verbal communication suggested that 55 percent of communication account for body language, 38 percent for voice and tone and only seven percent account for spoken words.

96 David Ludden, "Your Eyes Really Are the Window to Your Soul," Psychological Today, December 2015, https://www.psychologytoday.com/blog/talking-apes/201512/your-eyes-really-are-the-window-your-soul.

97 Catherine Steiner-Adair, Teresa H. Barker, The Big Disconnect: Protecting Childhood and Family Relationships in the Digital Age (New York: Harper 2014), p.204.

98 Amanda Lenhart, Aaron, Monica Anderson, "Teens, Technology and Romantic Relationships." Pew Research Center, October 2015, p. 51.

99 Amanda Lenhart, Aaron, Monica Anderson, "Teens, Technology and Romantic Relationships." Pew Research Center, October 2015, p. 53.

100 Prince Ea, Can We Auto-Correct Humanity, accessed August 5th, 2020, https://www.youtube.com/watch?v=dRl8EIhrQjQ For the sake of easier readability, the spelling of this comment has been edited.

101 Sherry Turkle, Reclaiming Conversation: The Power of Talk in a Digital Age, (New York: Penguin, 2015), p. 322.

102 John Joseph Powell, The Secret to Staying in Love, (New York: Thomas More 1994).

103 Marc G. Bermana, Walter Mischelb, Edward E. Smith, and Tor D. Wager, "Social Rejection Shares Somatosensory Representations with Physical Pain,", PNAS vol. 108, no. 15, April 12, 2011, p.1.

104 Erich Fromm, quoted in: Pamela Anderson. Shmuley Boteach, Lust for Love: Rekindling Intimacy and Passion in Your Relationship, p.273. (New York: Center Street, 2018), Kindle.

105 Chloe Watson, "The Key Moments from Mark Zuckerberg's Testimony to Congress, The Guardian, April 11, 2018, https://www.theguardian.com/technology/2018/apr/11/mark-zuckerbergs-testimony-to-congress-the-key-moments/

106 Olivia Solon, "Facebook says Cambridge Analytica may Have Gained 37m More Users' Data," The Guardian, April 4, 2018, https://www.theguardian.com/technology/2018/apr/04/facebook-cambridge-analytica-user-data-latest-more-than-thought

107 Olivia Solon, "'A Grand Illusion': Seven Days that Shattered Facebook's Façade," The Guardian, March 24, 2018, https://www.theguardian.com/technology/2018/mar/24/cambridge-analytica-week-that-shattered-facebook-privacy.

108 Natasha Singer, Mike Isaac, "Facebook to Pay $550 Million to Settle Facial Recognition Suit", The New York Times, January 29, 2020, https://www.nytimes.com/2020/01/29/technology/facebook-privacy-lawsuit-earnings.html.

109 "Facebook: Worldwide Quarterly Revenue 2011-2020", statista, August 10, 2020, https://www.statista.com/statistics/422035/facebooks-quarterly-global-revenue/.

110 Mike Allen, "Sean Parker Unloads on Facebook: God Only Knows What it's Doing to our Children's Brains," Axios, November 9th 2017, https://www.axios.com/sean-parker-unloads-on-facebook-god-only-knows-what-its-doing-to-our-childrens-brains-1513306792-f855e7b4-4e99-4d60-8d51-2775559c2671.html.

111 Scott Galloway, The Four: The Hidden DNA of Amazon, Apple, Facebook, and Google (New York: Random House, 2017), p. 266.

112 Roger McNamee, "How Facebook and Google Threaten Public Health – and Democracy," The Guardian, November 11, 2017, https://www.theguardian.com/commentisfree/2017/nov/11/facebook-google-public-health-democracy.

113 Sarah Frier, Nico Grant, "Instagram Brings in More Than a Quarter of Facebook Sales," Bloomberg, February 4th 2020, https://www.bloomberg.com/news/articles/2020-02-04/instagram-generates-more-than-a-quarter-of-facebook-s-sales?srnd=premium.

114 Emily McCormick, "Instagram Is Estimated to Be Worth More than $100 Billion," Bloomberg, June 25, 2018, https://www.bloomberg.com/news/articles/2018-06-25/value-of-facebook-s-instagram-estimated-to-top-100-billion.

115 Ibid.

116 Cam Adair, "Escaping Video Game Addiction," filmed September 2013 at TEDx Boulder, CO, https://tedxboulder.com/speakers/cam-adair.

117 Gary Wilson, Your Brain on Porn, 2014, para. 1015-1033, Kindle.

118 Gary Wilson, Your Brain on Porn, para. 1033, Kindle.

119 "Learning Addiction: Dopamine Reinforces Drug-Associated Memories," The Global Source for Science News, September 9, 2009, https://www.eurekalert.org/pub_releases/2009-09/cp-lad090309.php.

120 Research conducted at the Max Planck Institute in Germany discovered a connection between the amount of porn consumption (hours per week) and a reduction of gray matter in locations of the brain associated with the reward circuitry or striatum (motivation and decision-making). Less grey matter amounts to limited amount of nerve contacts. For further inquiries into this research, please see: Kühn, S.; Gallinat, J. (2014). Brain Structure and Functional Connectivity Associated with Pornography Consumption. The Brain on Porn, in: JAMA Psychiatry, 71 (7), pp. 827-834.

121 Gary Wilson, Your Brain on Porn, 2014, para. 169-177, Kindle.

122 Martin Walter, Felix Bermpohl, Harold Mouras, Kolja Schiltz, Claus Tempelmann, Michael Rotte, Hans Jochen Heinze, Bernhard Bogerts, Georg Northoff, „Distinguishing Specific Sexual and General Emotional Effects, fMRI-Subcortical and Cortical Arousal During Erotic Picture Viewing," Neuroimage 40, no. 4, February 7, 2008, pp. 1482-1494, 10.1016/j.neuroimage.2008.01.040.

123 Simone Kühn, Jürgen Gallinat, "Brain Structure and Functional Connectivity Associated with Pornography Consumption. The Brain on Porn," JAMA Psychiatr, 71, no. 7, July 2014, pp. 827-834. 10.1001/jamapsychiatry.2014.93.

124 Gary Wilson, Your Brain on Porn, 2014, para. 1015-1033, Kindle.

125 Sagal Mohammed, "Can a Millenial Date in Real Life? We Asked One to Ditch Her Beloved Dating Apps and Put it to the Test," Glamour Magazine, June 28, 2019, https://www.glamourmagazine.co.uk/article/can-a-millennial-date-in-real-life.

126 Tarazi F.; Baldessarini R., "Comparative Postnatal Development of Dopamine D(1), D(2) and D(4) Receptors in Rat Forebrain," International Journal of Developmental Neuroscience. February 18, 2000, pp. 29–37.
See also: Teicher et al., 2003, 339, 169–171.

127 Gary Wilson, Your Brain on Porn, 2014, para. 1202-1204.

128 Mariam Arain, Maliha Haque, Lina Johal, Puja Mathur, Wynand Nel, Afsha Rais, Ranbir Sandhu, Sushil Sharma, "Maturation of the Adolescent Brain," Dove Press Journal, Neuropsychiatric Disease and Treatment, April 2, 2013, p.449.

129 Ibid, p. 450-451.

130 Ibid, p. 453-454.

131 Ibid, p. 454.

132 Ibid, p. 455.

133 Ibid, p. 455.

134 Kevin McSpadden, "You Now Have a Shorter Attention Span Than a Goldfish," Time Magazine, May 14 2015, http://time.com/3858309/attention-spans-goldfish/.

135 Nicolas Carr, The Shallows: What the Internet is Doing to Our Brains, (New York: Norton & Company, 2011), p.16.

136 Norman Doidge, "The Brain That Changes Itself: Stories of Personal Triumph from the Frontiers of Brain Science Brain That Changes Itself," (New York: Penguin, 2007) p.317.

137 Nicolas Carr, The Shallows: What the Internet is Doing to Our Brains, (New York: Norton & Company, 2011), p. 34.

138 "Pornhub's 2017 Year in Review," Pornhub, January 9, 2018, https://www.pornhub.com/insights/2017-year-in-review.

139 Patricia Garcier, "Instagram Star Quits Social Media, Says It's Not Real Life," Vogue, November 2, 2015 https://www.vogue.com/article/instagram-star-essena-oneill-quits-social-media.

140 Essena O' Neill, "Why I Really am Quitting Social, November 5 2015," https://www.youtube.com/watch?v=gmAbwTQvWX8.

141 Lyra, "A Journal of Social Influencer Lifestyle, Fashion, & Fiction." Retrieved May 25, 2018, http://paperduchesses.com/essena-oneill/.

142 Ibid.

143 Aatif Sulleyman, "Ex-Facebook and Google Employees Form Group to Protect People from 'Harmful and Addictive' Tech Products," Independent, February 7, 2018, https://www.independent.co.uk/life-style/gadgets-and-tech/news/facebook-addiction-google-social-media-harmful-truth-about-tech-campaign-tristan-harris-a8197686.html.

144 Roger McNamee, "How Facebook and Google Threaten Public Health – and Democracy," The Guardian, November 11, 2017, https://www.theguardian.com/commentisfree/2017/nov/11/facebook-google-public-health-democracy.
145 Roger McNamee, "How to Fix Facebook—Before It Fixes Us," Washington Monthly, January 2018, https://washingtonmonthly.com/magazine/january-february-march-2018/how-to-fix-facebook-before-it-fixes-us/
146 Scott Galloway, The Four: The Hidden DNA of Amazon, Apple, Facebook, and Google (New York: Random House, 2017), p. 106.
147 Mike Allen, "Sean Parker Unloads on Facebook: 'God only knows what it's doing to our children's brains,'"axios, November 9, 2017, https://www.axios.com/sean-parker-unloads-on-facebook-god-only-knows-what-its-doing-to-our-childrens-brains-1513306792-f855e7b4-4e99-4d60-8d51-2775559c2671.html.
148 Allie Waxman, "Nancy Jo Sales Swipes Left on Tinder," accessed August 11, https://www.hbo.com/documentaries/swiped-hooking-up-in-the-digital-age/nancy-jo-sales-director-interview.
149 Paul Lewis, "'Our Minds can be Hijacked': the Tech Insiders who fear a Smartphone Dystopia," The Guardian, October 5, 2017, https://www.theguardian.com/technology/2017/oct/05/smartphone-addiction-silicon-valley-dystopia.
150 Lindsey Bever, "She Instagrammed her Exotic Drug-Smuggling Vacation. Now 'Cocaine Babe' is Going to Prison," Washington Post, April 18, 2018, https://www.washingtonpost.com/news/worldviews/wp/2018/04/18/she-Instagrammed-her-exotic-drug-smuggling-vacation-now-cocaine-babe-is-going-to-prison/?utm_term=.b49e7a15fd77.
151 Adam Alter, Irresistible: The Rise of Addictive Technology and the Business of Keeping Us Hooked, (New York: Penguin, 2017) pp. 117-118.
152 "Company Info," Facebook, July 20, 2018, https://newsroom.fb.com/company-info/.
153 Zephoria, "The Top 10 Valuable Snapchat Statistics – Updated August 2020", accessed August 16th 2020, https://zephoria.com/top-10-valuable-snapchat-statistics/.
154 A survey with 2084 subjects by Harris Interactive found that 56 percent of all social media users suffer from FoMo and 61 percent of all interviewed teens would rather not have sex than not having social media. "National MyLife.com® Survey Reveals More Social Networks And Message Services, More Problems: Users Are Increasingly Overwhelmed, Overloaded," PRNewswire, July 9th, 2013.

https://www.prnewswire.com/news-releases/national-mylifecom-survey-reveals-more-social-networks-and-message-services-more-problems-users-are-increasingly-overwhelmed-overloaded-214741101.html.

155 Eric Barker, "This Is the Best Way to Overcome Fear of Missing Out," Time Magazine, June 7th, 2016, http://time.com/4358140/overcome-fomo/.

156 Brian A. Primack, Ariel Shensa, Jaime E. Sidani, Erin O. Whaite, Liu yi Lin, Daniel Rosen, Jason B. Colditz, Ana Radovic, Elizabeth Miller, "Social Media Use and Perceived Social Isolation Among Young Adults in the U.S.", American Journal of Preventative Medicine 53, no. 1, July 1st, 2017, http://www.ajpmonline.org/article/S0749-3797(17)30016-8/fulltext. It turns out that the people who reported spending the most time on social media — more than two hours a day — had twice the odds of perceived social isolation than those who said they spent a half hour per day or less on those sites. And people who visited social media platforms most frequently, 58 visits per week or more, had more than three times the odds of perceived social isolation than those who visited fewer than nine times per week.

157 Jean M. Twenge, "Have Smartphones Destroyed a Generation?," September 2017, The Atlantic, https://www.theatlantic.com/magazine/archive/2017/09/has-the-smartphone-destroyed-a-generation/534198/.

158 "Top 10 Most Popular People on Social Media in 2018," TopTenZ, May 21, 2018, https://www.toptenz.net/top-10-most-popular-people-on-social-media-in-2018.php.

159 Ashley Spencer, "Selena Gomez's Sponsored Social Media Posts are Worth a Whopping $550,000 Each," July 20, 2016, https://celebrity.nine.com.au/latest/10-surprising-celebrity-social-media-stats/614544c5-c646-455f-9332-ce7757dce654.

160 Lilian Min, "Selena Gomez Covered Time To Talk About Making Social Media History," Cosmopolitan, September 8, 2017, https://www.cosmopolitan.com/entertainment/celebs/a12196579/selena-gomez-time-cover-social-media/.

161 Sarah Young, "Selena Reveals Why she Decided to Quit Instagram after Becoming most Followed User," Independent, March 16th, 2017, afterhttps://www.independent.co.uk/life-style/fashion/selena-gomez-Instagram-mental-health-vogue-cover-social-media-anxiety-a7634081.html.

162 Imran Amed, "Inside the Millennial Mind of Selena Gomez," Business of Fashion, September 11, 2017, https://www.businessoffashion.com/articles/people/inside-the-millennial-mind-of-selena-gomez.

163 Justina Vasquez, "In One Tweet, Kylie Jenner Wiped Out $1.3 Billion of Snap's Market Value," February 22, 2018, https://www.bloomberg.com/news/articles/2018-02-22/snap-royalty-kylie-jenner-erased-a-billion-dollars-in-one-tweet

164 American Meme, Bert Marcus and Cassandra Hamar Thornton, Bert Marcus Productions, 2018, www.bertmarcusproductions.com.
165 Amanda Lenhart, Aaron Smith, Monica Anderson, Maeve Duggan and Andrew Perrin, "Teens, Technology and Friendships." Pew Research Center, August, 2015, http://www.pewinternet.org/2015/08/06/teens-technology-and-friendships/, p.54.
166 Ibid, p.59.
167 Gail Dines, A presentation at the Nova Scotia Women's Summit on Porn Culture and its Affect on our Society and Violence Against women. November 16, 2012, https://quotecatalog.com/quote/gail-dines-in-our-society-P7vg05p/ https://www.youtube.com/watch?v=-Z5iANEfQUU.
168 Lyra, "A Journal of Social Influencer Lifestyle, Fashion, & Fiction." Retrieved May 25, 2018 from http://paperduchesses.com/essena-oneill/.
169 Shirley Cramer CBE, Chief Executive, Royal Society for Public Health, "Instagram Ranked Worst for Young People's Mental Health," Royal Society for Public Health, May 19, 2017, https://www.rsph.org.uk/about-us/news/Instagram-ranked-worst-for-young-people-s-mental-health.html.
170 Heather Saul, "Sexting' is Becoming the New Norm for Teenagers Growing up, Study Finds," Independent, October 7, 2014, http://www.independent.co.uk/news/science/sexting-is-becoming-the-new-norm-for-teenagers-growing-up-study-finds-9779356.html.
171 Catherine Steiner-Adair, Teresa H. Barker, The Big Disconnect: Protecting Childhood and Family Relationships in the Digital Age (New York: Harper, 2014), p. 213.
172 Paul Roberts, The Impulse Society. America in the Age of Instant Gratification, (New York: Bloomsbury, 2014).
173 Caitlin O'Kane, "Kylie Jenner Donates $1 million to Help Fight Australia," CBS News, January 9 2020, wildfireshttps://www.cbsnews.com/news/australia-fires-kylie-jenner-donates-1-million-to-help-fight-australia-brushfire-instagram-kardashians-celebrites/.
174 Susanna Schrobsdorff, "Teen Depression and Anxiety: Why the Kids Are Not Alright", Time Magazine, October 27, 2016, http://time.com/magazine/us/4547305/november-7th-2016-vol-188-no-19-u-s/.
175 Caroline Crosson Gilpin, "Why Are More American Teenagers Than Ever Suffering From Severe Anxiety?" New York Times, October 13, 2017, https://www.nytimes.com/2017/10/11/magazine/why-are-more-american-teenagers-than-ever-suffering-from-severe-anxiety.html.
176 "U.S. Loneliness Index," Cigna, https://www.multivu.com/players/English/8294451-cigna-us-loneliness-survey/docs/IndexReport_1524069371598-173525450.pdf, p. 6ff.

177 Monica Anderson and Jingjing Jiang, Pew Research Center, May 2018, "Teens, Social Media & Technology 2018, http://assets.pewresearch.org/wp-content/uploads/sites/14/2018/05/31102617/PI_2018.05.31_TeensTech_FINAL.pdf.

178 Amanda Lenhart, Aaron Smith, Monica Anderson, Maeve Duggan and Andrew Perrin, "Teens, Technology and Friendships." Pew Research Center, August, 2015. http://www.pewinternet.org/2015/08/06/teens-technology-and-friendships/p. 41.

179 Kim Parker, Juliana Menasce Horowitz, Pew Research Center, December 17, 2015, "Parenting in America: Outlook, Worries, Aspirations are Strongly Linked to Financial Situation", p.70.

180 Pew Research Center, May 2018, "Teens, Social Media & Technology 2018http://assets.pewresearch.org/wp-content/uploads/sites/14/2018/05/31102617/PI_2018.05.31_TeensTech_FINAL.pdf.

181 Amanda Lenhart, Aaron Smith, Monica Anderson, Maeve Duggan and Andrew Perrin, "Teens, Technology and Friendships." Pew Research Center, August, 2015. http://www.pewinternet.org/2015/08/06/teens-technology-and-friendships/, p. 21.

182 Tom Wijman, "The Global Games Market Will Generate $152.1 Billion in 2019 as the U.S. Overtakes China as the Biggest Market," newzoo, June 18, 2019, https://newzoo.com/insights/articles/the-global-games-market-will-generate-152-1-billion-in-2019-as-the-u-s-overtakes-china-as-the-biggest-market/.

183 Eric Geissinger, Gamer Nation: The Rise of Modern Gaming and the Compulsion to Play Again (New York: Prometheus, 2018), p. 127.

184 Aeijeta Lajka, "Esports Player Burn Out Young as the Grind Takes Mental and Physical Toll," CBS News, December 21, 2018, https://www.cbsnews.com/news/esports-burnout-in-video-gaming-cbsn-originals/.

185 Lauren Larsen, "DanTDM Net Worth 2020: Age, Height, Weight, Wife, Kids, Bio-Wiki, Wealthy Persons," May 25, 2020, https://www.wealthypersons.com/dantdm-net-worth-2020-2021/.

186 "Popular PC Gaming Store Hosts Candy Crush with Porn"-style Video Game," January 16, 2020, https://endsexualexploitation.org/articles/popular-pc-gaming-store-hosts-candy-crush-with-porn-style-videogame/.

187 Meghan Gestos, Jennifer Smith-Merry, and Andrew Campbell. Cyberpsychology, Behavior, and Social Networking 21, no. 9, September 1 2018. pp.535-541, http://doi.org/10.1089/cyber.2017.0376.

188 Mark Aguiar, Mark Bils, Kerwin Kofi Charles, Erik Hurst, "Leisure Luxuries and the Labor Supply of Young Men," July 4, 2017, https://scholar.princeton.edu/sites/default/files/maguiar/files/leisure-luxuries-labor-june-2017.pdf.

189 The Economist, "The Link Between Video Games and Unemployment," March 30, 2017, https://www.economist.com/the-economist-explains/2017/03/30/the-link-between-video-games-and-unemployment.

190 Fry, Richard. Pew Research Center, May 2016. "For First Time in Modern Era, Living with Parents Edges Out Other Living Arrangements for 18- to 34-Year-Olds."

191 Cam Adair, "Escaping Video Game Addiction," filmed September 2013 at TEDx Boulder, CO, https://tedxboulder.com/speakers/cam-adair.

192 Adam Alter, Irresistible: The Rise of Addictive Technology and the Business of Keeping us Hooked (New York: Penguin: 2017) p. 9.

193 Charlotta Hellström, Kent W Nilsson, Jerzy Leppert, Cecilia Åslund, "Effects of Adolescent Online Gaming Time and Motives on Depressive, Musculoskeletal, and Psychosomatic Symptoms," Upsala Journal Medical Sciences, 120, no. 4, November, 2015; pp. 263–275.doi: 10.3109/03009734.2015.1049724.

194 Brené Brown, Dare to Lead: Brave Work. Tough Conversations. Whole Hearts, (New York: Random House, 2018), p. 126.

195 Haley Sweetland Edwards, "You're Addicted to Your Smartphone. This Company Thinks It Can Change That," Time Magazine, April 12, 2018 http://time.com/5237434/youre-addicted-to-your-smartphone-this-company-thinks-it-can-change-that/.

196 Tom Huddleston, "Prince Harry Says Video Game Fortnite is 'Irresponsible' and Should be Banned," cnbc, April 5, 2019, https://www.cnbc.com/2019/04/05/prince-harry-says-video-game-fortnite-should-be-banned.html.

197 Ramin Shokrizade, "Monetizing Children," accessed August 20, 2020, https://www.gamasutra.com/blogs/RaminShokrizade/20130620/194429/Monetizing_Children.php.

198 Cecilia D'Anastasio, "How Video Game Addiction Can Destroy Your Life," vice, January 6, 2015, https://www.vice.com/en_us/article/vdpwga/video-game-addiction-is-destroying-american-lives-456.

199 Shlam, Shosh, Hilla Medalia, Neta Zwebner-Zaibert, and Enat Sidi. 2014. Web junkie.

200 Ibid.

201 Ibid.

202 Cam Adair, "Escaping Video Game Addiction," filmed September 2013 at TEDx Boulder, CO, https://tedxboulder.com/speakers/cam-adair.

203 David Kinnaman, "The Porn Phenomenon," Barna, February 25, 2016, https://www.barna.com/the-porn-phenomenon/.

204 Pamela Anderson. Shmuley Boteach, Lust for Love: Rekindling Intimacy and Passion in Your Relationship, (New York: Center Street, 2018), Kindle-Version, p. 47.

205 Matt Fradd, The Porn Myth. Exposing the Reality Behind the Fantasy of Pornography (San Francisco: Ignatius, 2017), p.160.
206 Kirk Doran, "Industry Size, Measurement, and Social Costs," (presentation, Princeton University, Princeton, New Jersey, December 11-13, 2008), posted on the Social Costs of Pornography, http://wwww.socialcostsof pornography.com/Doran_Inustry_Size_Measurement_Social_Costs.pdf.
207 Kammeyer, K.C.W., "A Hypersexual Society. Sexual Discourse, Erotica and Pornography in America Today." (New York: Palgrave Macmillan, 2008), p. 184.
208 Nathan McAlone, "Here's how Janet Jackson's Infamous 'Nipplegate' Inspired the Creation of YouTube," Business Insider, Oct 3, 2015, https://www.businessinsider.com/idea-for-youtube-came-from-janet-jackson-nipplegate-2015-10.
209 Pornhub's 2017 Year in Review, Pornhub, http://www.pornhub.com/insights/2017-year-in-review Accessed April 20, 2018.
210 NBC News, "Things Are Looking Up in America's Porn Industry", NBC News, January 20, 2015, https://www.nbcnews.com/business/business-news/things-are-looking-americas-porn-industry-n289431
211 Wendy Waltz; Larry Waltz, The Porn Trap: The Essential Guide to Overcoming Problems Caused by Pornography, (Harper Collins, New York, 2008), p. 17.
212 Donald Hilton, "Slave Master: How Pornography Drugs and Changes Your Brain", Salvo 13, no. 34.
213 "ICT Facts and Figures 2017," accessed August 22, 2020, https://www.itu.int/en/ITU-D/Statistics/Documents/facts/ICTFactsFigures2017.pdf.
214 Wendy Waltz; Larry Waltz, The Porn Trap: The Essential Guide to Overcoming Problems Caused by Pornography, (Harper Collins, New York, 2008), p.4.
215 "The 'Porn Genie' is Out of the Bottle: Understanding and Responding to the Impact of Pornography on Young People," Australian Psychological Society, April 2015, Vol 37, Issue 2 https://www.psychology.org.au/inpsych/2015/april/pratt/.
216 Dr. Anthony Jack is a Professor of Philosophy, Psychology, Neurology and Neuroscience and Research Director at the Inamori International Center for Ethics and Excellence, Case Western Reserve University, USA. This quote can be found in: Wilson, 2014, para. 62-66.
217 Gail Dines, Pornland: How Porn Has Hijacked Our Sexuality, (Boston: Beacon Press, 2010), p. 47.
218 "Pornhub's 2016 Year in Review," Pornhub, http://www.pornhub.com/insights/2016-year-in-review Accessed 30 February 2017).
219 Pornhub's 2017 Year in Review, Pornhub, http://www.pornhub.com/insights/2017-year-in-review

220 Patrick Wood, "Australia's Porn Problem," ABC News, July 7, 2019, https://www.abc.net.au/news/2019-01-16/australias-porn-problem/10668940.

221 Patrick Wood, "Australia's Porn Problem," ABC News, July 7, 2019, https://www.abc.net.au/news/2019-01-16/australias-porn-problem/10668940.

222 Ana Bridges; Robert Wosnitzer, Erica Scharrer, Chyng Sun, Rachael Liberman, "Aggression and Sexual Behavior in Best-Selling Pornography Videos. A Content Analysis Update," *Psychology of Women Quarterly, 32*(3), 312–325.

223 ibid.

224 John Foubert; Matthew Brosi; Sean Bannon, "Pornography Viewing Among Fraternity Men. Effects on Bystander Intervention, Rape Myth Acceptance and Behavioral Intent to Commit Sexual Assault, in: Sexual Addiction & Compulsivity." The Journal of Treatment & Prevention 18, no.4, 2011, pp. 212-213.

225 "Pornhub's 2017 Year in Review," Pornhub, http://www.pornhub.com/insights/2017-year-in-review.

226 Ibid.

227 Martin Dubney, "Experiment that Convinced me Online Porn is the Most Pernicious Threat Facing Children Today: by Ex-Lads' Mag Editor," Daily Mail, September 25, 2013, http://www.dailymail.co.uk/femail/article-2432591/Porn-pernicious-threat-facing-children-today-By-ex-lads-mag-editor-MARTIN-DAUBNEY.html.

228 Catherine Steiner-Adair, Teresa H. Barker, The Big Disconnect: Protecting Childhood and Family Relationships in the Digital Age (New York: Harper 2014), p. 219.

229 Julie Bindel, "The Truth about the Porn Industry," The Guardian, July 2, 2010, https://www.theguardian.com/lifeandstyle/2010/jul/02/gail-dines-pornography.

230 Amanda Lenhart, Aaron, Monica Anderson, "Teens, Technology and Romantic Relationships. "Pew Research Center, October 2015, p. 64.

231 Paul J. Wright, Robert S. Tokunaga, Ashley Kraus, 29 December 2015, "A Meta Analysis of Pornography Consumption and Actual Acts of Sexual Aggression in General Population Studies" Journal of Communication 66, no. 1. 29 December 2015. https://doi.org/10.1111/jcom.12201.

232 "Kids at Risk: Sexualised Behaviour 'Normal,'" The Australian, May 30, 2015, https://www.theaustralian.com.au/news/nation/kids-at-risk-sexualised-behaviour-normal/news-story/78edb3003412e1f962e380f13f8e37f8.

233 Kate Julian, "Why Are Young People Having So Little Sex?" The Atlantic, November 13, 2018, https://www.theatlantic.com/feed/author/kate-julian/.

234 Ibid.

235 Weiss, "Can Porn Addiction Cause Male Sexual Dysfunction?" 2015, https://www.addiction.com/expert-blogs/can-porn-addiction-cause-male-sexual-dysfunction/.
"Could Porn Cause ED? Why Clearing Your History May Leave you Limp," Men's Health, 2017, http://www.menshealth.com/sex-women/porn-erectile-dysfunction).

236 Quote was found in: Gary Wilson, Your Brain on Porn, 2014, para. 200-203. Kindle.

237 Lucia F O'Sullivan, Lori A Brotto, Sandra Byers, Jo Ann Majerovich, Judith A Wuest, "Prevalence and Characteristics of Sexual Functioning among Sexually Experienced Middle to Late Adolescents," International Society for Sexual Medicine 11, January 12, 2014, p. 636. 10.1111/jsm.12419.

238 Brian Y Park, Gary Wilson, Jonathan Berger, Matthew Christman, Bryn Reina, Frank Bishop, Warren P Klam, Andrew P Doan, "Is Internet Pornography Causing Sexual Dysfunctions? A Review with Clinical Reports," Behavioral Sciences, 6, no. 3, 2016, pp.16-17.

239 Donna Freitas, The End of Sex: How Hookup Culture is Leaving a Generation Unhappy, Sexually Unfulfilled, and Confused About Intimacy (New York: Basic Books, 2013), pp. 318-321. Kindle.

240 Pamela Anderson. Shmuley Boteach, Lust for Love: Rekindling Intimacy and Passion in Your Relationship, (New York: Center Street, 2018), Kindle-Version, pp.28.

241 Donna Freitas, The End of Sex: How Hookup Culture is Leaving a Generation Unhappy, Sexually Unfulfilled, and Confused About Intimacy (New York: Basic Books, 2013), Kindle.

242 Yona, Lihi, Politicalizing Health, Medicalizing Porn. Rethinking Modern Pornography, in: Marquette Elder's Advisor, 16, no. 1, 2014, p. 130.

243 Simone Kühn, Jürgen Gallinat, "Brain Structure and Functional Connectivity Associated with Pornography Consumption. The Brain on Porn," JAMA Psychiatry, 71, no. 7, pp. 827-834.

244 Gary Wilson, Your Brain on Porn, 2014, para. 1015-1033, Kindle.

245 Yona Lihi "Politicalizing Health, Medicalizing Porn. Rethinking Modern Pornography," Marquette Elder's Advisor 16, no. 1, 2014, p. 131.

246 Ibid.

247 Dewsbury, D. A., "Effects of Novelty of Copulatory Behavior: The Coolidge Effect and Related Phenomena," Psychological Bulletin 89, no. 3, 1981, pp. 464-482.
James R. Wilson, Robert E. Kuehn und Franka A. Beach: Modifications in the Sexual Behavior of Male Rats Produced by Changing the Stimulus Female. In: Journal of Comparative and Physiological Psychology 56 (1963), S. 636–644,

248 Eric Koukounas, E; Overb, R., "Changes in the Magnitude of the Eyeblink Startle Response During Habituation of Sexual Arousal, Behavior," Research and Therapy 38, 2000, pp. 573-584.

249 John Salamone, Merce Correa, The Mysterious Motivational Functions of Mesolimbic Dopamine, in: Neuron 76 (3), pp. 470–485.Salamone, J.D.; Correa, M., 2012, 2012, pp. 470–485.

250 Gary Wilson, Your Brain on Porn, 2014, para. 1136-1139.

251 Paul Kenny, George Voren, Paul Johnson, P.M. "Dopamine D2 Receptors and Striatopallidal Transmission in Addiction and Obesity," Current Opinion in Neurobiology, 23, no. 4, 2013, pp. 535-538.

252 Gary Wilson, Your Brain on Porn, 2014, para. 1152-1157.

253 Wendy Waltz; Larry Waltz, The Porn Trap: The Essential Guide to Overcoming Problems Caused by Pornography, (Harper Collins, New York, 2008), p.187.

254 Ibid. p. 20.

255 Twenge, Jean M., et al. "Declines in Sexual Frequency among American Adults, 1989–2014." Archives of Sexual Behavior, June 2017, doi:10.1007/s10508-017-0953-1.

256 http://www.socialcostsofpornography.com/Bridges_Pornographys_Effect_on_Interpersonal_Relationships.pdf

257 Pamela Anderson, Shmuley Botech, Lust for Love: Rekindling Intimacy and Passion in Your Relationship (p.41). Center Street. Kindle-Version.

258 Ran Gavrieli, "Why I stopped Watching Porn," filmed October 2013, TEDx Jaffa, https://www.youtube.com/watch?v=gRJ_QfP2mhU.

259 Elizabeth M. Morgan, "Associations between Young Adults' Use of Sexually Explicit Materials and Their Sexual Preferences, Behaviors, and Satisfaction", The Journal of Sex Research, November 2011, 48:6, pp.520-530. https://www.researchgate.net/publication/49778278_Associations_between_Young_Adults'_Use_of_Sexually_Explicit_Materials_and_Their_Sexual_Preferences_Behaviors_and_Satisfaction

260 Kevin B. Skinner, "Is Porn Really Destroying 500,000 Marriages Annually?" December 12, 2011, https://www.psychologytoday.com/us/blog/inside-porn-addiction/201112/is-porn-really-destroying-500000-marriages-annually

261 Wendy Waltz; Larry Waltz, The Porn Trap: The Essential Guide to Overcoming Problems Caused by Pornography, (Harper Collins, New York, 2008), p. 42.

262 Dolf Zillmann and Jennings Bryant, "Psychology's Impact on Sexual Satisfaction", Journal of Applied Social Psychology 18, 5 (Found in Porn Myth p. 154)

263 Amanda Barrell, "Do Penis Enlargement Methods Work, Medical News Today, January 12, 2020, https://www.medicalnewstoday.com/articles/323688.php

264 Wendy Waltz; Larry Waltz, The Porn Trap: The Essential Guide to Overcoming Problems Caused by Pornography, (Harper Collins, New York, 2008), p. 35.

265 Tom Usher, "Want a Larger Penis? Then your Problems May be Upstairs, not Downstairs", The Guardian, April 16, 2019, https://www.theguardian.com/commentisfree/2019/apr/16/penis-enlargement-surgery-masculinity-papua-new-guinea.

266 Morgan Griffin, "Penis Enlargement: Does It Work?" WebMD, accessed August 22,2020, https://www.webmd.com/men/guide/penis-enlargement-does-it-work#1.

267 Colin Drury,"'I Wanted a Truncheon in my Pants': the Rise of the Penis Extension," The Guardian, September 22, 2018, https://www.theguardian.com/lifeandstyle/2018/sep/22/penis-extension-wanted-truncheon-in-pants-rise.

268 Brené Brown, Dare to Lead: Brave Work. Tough Conversations. Whole Hearts (New York: Random House, 2018), p. 120.

269 Martin Daubney, "Experiment that convinced me online porn is the most pernicious threat facing children today," DailyMail,. Sept. 25, 2013. http://www.dailymail.co.uk/femail/article-2432591/Porn-pernicious-threat-facing-children-today-By-ex-ladsmag-editor-MARTIN-DAUBNEY.html.

270 Patricia M. Greenfield, "Inadvertent exposure to pornography on the Internet: Implications of peer-to-peer file-sharing networks for child development and families," Journal of Applied Developmental Psychology 25 (Nov/Dec 2004), pp. 741–750.

271 Ibid.

272 Nicola Lucchi, "Internet Content Governance and Human Rights," Vanderbild Journal Entertainment & Technology Law 16, no.4, p. 812.

273 UN General Assembly, Universal Declaration of Human Rights, 10 December 1948, 217 A (III).

274 UN General Assembly, Universal Declaration of Human Rights, 10 December 1948, 217 A (III).

275 UN Human Rights Committee (HRC), General comment no. 34, Article 19, Freedoms of opinion and expression, 12 September 2011, CCPR/C/GC/34, para. 2.

276 Benjamin Franklin, Monday July 2. to Monday July 9. 1722, https://www.ushistory.org/franklin/courant/issue49.htm.

277 Melissa Castan, Sarah Joseph, Jenny Schultz, The International Covenant on Civil and Political Rights, Cases, Materials and Commentary (Oxford: Oxford University Press, 2013), p. 590.

278 "Global Digital Population as of July 2020," Statista, August 20, 2020, https://www.statista.com/statistics/617136/digital-population-worldwide/#:~:text=How%20many%20people%20use%20the,in%20terms%20of%20internet%20users.

279 Dragoş Cucereanu, Aspects of Regulating Freedom of Expression on the Internet (Antwerpen, Oxford and Portland: Intersentia, 2008) p. 138.

280 Sonia Livingstone & Magdalena Bober, "Taking Up Opportunities? Children's Uses of the Internet for Education, Communication and Participation, (London: LSE Research, 2004), http://eprints.lse.ac.uk/archive/00000418, pp. 20-21.

281 William Dutton; Anna Dopatka, Ginette Law, Victoria Nash, "Freedom of Connection. Freedom of Expression. The Changing Legal Regulatory Ecology Shaping the Internet," United Nations Educational, Scientific and Cultural Organization, (Paris: UNESCO Publishing, 2011), p. 59.

282 Cucereanu, Aspects of Regulating Freedom of Expression on the Internet, 2008, p. 140.

283 Ibid.

284 Alfred Maskeroni, "Pornhub Erects Huge Billboard in Times Square After Long Search for a Great Non-Pornographic Ad," Adweek, October 8, 2014, https://www.adweek.com/creativity/pornhub-erects-huge-billboard-times-square-after-long-search-great-non-pornographic-ad-160632/,

285 " Sexual Violence is Preventable," Centers for Desease Control and Prevention, August 22,2020 https://www.cdc.gov/injury/features/sexual-violence/index.html.

286 UN Women, "Facts and Figures: Ending Violence Against Women" August 22,2020, https://www.unwomen.org/en/what-we-do/ending-violence-against-women/facts-and-figures.

287 Auto Alliance, "How Automakers Are Driving Innovation," Strategy&, The 2018 Global Innovation 1000 Study, https://autoalliance.org/innovation/.

288 Ran Gavrieli, "Why I stopped Watching Porn," filmed October 2013, TED x Jaffa, https://www.youtube.com/watch?v=gRJ_QfP2mhU.

289 Exodus Cry, "One Million People Sign Petition to Shut Down Pornhub for Alleged Sex Trafficking Videos," June 9, 2020, https://www.prnewswire.com/news-releases/one-million-people-sign-petition-to-shut-down-pornhub-for-alleged-sex-trafficking-videos-301072809.html.

290 Megha Mohan, "'I was Raped at 14, and the Video Ended up on a Porn Site'", BBC, February 10, 2020, https://www.bbc.com/news/stories-51391981.

291 Frances Gragg, Ian Petta, Haidee Bernstein, Karla Eisen, Liz Quinn, "New York Prevalence Study of Commercially Sexually Exploited Children.," WESTAT, April 18, 2007.

292 David Finkelhor, Gerald Hotaling, I.A. Lewis, & Christine Smith, Sexual Abuse in a National Survey of Adult Men and Women. Prevalence, Characteristics and Risk Factors. Child Abuse & Neglect 14, 1990, pp. 19-28.

293 Smith, S.G., Chen, J., Basile, K.C., Gilbert, L.K., Merrick, M.T., Patel, N., Walling, M., & Jain, A. (2017). The National Intimate Partner and Sexual Violence Survey (NISVS): 2010-2012 State Report. Atlanta, GA: National Center for Injury Prevention and Control, Centers for Disease Control and Prevention.

294 Donna M. Hughes, "Sex Trafficking of Women for the Production of Pornography," Citizens Against Trafficking, 2010, https://www.academia.edu/4847671/Sex_Trafficking_of_Women_for_the_Production_of_Pornography.

295 Ibid.

296 Ibid.

297 "Press Release from The Pink Cross Foundation." September 15, 2009, http://www.shelleylubben.com/.

298 "Attempts to Justify Slavery," BBC, August 23, 2020, http://www.bbc.co.uk/ethics/slavery/ethics/justifications.shtml

299 Harriet N. Jacobs, "Incidents in the Life of a Slave Girl," http://slaverystories.org/harriet-jacobs/1.

300 "Attempts to Justify Slavery," BBC, August 23, 2020, http://www.bbc.co.uk/ethics/slavery/ethics/justifications.shtml

301 United States Declaration of Independence.

302 Linda Smith, Samantha Healy Vardaman, Melissa Snow, Smith, Healy Vardaman, Snow, "The National Report on Domestic Minor Sex Trafficking," Center for Victim Research, p. 4, https://ncvc.dspacedirect.org/handle/20.500.11990/907.

303 "Pornhub's Darkly Ironic Claims About Racism and Social Injustice," End Sexual Exploitation, June 19, 2020, https://endsexualexploitation.org/articles/pornhubs-darkly-ironic-claims-about-racism-and-social-injustice/.

304 Carolyn West, "Race and Porn," interview by Gail Dines, Culture Reframed, June 10, 2020, video, 30:53. https://www.facebook.com/culturereframed/.

305 Ibid.

306 Ibid.

307 Ibid.

308 Carolyn West, "Race and Porn," interview by Gail Dines, Culture Reframed, June 10, 2020, video, 30:53. https://www.facebook.com/culturereframed/.

309 Brian Fung, Twitter labeled Trump Tweets With a Fact Check for the First Time, CNN, May 27, 2020, https://www.cnn.com/2020/05/26/tech/twitter-trump-fact-check/index.html.

310 Brian Flood, "What is Section 230 of the Communications Decency Act, and why is it under fire?", Fox News, June 17, 2020, https://www.foxnews.com/media/what-is-section-230-and-why-is-it-under-fire.

311 47 U.S.C. § 230

312 Brian Flood, "What is Section 230 of the Communications Decency Act, and why is it under fire?", Fox News, June 17, 2020, https://www.foxnews.com/media/what-is-section-230-and-why-is-it-under-fire.
313 Ibid.
314 Jeff Kosseff, The Twenty-Six Words That Created the Internet (New York: Cornell University Press, 2019).
315 "New Zealand Government Keeps it Real, Uses Actors Portraying Naked Porn Stars in Viral Internet Safety Video," National Post, June17, 2020, https://nationalpost.com/health/sexual-health/new-zealand-government-keeps-it-real-uses-famous-porn-stars-in-viral-internet-safety-video.
316 U.S. Department of Justice. Post Hearing Memorandum of Points and Authorities, at 1, ACLU v. Reno, 929 F. Supp. 824, 1996.
317 Supreme Court, Reno v. American Civil Liberties Union 521 U.S. 844 (1997)
318 Communication Decency Act (CDA) P.L. 104-104, Title V, 47 U.S.C.S § 994 nt. (1996). The CDA was designed with the aim to regulate a minor's access to pornographic material online by creating laws, which obligated internet service providers, industry, and consumers to avoid sharing pornographic material online in a way that is accessible to children.
319 U.S. Constitution Amend. I.
320 "Founding Fathers on Freedom, Liberty and American Exceptionalism," January 26, 2018, https://www.insearchofliberty.com/founding-fathers-on-freedom-liberty-and-american-exceptionalism/
321 U.S. Constitution Amend. I.
322 Herbert Lin, Dick Thornburgh, Youth Pornography and the Internet (Washington: National Academies Press, 2002), p. 85.
323 Ibid, p. 68.
324 Ibid, p. 68. See also: Roth v. United States, 354 U.S. 476 (1957)
325 Chaplinsky v. New Hampshire, 315 U.S. (568/1942).
326 Chaplinsky v. New Hampshire, 315 U.S. (568/1942), para. 11.
327 End Sexual Exploitation, accessed August 22, 2020, https://endsexualexploitation.org/faqs/.
328 Butler v. Michigan (380 /1957), supra, pp. 508-509.
329 "Porn Sites Could be Blocked by ISPs Under New UK Rules," BBC, 2016, http://www.bbc.com/news/technology-38062660.
330 David Barstow, "India Blocks 857 Pornography Websites, Defying Supreme Court Decision." New York Times, August 3, 2015, https://www.nytimes.com/2015/08/04/world/asia/india-orders-blocking-of-857-pornography-websites-targeted-by-activist.html?_r=0.
331 "Russia Blocks Access to Adult Site Pornhub, The Moscow Times, September 14, 2016 https://themoscowtimes.com/news/russia-blocks-access-to-pornhub-55334.

332 John Tobin, Fixed Concepts but Changing Conceptions: Understanding the Relationships Between Children and Parents under the CRC. In: Handbook of Children's Rights: Global and Multidisciplinary Perspectives, edited by Martin D. Ruck, Michele Peterson-Badali, Michael Freeman (New York, London: Routledge, 2017), p. 58.

333 John Tobin, "Justifying Children's Rights," International Journal of Children's Rights, January 1, 2013, Vol 21, no. 3, 2013, p. 428.

334 Art. 19, ICCPR

335 Initial reports of States parties due in 1993. International Covenant on Civil and Political Rights, HRC, UN Doc. CCPR/C/81/Add.4, (1994), para. 589.

336 Renton v. Playtime Theaters, Inc., 475 U.S. 41, 89 L. Ed. 2d 29, 196 S Ct. 925 (1986).

337 Wayne Sutton, "14 Dr. Martin Luther King Jr. Quotes To Inspire Change in 2016," January 18, 2016, https://medium.com/@waynesutton/14-dr-martin-luther-king-jr-quotes-to-inspire-change-in-2016-722be51e564

338 David Cameron, "The Internet and Pornography: Prime Minister Calls for Action," July 22, 2013, https://www.gov.uk/government/speeches/the-internet-and-pornography-prime-minister-calls-for-action#:~:text=Speech-,The%20internet%20and%20pornography%3A%20Prime%20Minister%20calls%20for%20action,children%20on%2022%20July%202013.&text=This%20is%2C%20quite%20simply%2C%20about,our%20children%20and%20their%20innocence.

339 "2018 Impact Report," National Center in Sexual Exploitation, https://endsexualexploitation.org/wp-content/uploads/NCOSE-2018-Impact-Report-Final.pdf, p.18-19.

340 Ibid.

341 The relationship between frequency of family dinner and adolescent problem behaviors after adjusting for other family characteristics, Journal of Adolescence 33, no. 1, February 2010, pp.187-196, https://www.sciencedirect.com/science/article/abs/pii/S0140197109000372?via%3Dihub.

342 Marla E. Eisenberg; Rachel E. Olson, Dianne Neumark-Sztainer, Mary Story, Linda H. Bearinger, "Correlations Between Family Meals and Psychosocial Well-being Among Adolescents," Jama Pediatrics 158, no.8, 2004, pp.792-796. doi:10.1001/archpedi.158.8.792.

343 Judith Newman, 'Hygge is where the Heart is," New York Times, February 24, 2017, https://www.nytimes.com/2017/02/24/books/review/hygge-is-where-the-heart-is.html.

344 Anne Fishel, "The Most Important Thing You Can Do with Your Kids? Eat Dinner with Them," Washington Post, January 12, 2015. https://www.washingtonpost.com/posteverything/wp/2015/01/12/the-most-important-thing-you-can-do-with-your-kids-eat-dinner-with-them/.

345 Danah Boyd, It's Complicated: The Social Lives of Networked Teens (Connecticut: Yale University Press, 2014), p. 113.

346 Inspired by Thich Nhat Hanh's "At Home in the World: Stories and Essential Teachings from a Monk's Life. (Berkeley: Parllax Press, 2016)."

347 "Cellphone Use in America, Sure Call, https://www.surecall.com/docs/20180515-SureCall-Attachment-Survey-Results-v2.pdf.

348 "Mobile Professional Report 2017," iPass, accessed August 25, 2020, https://www.ipass.com/wp-content/uploads/2017/11/iPass-Mobile-Professional-Report-2017.pdf.

349 Twenge, Jean M.,Martin, Gabrielle N.,Campbell, W. Keith, "Decreases in psychological well-being among American adolescents after 2012 and links to screen time during the rise of smartphone technology," Emotion 18, no.6, Sep 2018, pp. 765-780.

350 Sean Gregory, "This College Basketball Team Banned Smartphones. Now It's in the Final Four," Time Magazine, April 5, 2019, https://time.com/5565272/college-basketball-team-ban-cellphones/.

351 Brooks, David. The Social Animal: The Hidden Sources of Love, Character, and Achievement Random House Publishing Group, p.123, Kindle.

352 Ibid. p. 127, Kindle.

353 Yalda T. Uhls, Minas Michikyan, Jordan Morris, Debra Garcia, Gary W.Small, Eleni Zgourou, Patricia M.Greenfield, "Five days at Outdoor Education Camp Without Screens Improves Preteen Skills with Nonverbal Emotion Cues," Computers in Human Behavior 39, October 2014, pp. 387-392. https://www.sciencedirect.com/science/article/pii/S0747563214003227.

354 Jingjing Jiang, "How Teens and Parents Navigate Screen Time and Device Distractions," Pew Research Center, August 2018.

355 Brené Brown, Dare to Lead: Brave Work. Tough Conversations. Whole Hearts (New York: Random House, 2018), p.189.

356 Abby Ohlheiser, "YouTube is the Way to Get Famous. At VitCon the Teens Want to be Next in Line," Washington Post, June 25, 2018, https://www.washingtonpost.com/news/the-intersect/wp/2018/06/25/they-became-famous-youtubers-a-new-generation-of-kids-wants-to-take-their-place/.

357 Amy Morin, „The 1 Skill College Students Wish Their Parents Had Taught Them," Psychology Today, August 17, 2017, https://www.psychologytoday.com/intl/blog/what-mentally-strong-people-dont-do/201708/the-1-skill-college-students-wish-their-parents.

358 "The Implication of Dunbar's Number: Network Size and Social Ties," College of Communication, https://sites.bu.edu/cmcs/2018/10/01/the-implications-of-dunbars-number-network-size-and-social-ties/.

359 Gretchen Livingston, Andrea Caumont, "5 Facts on Love and Marriage in America." Pew Research Center, 13 February 2017, www.pewresearch.org/fact-tank/2017/02/13/5-facts-about-love-and-marriage/.

360 Based on a compilation of teenage stories.

Made in USA - North Chelmsford, MA
1198932_9781735910000
09.06.2022 1418